Competitive Sensemaking

Un Autre Monde, J.J. Grandville (1844)

Competitive Sensemaking:

An Upgrade to Common Sense on Disagreement

John Nerst

Everything Studies Press

2026

Competitive Sensemaking: An Upgrade to Common Sense on Disagreement

Published by Everything Studies Press
www.everythingstudies.com
everythingstudies.substack.com

ISBN: 978-91-531-4929-3

Cover design by John Nerst
Interior design by John Nerst

To my readers

Contents

Prelude

What You Are About to Read

The single biggest problem in communication is the illusion that it has taken place.

— George Bernard Shaw

Any respectable book must have a thesis. This does have one, but it is not one simple enough to be captured in an elevator speech. It is designed to slowly accustom you to a certain way of thinking, one that requires many interlocking components who need each other for their full significance to be apparent. I will go through them in turn, later pieces building on earlier in an increasingly dense web, like a novel where parallel stories eventually come together. It tells us how disagreement works, as in how and why people have different beliefs, and what happens when they negotiate them.

Thinking about the philosophical and psychological complexities of disagreement has been unnecessary for the great majority of us who don't engage in theoretical discussions on a daily basis. But this has changed. Now everybody has a voice, the voices can reach each other, and with that have the capacity to cultivate their differences, and to access any intellectual resource they need to do so, from the writing of tenured academics to those of schizotypal cranks.

The resulting diversity is beautiful, in a way, but also causes problems, including but not limited to toxic political polarization, social disintegration, decay of trust and goodwill, as empathy requires both comprehension and charity. We have old, venerable conventional wisdom of how to have civilized discussion and debate, but it is increasingly irrelevant. There's a notable absence of awareness what people disagreeing in public actually do instead of behaving like formal debaters — because it's definitely something else. Rather than throw up our hands at the everyman's eternal failure to behave like a philosopher's ideal just because he is exhorted to, we should seek to understand what is really happening, and why. There is method to the madness: if people are debating badly, what are they doing well? The first step to treatment is diagnosis.

Public disagreements have become vastly more complex in recent decades (for reasons explained in chapters 2 and 3) and require more competence to navigate. Such competence, I believe, comes from internalizing some insights. "Competitive sensemaking" is a two-word description of what public disagreement, discourse, and "debate" actually is. *Sensemaking* is the process by which we turn a vast array of unorganized concrete details about the world into stories and belief systems that we can comprehend and use. We also like these stories and belief systems to support us and our friends in our social and political goals—that's the "competitive" part.

Sensemaking uses a range of philosophical, social, and psychological mechanisms that are not logical argumentation. A key element for understanding it is that language differs entirely from the reality it supposedly depicts, which throws a wrench into simplistic notions of true and false. Another is the multifaceted, yet foundational role linguistic ambiguity plays in rhetoric. Also, it cannot be understood without considering that coordinating around shared belief systems for power is a core function of building and maintaining them.

Under these conditions, communication would be difficult enough if all people were alike, but we are not. We subscribe to different, incompatible, often mutually incomprehensible belief systems partly because we perceive the world differently on an intellectual, emotional, and even physiological level. Add to the mix a subconscious mind with ulterior motives we don't notice, and the side effects of having social instincts made for navigating a small, local social circle but now confronted with an endless mass of disembodied potential friends, rivals, and enemies, and then you have, well, today.

Think about what you are about to read as a gymnast's vault, where the first third is all run-up, the middle jumps off the spring-board and flips over the vault table, and in the last third we're spinning in the air and—hopefully—stick the landing.

PART I

Groundwork

Chapter 1

A Tale of Two Realities

Their language and the derivations of their language—religion, letters, metaphysics—all presuppose idealism. The world for them is not a concourse of objects in space; it is a heterogeneous series of independent acts. It is successive and temporal, not spatial.

— Jorge Luis Borges, *Tlön, Uqbar, Orbis Tertius*

According to stereotypes, we engineers are expected to hold certain opinions on the quality of humanities scholarship. In return, humanists are expected to hold certain opinions on the quality of engineers' personalities. As often, there's truth to the joke: there is a rich broth of intellectual, social, and temperamental hostilities between STEM fields and the humanities. The observation is not new; chemist-cum-novelist CP Snow wrote about what he called *The Two Cultures* back in 1959:

> Literary intellectuals at one pole—at the other scientists, and as the most representative, the physical scientists. Between the two a gulf of mutual incomprehension—sometimes (particularly among the young) hostility and dislike, but most of all lack of understanding.

My degree program in *Sociotechnical Systems Engineering* was set up as an attempt to bridge the gulf. It brought social science and humanities to an engineering education, hoping to produce well-rounded graduates capable of taking multiple perspectives on technology. We took courses from a wide range of departments and disciplines, including physics, history, philosophy, geography, and economics.

Those given by the History of Science department introduced us to a few schools of thought[1], like *STS*—"science and technology studies", *SSK*—"the sociology of scientific knowledge", and *SCOT*—"the social construction of technology". They're distinct but share a broadly relativist, *problematizing* attitude towards science and its role in society. Had I known in advance how much of this literature I would have to read, I might have picked a more traditional engineering path, because I was familiar with this stance and didn't like it one bit. I'm the sort who grew up devouring popular science books. I liked puzzles, systems, details, and the satisfaction of correct answers. My exposure to *social constructionism* was through hard-nosed, analytical thinkers with a scientific background and disposition like Richard Dawkins, Steven Pinker and Daniel Dennett, as well as the physicists Alan Sokal and Jean Bricmont, authors of the 1998 polemic *Fashionable Nonsense: Postmodern Intellectuals' Abuse of Science*. In it, they skewered relativists and their acolytes, setting off "The Science Wars", a controversy where scientists and humanist theorists of science and knowledge came to blows over the latter's allegedly anti-scientific pronouncements.

I agreed with the scientists, of course. Constructionists and, more broadly, relativists and "postmodernists" were the enemy—all insisting that claims of truth, objectivity and rationality are nothing but tools of oppression. I came inoculated, my intellectual immune system trained on weak strains, channeled through hostile scientist intermediaries. On my guard against any sign of contempt for science and objectivity coming from my professor and the texts he assigned us[2], I scanned the lines with suspicion. And sure, I found what I was looking for. The message we were supposed to take home did look a lot like "taking those arrogant scientists down a peg".

---

[1] A "school of thought" is a small number of academics writing papers mostly at each other.

[2] We were given materials by prominent scholars in these fields, e.g. David Bloor, Wiebe Bijker and Trevor Pinch, Bruno Latour, Harry Collins, Donna Haraway, Langdon Winner, Dorothy Nelkin, Andrew Pickering and Sharon Traweek.

The "Strong Programme" in the sociology of science, primarily associated with the British sociologist David Bloor, aimed to explain scientific knowledge purely in social, rhetorical terms. Experiments, evidence, and the force of logical argument didn't settle controversies, it was said. Claims did not become scientific consensus because they were true, but because scientists were convinced of them for largely social reasons. In line with this, scientific theories and their interpretation were evaluated and criticized more for their supposed social and political assumptions and implications, and less for their correspondence to the facts. Similarly, the alleged ideological motives and biases of scientists were considered more significant and interesting than the accuracy of their theories.

This wasn't easy. It's exasperating to work your way through the reasonings of writers whose underlying assumptions, preoccupations, and goals are radically different from yours. Every other sentence you want clarification, you want to know what a word does and doesn't mean, you want your objections acknowledged and addressed, and you want to know why their train of thought is going where it's going and not where it would be going if it were yours[3].

This would've been hard enough if such contrasting assumptions, preoccupations and goals were stated explicitly at the beginning, but of course they weren't. Such things are taken for granted because it's so easy to forget that not everyone shares them, especially when you work in a narrow academic field and speak mostly to your peers. There is little incentive to accommodate outsiders, and when your collective self-image is to be the leading experts on the topic you study, your shared assumptions, interests and priorities may to you look like nothing but basic truths, and disagreement nothing but ignorance.

Our professor could've made a better effort helping us with this. I assume he didn't in part because he was used to teaching humani-

---

[3] My molecular-biology-PhD-holding wife had similar complaints when she decided to get a teaching certificate and had to take a year of pedagogy and read that scholarship.

ties students who need less "translation" than we did. It may also just have been me, personally, who had the biggest problem with it, given my personal background with these theories (I was certainly the one speaking out the most against it). And if I'm honest, in retrospect, the reason I found much of it not just wrong or uninteresting but *offensive* was that it collided head-on with my personality and values. As a natural know-it-all, a systematizing stickler for whom knowing the right answers was the primary source of self-worth, I did not care for the message that objectivity and rationality are illusions—a combination of philosophical naivety and tools of political domination.

I know what you're thinking. This is set up, all in the past tense, as if there is a turnaround where I realize that I've been wrong all along, and with the fervor of the newly converted embrace constructionism and denounce the misrepresentations my former intellectual heroes had fed me. This is not that kind of story. I have not switched sides. I *have* come to understand that the constructionists were right about some things, even when I would prefer that they weren't. I still dislike their attitudes and priorities, but personal dislike is not an argument. They have valid points about science in practice not working as it's supposed to, about institutionalized knowledge not being equal to objective truth, and about the ways we codify knowledge having political influences and consequences. Scientific knowledge being contingent does not imply that there's no true nature to reality, but that social factors affect what sort of questions we ask, what sort of answers we're looking for, and which ones get noticed and recognized by society.

My teenage self's brothers-in-arms made it too easy for themselves when they threw the baby of reasonable problematization out with the bathwater of vulgar relativism. There's absolutely a middle ground where the constructionists' points can be integrated into a pro-science, pro-rationality, and pro-objectivity story (and this is a big part of what this book is trying to do). Then why the mudslinging, snark, and mutual hostility? Why did "The Science Wars" happen? Aren't academics supposed to be able to disagree constructively? They are, but can only manage it (at best) within fields, where there are shared foundational assumptions and specialized vocabulary allowing everyone to understand what is being said on complex topics. Between fields, especially distant fields, that is not the case and they struggle to even communicate, let alone resolve conflicts. You need to do hard work to not talk past each other, and it's work you're not used to having to do—hell, not having to do that is one of the main perks of isolating yourself in a bubble of specialists! Having to be explicit about the underlying assumptions, interests, and priorities that you usually just take for granted, and accurately inferring the corresponding assumptions, interests, and priorities that others in turn take for granted, is a tall order. Much of it is embedded in the language we use, and whose ambiguity we underestimate since we disproportionately wield and encounter language we're familiar with, giving us unearned confidence in our ability to interpret unfamiliar vocabulary.

"Reality" vs. reality

What exactly was the difference that was so hard to navigate? There are many, of course, but there is a key one, which we strangely enough weren't directly told about. To illustrate it, we can use a phrase central to this whole controversy, and a perfect example of verbiage causing trouble. You may have heard that "reality is socially constructed". What does it mean? It's complicated. Let's consider "socially constructed" and "reality" separately. "Constructed" implies artifice, something created through human effort and intention, and "socially" implies by a social process. Calling something socially constructed suggests that it's been created by human social processes. That's the easy part, and the difficulty comes with "reality". Isn't it obvious what "reality" means? No, it isn't. I said I grew up on science books, and for a scientist it *is* obvious; "reality" means the physical universe. It is made of physical things: objects, substances, forces, motion, and beneath that, molecules, atoms, elementary particles, and fundamental forces. Human social affairs are not the central feature of the universe and understanding reality is not about understanding them on their own terms[4].

I have never believed anything other than this. Before I had any knowledge of science, I had no beliefs about the world I can remember. I knew that not everyone's worldview was based on physical science, of course, but I did at one point believe that virtually everyone educated, certainly educated enough to work in a university and have standing as an intellectual, would be roughly on the same page about this. Theologians and such notwithstanding, I expected everyone working to make sense of the world using roughly scientific principles—and claiming the authority resulting from the tremendous success of those principles—to accept this. Some scientists might be religious in their personal lives, but surely not dispute that scientific knowledge has no room for religious or magical elements.

It was a rude awakening to find out that large parts of the humanities, some parts of the social sciences, and virtually all thought under the constructionist umbrella, are not on this page and do not start their intellectual explorations from that base camp. I don't mean to say that they're religious or believe in the supernatural, per se, I mean that they haven't internalized scientific materialism as the basis of authoritative knowledge the way scientists have. They do not believe that knowledge must be rooted in and expressed in terms compatible with a material understanding of the world. The philosopher Ian Hacking covered these issues in his 1999 book *The Social Construction of What?*, putting it plainly, in a way 23-year-old me needed to hear:

> Politics, ideology and power matter more than metaphysics to most advocates of constructionist analyses of social and cultural phenomena.

[4] There are attempts to study human affairs scientifically, but it's difficult and not anywhere near as successful as studying matter. It's also not how the notion of science came about. Rather, *social* science is the attempt to use matter-appropriate methods on human-stuff, with mixed results.

When I first read Hacking I considered this a pointed criticism. It was an accusation that constructionists were shirking their responsibilities as scholars to be politically disinterested in a monk-like, quasi-autistic pursuit of truth. When my professor calmly agreed with Hacking when I presented the quote to him, and didn't consider it much of a problem, it meant a dramatic shift in my understanding of academia and what it means to be an intellectual.

It isn't just a matter of methodology, but a core difference in what we mean when we say "reality". I once reacted with great surprise when someone told me the humanities were more interesting than science because science deals with such a narrow slice of reality. What an absurd thing to say! It's obviously the humanities that deal with an extraordinarily narrow slice of reality. Science is about understanding the *universe*, while the humanities concern, in excruciating particularity, the activities of one species of featherless biped on a small planet in one of the less fashionable spiral arms of the galaxy. Of course, by "narrow slice of reality", this person meant "narrow slice of human experience", not of the physical universe. Keep that in mind when considering this proclamation, taken from the Wikipedia article on social constructionism:

> language does not mirror reality; rather, it constitutes [creates] it.

To a physical scientist it is just nonsense. There's material reality, ultimately a manifestation of the laws of physics, and then there is the mere overlay that is our apprehension of it, conceptualized and communicated with language. One is downstream from the other and it certainly isn't physics from language. Alan Sokal said:

> Anyone who believes that the laws of physics are mere social conventions is invited to try transgressing those conventions from the windows of my apartment. (I live on the twenty-first floor.)

However, if someone says something crazy, we should consider if they mean something other than what we think they mean. For the proclamation to make sense, "reality" cannot mean what scientists mean by it. To make sure, I went back to the source of the phrase "social construction", which is the 1966 book *The Social Construction of Reality* by sociologists Peter Berger and Thomas Luckmann. Despite its title, it isn't about reality. It's explicitly *not* about reality. There's nothing in it about what a physical scientist studies; it's about what society collectively treats as knowledge.

Starting from the idea that we experience reality mediated by concepts and beliefs instead of directly, they point out that what comes across as plain, manifest truth to us is in fact a set of beliefs. Since what is considered to be knowledge varies between cultures, there's room, and a need, they argue, for a field of study that examines the social factors that lead to different communities having different sets of beliefs ("realities"). Note the qualification: that *which is considered to be* knowledge. Right away in the introduction they point out that both "knowledge" and "reality" ought to be used in quotes every time, since otherwise they would refer to what they normally refer to, i.e. that which is true and real.

> If we were going to be meticulous in the ensuing argument, we would put quotation marks around the two aforementioned terms every time we used them, but this would be stylistically awkward. To speak of quotation marks, however, may give a clue to the peculiar manner in which these terms appear in a sociological context.
>
> One could say the sociological understanding of 'reality' and 'knowledge' falls somewhere in the middle between that of the man in the street and that of the philosopher. The man in the street does not ordinarily trouble himself about what is 'real' to him and about what he 'knows' unless he is stopped

> short by some sort of problem. He takes his 'reality' and his 'knowledge' for granted. The sociologist cannot do this, if only because of his systematic awareness of the fact that men in the street take quite different 'realities' for granted as between one society and another. /---/
>
> The philosopher, on the other hand, is professionally obligated to take nothing for granted, and to obtain maximal clarity as to the ultimate status of what the man in the street believes to be 'reality' and 'knowledge'. Put differently, the philosopher is driven to decide where the quotation marks are in order and when they may safely be omitted, that is to differentiate between valid and invalid assertions about the world. This the sociologist cannot possibly do. Logically, if not stylistically, he is stuck with the quotation marks.

That is, since sociologists of knowledge can't claim to know what is really true, they, when they talk about "knowledge" and "reality", take culture at its word and refer only to *that which is socially accepted as such.* It's important enough to be worth repeating, and Strong Programme strongman Bloor does so in *Knowledge and Social Imagery* from 1991:

> Instead of defining it as true belief—or perhaps, justified true belief—knowledge for the sociologist is whatever people take to be knowledge. It consists of those beliefs which people confidently hold to and live by. In particular the sociologist will be concerned with beliefs which are taken for granted or institutionalised, or invested with authority by groups of people. Of course knowledge must be distinguished from mere belief. This can be done by re-

> serving the word "knowledge" for what is collectively endorsed, leaving the individual and idiosyncratic to count as mere belief.

What separates "knowledge" from "belief" in Bloor's eyes is not truth, but collective endorsement. *This is not a small difference from what the word is usually understood to mean.* Later scholars (and teachers[5]) don't always bother making this clear.

The constructionist notion of reality, or "reality", as it ought to be written, isn't made of physical stuff at all. It's concepts, not things. Thus, when a constructionist talks about the "construction" of this or that—like elementary particles in Andrew Pickering's book *Constructing Quarks* from 1984—they're talking about the concepts we use to refer to things, not the actual things[6].

This is how you get claims suggesting (and people have personally said this to me) that romantic love, child abuse or homosexuality (which predates the human species) were invented at a certain point in history. What *was* "invented" were certain socially recognized concepts, which to a more scientific, materially minded person is clearly distinct from, and less important than, the feelings and behaviors themselves.

This feels upside down to scientists, but there is a logic to it, since it can be argued that the system of culturally accepted beliefs governs our lives much more tangibly than esoteric, unintuitive laws of physics do[7]. Many of our most socially impactful concepts like

---

[5] Both these explanatory quotes come from sources I looked up myself; none of them were assigned reading.

[6] The implied justification (going back all the way to Immanuel Kant and arguably further) is that we can't experience things directly, so concepts is the only thing we can talk reliably about.

[7] It's easy to think this way if you are not only uninterested in physical science but also live in an environment entirely built by humans (like a city) and work a job that isn't about negotiating physical reality like agriculture, construction, engineering or resource extraction, but rather concepts and relationships (you produce texts, images, messages, documents, "projects" etc.). *Of course* it feels like raw physical reality unmediated by social concepts is, to the extent it exists at

roles, expectations, institutions, customs and norms, value judgments, habits and practices, relationships and social structures, don't represent any material objects, phenomena or states of affairs the way scientific concepts and taxonomies do. They are genuinely better understood in terms of how they regulate people's social behavior than their relationship to physical matter.

It follows that if these concepts are what reality is made of, then their essential natures are their social functions, and it is perfectly appropriate to evaluate them by that—and thus to consider claims of objective correctness as ideologically self-serving power grabs, since the *social function* such claims perform is to establish and justify certain beliefs as collectively endorsed.

While it makes a lot of sense for most everyday "knowledge", when applied to science it yields the odd result you inevitably get when you describe something but leave out its defining, essential feature. No wonder it raises the ire of scientists when sociologists ignore correspondence to objective reality as a feature of scientific knowledge[8]. Not only is it the most important thing to them, it is also the exact one that justifies the special status science holds.

From what ground up?

We can think of both the scientific and the constructionist worldviews as built from the ground up, but with opposite ideas about what "the ground" is. In the scientific view, everything is made of atoms, and what happens is nothing but the laws of physics mani-

---

all, irrelevant to your life and to society. When virtually all matter you do interact with is shaped by people, in a very real sense "socially constructed", it's natural to think that the properties of matter itself are downstream of social processes instead of the other way around.

[8] In theory it's reasonable and respectful to avoid judging the truth and validity of others' beliefs when discussing them, but having read research that does — implicitly — follow that rule (and having learned to spot it), it certainly doesn't come across that way most of the time. E.g. going out of your way to describe how people do X because they *believe* Y is true when they clearly do X because Y *is* true, will never not sound condescending.

festing in complicated ways. As you move away from basic physics to more complex and opaque processes, you get further away from physics-like, rule-bound behavior, and the everything-as-particles-in-motion model becomes not strictly untrue, but unworkable.

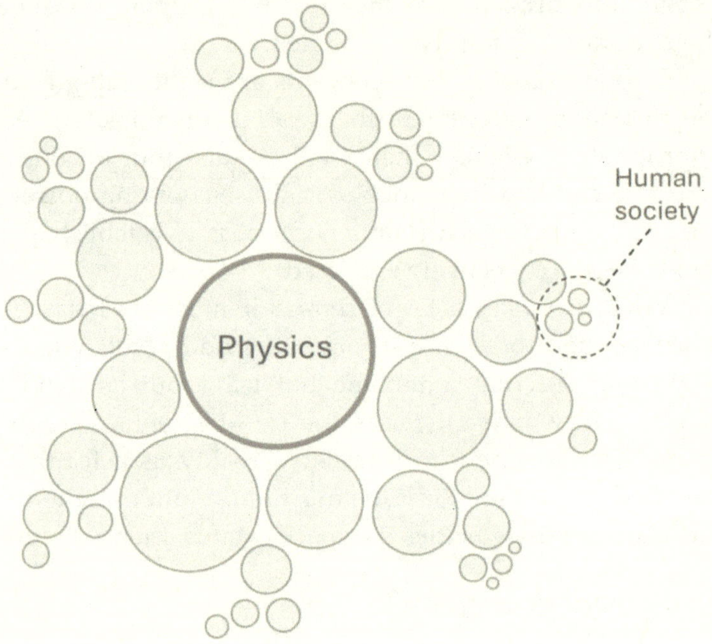

Figure 1, the worldview of physics.

It's strictly true that the second world war was a vast number of elementary particles moving in a rather complicated pattern, but that's not a way to describe it that we find meaningful. WW2 wasn't non-physical, but neither is it a suitable object of study for physicists.

Conversely, to the constructionist, the ground is everyday human experience. Rather than adopting science's view from nowhere it centers the perspective of a human being in a social milieu. Every person's internal reality is a stew of facts and values, of objects and agents, of causes, functions, purposes, expectations and possibilities, rights, responsibilities, blame, virtue, vice, hierarchies, judgments, friends and foes. These internal "realities" are created by and in turn take part in (re)creating and maintaining the norms, habits and practices that constitute the social order.

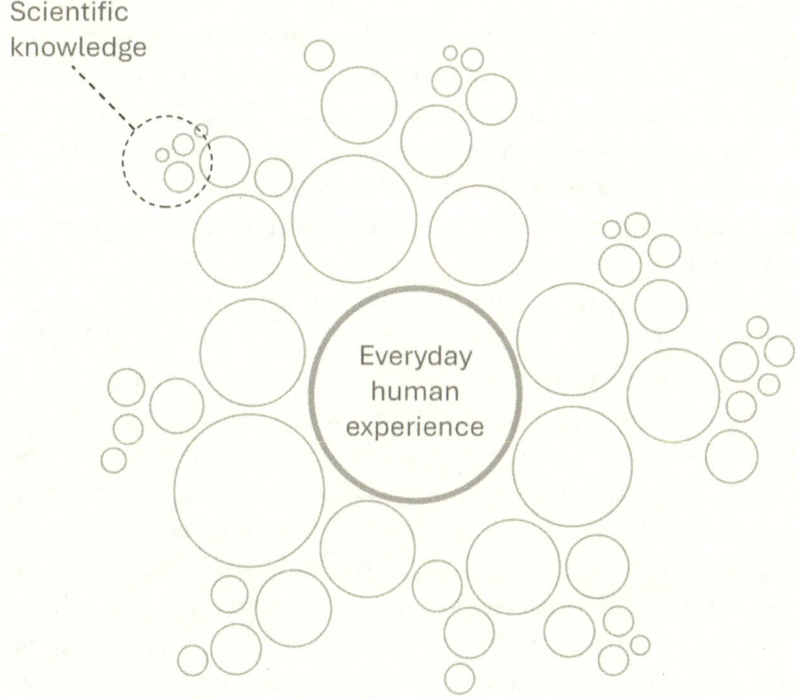

Figure 2, the worldview of constructionism.

Taking normal experience as the starting point makes the rarefied, historically novel institution of science merely one peculiar outgrowth on the periphery of normal human "knowledge"-creating processes. As such, its output gets described the same way as everything else that passes for knowledge. But just like physics becomes less useful when applied to human society, the constructionist model is less applicable to "knowledge" where there are mechanisms set up to make it actually represent reality correctly, i.e. where the features that their perspective rounds down to insignificance becomes big enough to be important, even dominant.

The messy middle

This is relatively easy to see at the ends of the spectrum, but the real action is in the middle. Concepts play dual roles, referring to material reality on the one hand and regulating human behavior and relations on the other. Some concepts (like "hydrogen") lie at one end and are scientists' typical objects of study, while others (like "capitalism") lie at the other and are social theorists' typical objects of study. Between these extremes is a stretch of disputed territory, to which both scientists and social theorists bring methods and habits appropriate for their own end.

To pick an example smack in the middle between "concrete physical phenomenon" and "concept regulating human social behavior": *gender*. There are two stories being told, with each side looking at the middle from opposite ends and seeing different things. The scientific realist says that gender, as in "the concepts representing masculinity and femininity with associated attributes", are to be understood as depictions of average sex differences as natural phenomena[9]. The constructionist, however, thinks they are to be understood as formed by social processes—not mere observation—to regulate behavior and thereby *create* the sex differences they are said to depict.

Note how this creates a *factual* disagreement over what is actually true about sex differences out of a *philosophical* divide over whether material objects or concepts are the basic units of reality. It can be funny when people learn to parrot these slogans without understanding the philosophical and methodological background behind their use. A coworker of mine once said "don't you know that the sexes are social constructs?" to get a rise out of me. I asked him what it meant and he said "that they're just something we made up". I didn't have the presence of mind to say anything better than it being a lot more complicated than that, but I should have asked him why he didn't simply say that then. He didn't say that the sexes are just something we made up because he, like everyone else, knows it's not true. What is true is that the exact form of the *concepts* associated with maleness

---

[9] Or ultimately stemming from natural phenomena.

and femaleness are to some extent the contingent result of social processes. It's by confusing the two interpretations that the phrase becomes impactful.

That's not to say that philosophical and factual beliefs don't influence each other. They very much do! Our philosophical assumptions steer us towards making certain interpretations of evidence, finding certain things prima facie plausible or implausible, and more easily integrating certain ideas into our existing belief system. They also imply different norms of evaluation: for the scientific realist assuming that concepts in essence depict reality, claims should be evaluated by the accuracy of the depiction; for the constructionist, assuming that concepts in essence govern social relations, it's more pertinent to evaluate them by the manner in which they do this. Note finally that this sort of disagreement can't be settled by appealing to evidence and facts, because it is less about specific facts than it is about the validity of whole frameworks of understanding. Both sides have enough material to work with to produce reasonable yet one-sided accounts, which, by the nature of the frameworks they use, will magnify some facts and ignore others.

My knowledge subsumes yours

Who has explanatory authority over the messy middle? Without agreed-upon standards of dispute resolution, which distant academic fields do not have, disagreements deteriorate into power struggles. It seems impossible to make sense of the disordered animosity between scientists and constructionists over the nature of knowledge without thinking of it as a battle of rightful authority.

There's a scene in the sitcom *The Big Bang Theory* where Sheldon, a theoretical physicist, and Amy, a neurobiologist, argue about whose research is more fundamental. Sheldon says he studies the laws of the universe, which enable the existence of brains, so the answer is obviously his. Amy retorts that since his brain comes up with his theories, the content of his research is a result of brain function, which she studies—so her research subsumes his. The short exchange is played for laughs but is quite profound. It mirrors the situation between scientists and constructionists arguing over whether reality itself or our beliefs about it are more fundamental and which can account for the other.

Calling something socially constructed is primarily not a factual claim that can be true or false, but an exhortation to apply a certain perspective to it. It's a *normative* claim about what kind of explanatory stories we should tell about the thing in question, and who gets to tell them. Once you think of it as a matter of establishing legitimate authority, the mantras of the historians and sociologists of science and technology that I once read start to make more sense. My teachers were explicit that Science and Technology Studies had a corrective or even polemic mission to criticize what they called "technological determinism". That viewpoint, which isn't explicitly pushed by any scholars (I asked) supposedly claims that the nature of scientific knowledge and technological systems is determined by a strictly internal logic of scientific and technological development, i.e. some scientific theories are just true, and some technological solutions are just better.

While such "technological determinism" is incomplete, which they did demonstrate even to my satisfaction, treating it as nothing but an effigy to tear down and not as an equal half of a full, balanced account suggests a, for lack of a better word, *fundamental ideological opposition*, rather than a desire to improve an incomplete picture. The greatest crime of technological determinism, it seemed, was the implication that if science and technology are independent of social factors, then they exist outside the jurisdiction of humanist scholars. A notably large proportion of this scholarship consisted of various repetitions and rearticulations of the general claim that technology was "systemic" and that technological systems were "inextricably" tied to the social and political conditions of their creation and the social habits around their use. "The seamless web" was a central phrase, and with it they were eager to establish that science and technology could not legitimately be considered in isolation, evaluated by their own internal standards. Putting the core idea to productive use pursuing further, more complete understanding of the mechanics of technological development often seemed less of a priority than simply hammering it home.

Academic conflict surely *could've* been softened by a better understanding of the assumptions, interests, and interpretative habits on the other side. My professor wasn't entirely wrong in his one-sentence dismissal of the Science Wars as scientists simply misunderstanding constructionists. The pro-science faction was indeed quick to judge, mistook their own interpretation for the intended meaning, and exhibited an ungenerous defensiveness and poor understanding of how standards of good scholarship differ between the sciences and the humanities. But it wasn't all innocent mistakes. Those on the other side have often seemed less than interested in avoiding these misunderstandings. Those following in Berger and Luckmann's footsteps did not take the same care to point out that omitting the quotes around "reality", "knowledge" was purely a stylistic choice. Once you don't have to make that distinction every time, it's easy to forget it and pretend that there really is no meaningful difference between a concept and the thing it represents. In fact, like when my colleague talked about gender, such rhetoric often relies on precisely that confusion to sound interesting and meaningful.

Let's look at that quote again.

> language does not mirror reality; rather, it constitutes [creates] it.

It refers to "reality" twice, the second time by "it" at the end. If it both times referred to "reality" quoted, as Berger and Luckmann used it, it wouldn't say much of anything:

> language does not mirror collectively endorsed belief; rather it constitutes [creates], collectively endorsed belief.

And we already know that if it meant unquoted both times it'd be magical nonsense:

> language does not mirror objective physical reality; rather, it constitutes [creates], objective physical reality

We're supposed to take it to mean unquoted reality the first time and quoted "reality" the second.

> language does not mirror objective physical reality; rather, it constitutes [creates], collectively endorsed belief

It is true that language does not straightforwardly mirror objective physical reality, but by deceptively using "reality" in two different senses you're pretending at a profound revelation—that reality itself is actually nothing more than collectively endorsed belief—with only the mundane observation that we often take accepted representations of reality for reality itself.

Why would you do this? It's not meant to tell us a truth (which is important but would be far easier to comprehend if expressed differently), but to establish a certain meaning of "reality" above another, and with it grant social theory authority above science. It's surreptitiously reengineering a concept to establish dominance for a particular belief system, something we might call "competitive sensemaking".

Alright, I'm convinced: sometimes claiming to be correct *is* a power play. Hacking suggests that while Berger and Luckmann did nothing wrong, some of their followers abandoned their honesty and caution exactly because cheating just a little bit with words offered a way to get one over on scientists, and the paradigm thus attracted people who wanted to do just that. Hacking:

> What is true is that many science-haters and know-nothings latch on to constructionism as vindicating their impotent hostility to the sciences. Constructionism provides a voice for that rage against reason.

> And many constructionists do appear to dislike the practice and content of the sciences.

Using the same word for related but different things, by metaphor or extension, is an essential part of language. It would not work without it. But it can be abused, and frequently is, to strategically alter the commonly accepted meanings of words. Once you start taking note of it in everyday rhetoric, you'll realize how astoundingly common it is. You'll notice how it is in fact the standard way to do rhetoric, as opposed to the logic of formal debate. Making awareness of this into second nature for the educated public is essential to improved understanding of disagreement.

Where we go from here

If you're not passionate about the philosophy of social constructionism, this first chapter may have been a lot to get through. I chose to start with it because this single case study touches on most ideas to be covered in the rest of the book (in fact, I recommend rereading it once you've finished). It shows the importance of the ambiguity of language and how it both causes honest confusions and gets used strategically. It also shows how there are two ways we evaluate ideas: on the one hand it matters whether something is true, and on the other hand it matters what it *does* as a collectively endorsed belief. Which aspect should take precedence in a given case is a major source of disagreement.

It shows how we simplify to make sense of the world when we can't represent it in full detail. Some things get focused on, magnified and put center stage, while others get sidelined, minimized and ignored. Such frameworks are optimized to work in a particular setting but are often applied elsewhere, with mixed results. And we risk—as constructionists are eager to point out—confusing the stories they produce for reality itself. It further serves as an example of how difficult it can be to navigate complex disagreements that are not just about the truth of a fact, or the desirability of an outcome, but where no critical point of dispute can be identified, focused on, and discussed because the disagreement is distributed throughout a whole system of beliefs, interests, judgments, priorities, and implicit philosophical commitments that we struggle to articulate.

As we move further into the 21st century, in an era of social media, filter bubbles, ideological inoculation, and not just alternative facts but alternative systems of sensemaking, philosophically complex academic controversies that laypeople didn't need to concern themselves with in the past, become more and more the model for navigating ordinary debates.

Chapter 2

Popular Erisology

Everything that needs to be said has already been said. But since no one was listening, everything must be said again.

— André Gide

The first chapter threw us in at the deep end. Well done for getting through it—it's the heaviest lifting you'll be asked to do. Now it's time to back up a little and talk about what it meant and why we're here.

What is "erisology"?

This book is about providing us with an improved *popular erisology,* which means conventional wisdom (popular) about how disagreement works (erisology). "Erisology" means "the study of disagreement" and comes from the name of the Greek goddess of discord, Eris, mostly known for smuggling in a golden apple labeled "for the fairest" to a wedding, making the goddesses turn on each other over who gets it. "Disagreement" refers to both the *process of disagreement,* i.e. arguing and other ways to assert and express beliefs that may be in conflict with those of others, and the *phenomenon of disagreement,* the mere fact that people have different beliefs, values and opinions, make different judgments, and react differently to things.

I made the word up back in 2015, and the short explanation is that I needed it for a story. I had a plan for a novel where one of the main characters was a grad student in an academic field dedicated to exactly the idiosyncratic, loosely connected collection of ideas on science, language, philosophy, politics, and the mind that I found important and interesting. This didn't exactly correspond to any existing body of knowledge—or at least it was easier to make up a fake academic field than trying to represent a real one correctly. The subject around which it was possible to unite most of these ideas and turn them into something resembling a coherent whole turned out to be "disagreement". Thus: the fictional discipline of "erisology".

I never wrote the novel. Instead I wrote a blog, exploring the same topics in essay form[10]. Nevertheless, the label "erisology" stuck around, because I couldn't find a better one. Did I write about philosophy? Yes. Language? Yes. Politics? Yes. Rhetoric? Yes. Sociology, economics, and psychology? Informed a lot by the statistics, data analysis, programming and narrative crafting that I do for a living? Yes, to all of those. Did I write about them "orthodoxly", taking care to situate them within these fields? No, I was playing pick and choose. But coherently.

None of this mattered, of course. I was just thinking out loud, writing to an empty room. But people liked it. My readership grew in fits and starts; I got hits, shares, Twitter followers, and invitations to some podcasts. It was great. However, as things got more serious, my idle musings got taken more seriously than had I expected. When the article *Erisology: The Science of Arguing About Everything* appeared in *The Atlantic* in spring 2019 I was pleased for the most part—getting written up like this in a serious magazine was exciting! The title did concern me, as I had never called or considered erisology a *science* (if anything it's a branch of the humanities). Part of how it was presented, a lot of which was my fault because of how I had expressed myself carelessly, made some believe I was saying that disagreement and argumentation hadn't been studied by any academic field, and that my playful fantasy that the discipline I had once imagined as part of a fictional story would be real, amounted to a serious, thought-through proposal to the academic community. As a result of

[10] I called that "Everything Studies" instead of "Erisology" to give myself more flexibility, but erisology turned out to be the main topic.

some unpleasant fallout from that, I'm taking some extra care to explain things now.

There's plenty of erisology in the world, it's just spread out across many disciplines and not called that[11]. No known field, as far as I can see, study *only* erisology and *all* of erisology, so a new word is justified. For a non-exhaustive list of relevant disciplines: *philosophers* study concepts, definitions and knowledge, *rhetoricians* study argumentation, *political scientists* study opinions, *psychologists* study thought and feeling, *historians* study beliefs and ideas through time and *anthropologists* study their variations in space; *cognitive scientists* and *machine learning researchers* study the nature of intelligence, *sociologists* study the social dynamics of shared beliefs, *programmers* create their own worlds that partially represent ours, *statisticians* study how to properly form beliefs from experience, *economists* study the incentives we're under when we do so, and *evolutionary biologists* can tell us why they are incentives in the first place.

Taking insights belonging to these fields, plus others, and internalizing them is necessary to understand something as deceptively simple as how and why people think differently. In theory, all relevant research, existing and merely possible, could be brought together, in full detail, in a single book. It would have to be a very large book, taking decades to write and far too long to read. Therefore it is not *this* book. This is my mild guess at what a for-dummies summary of that hypothetical book's key points would look like.

It's inescapable that it will mean biting off more than I can chew. The following 370-ish pages contain ideas that whiz by in a paragraph but deserve—and has, elsewhere—book length treatments. That is by design.

"Popular" how?

Imagining that "erisology" were a recognized field doesn't mean wishing there were a group of a dozen scholars that share an email

[11] Some have told me that the field already exists, but since they gave different answers to exactly which one it is I don't think they were right.

list, write dense, theoretical papers and get drunk together at conferences twice a year to forget their irritation over how nobody in their family understands what they do. For all I know that may even exist already, which is part of the problem. Narrow specialist fields are not of much use if they keep their knowledge to themselves.

Aiming at "*popular* erisology" is my way of saying that this book isn't designed to fit into specialist discourse. It will not have the customary detail, it will not subject you to a deluge of citations, and it will not contain a serious attempt at rigor. I will not even try to convince you of many facts, because I don't think that's what we most need for a better popular understanding of disagreement. The point is that there should be a commonly understood word for "knowledge about disagreement" the way there is one for knowledge about living things ("biology"), knowledge about language ("linguistics"), about the mind ("psychology"), about the properties and behavior of substances ("chemistry"), about the management of limited resources ("economy"), about mapping the Earth ("geography"), and about what we can see in the sky ("astronomy"). These are taught in schools, they have their own sections in well-stocked bookstores, and most know *something* about them. If nothing else, people know these bodies of knowledge exist and that they concern something about which it is possible and worthwhile to learn.

There's nothing new to the world in here. There are no groundbreaking findings that would make a specialist sit up straight and pay attention. There are only things most of us already understand on some level and will recognize when pointed out to us, but don't think about and have not put together into a whole. I want to lift truths plain to see up into conscious awareness, all at once, light a spark to get them to react with each other and fuse into a mental framework through which a lot of confusing and unwieldy disagreements line up to make perfect sense.

Consider this book an installation program for the mind. It establishes a particular way of looking at differences in ideas, the mechanics of arguing, and the relationship between concepts, words and the world. It's supposed to become a set of active ideas in your mind.

Passive ideas come only when asked, like tools that you go and get when you think of using them. They're used rarely, intentionally, and selectively, and if you don't use them often you'll eventually forget them like those trigonometric operations you may have learned in school once. Active ideas speak without being spoken to first. We "use" them without effort or intention, because they become part of perception. "Once you hear it, you see it everywhere" or "you can't unsee it" describe the experience of acquiring active ideas. I've had a few people say this about some of my articles and I consider it the highest praise.

This means there will be some repetition, as I describe the same things from slightly different directions. It's on purpose, in service of building a sturdy structure from layering, like papier-mâché.

A generalist's passion project

In medicine it's said that generalism is a specialty too, and I think the same applies to disagreement. I'm not a professional philosopher, rhetorician or psychologist, but for years I *have* been a professional at something else: diving into a topic to learn the most important things, find something meaningful to say about it, and present the result to non-specialists in a comprehensible, appealing package.

Such cultivated generalism especially helps if your topic of discussion is *difference*—which is what disagreement boils down to. When you're interested in so many things that you spend your life moving from topic to topic, consuming the basics until the cost-benefit ratio of continuing starts to drop, and then move on like a swarm of non-destructive locusts, you'll sample a lot of thought. Moving through physics, language, economics, philosophy, evolution, physics, mathematics, art, music, religion, social science, astronomy, history, and architecture, you notice how they all work in different ways, and how the controversies within each break down along different but related lines. You notice how they use different terms, have different ways of representing knowledge, are interested in different problems, valorize different feelings and have different standards for success. You develop an eye for difference.

Not only can ideas be so interestingly different, but so can people! You can have a meeting at work discussing the time table for the latest deliverable whatevers, where one person believes the world was created by God 6000 years ago and it's paramount that we resist sin with our divine spark of free will, while another believes the world is made of atoms and our brains simply follow the laws of physics, and a third is trying to manifest loving vibrations from the great pan-universal Mother Spirit. How we can navigate the same everyday world and seem normal to each other with drastically different beliefs about the fundamental nature of reality is nothing short of astonishing. It's as if there were different types of cars, some regular ones made of metal, some entirely marshmallows and rubber bands, others running on little gnomes carrying clipboards, and they all still somehow looked and worked just like regular cars.

Other people's minds are foreign countries. We get news reports from there, but we don't always understand them. Not really. We don't know their history, their customs, their core beliefs, or their political system. They surprise us with how differently they function and react. You hate my favorite movie; that book you love bores me to tears; that to me perfect example of everything that is wrong with society elicits nothing but a shrug from you, in turn provoking anger and frustration in me.

There's a deep joy in clearing up messy disagreements. It involves figuring out other people's underlying mental architectures that they themselves take for granted enough to be unwilling or unable to articulate in communication. You have to look for clues and draw careful, tentative conclusions about how another's mind is constructed: which ideas are connected and which aren't, what supports and justifies what, and so forth. It's like being a detective.

The book is organized into seven parts. The first introduces some overarching ideas about disagreements: why and how they are complicated and in my view often dysfunctional, and what we should try to do about it. The second goes into language, and how the ambiguity of language and its relationships to reality introduces an instability in the meaning of seemingly simple phrases. After that, part three is about how that instability is the substrate for our fights over the right to dictate our shared understanding of the world.

Part four moves the discussion to the stories we tell each other and ourselves about reality—and easily confuse for said reality. Part five takes a detour to discuss how minds can be different and the critical role this plays in disagreements. In part six, we talk about the deep influence of politics and coalitional instincts on our thinking, and the social and psychological forces that make us act dishonestly and uncharitably towards others. The final, seventh part introduces the concept coming from my blog that's had the most influence and spread, for better and worse.

Before moving on: there's a voice in my head that makes me want to qualify everything I say. Being wrong or overconfident embarrasses me deeply and I make my claims weaker and harder to criticize by using tic phrases like "most of", "some of", "in my opinion", "it seems like", "apparently", "I suspect", or "you could say that...". I've forced myself to remove *most* of them to save you all from tedium and instead put them here. So, whenever you notice something overstated, simplified, or a little strong that you want to criticize for stupidity and arrogance, please refer back to this section. Thank you.

I think, I think, I think, I think, I think, I think, I think, I think, in my opinion, in my opinion, in my opinion, in my opinion, in my opinion, in my opinion, in my opinion, in my opinion, some of, some of, some of, some of, some of, some of, some of, some of, some of, some of, most of the time, most of the time most of the time, most of the time, on average, on average, on average, on average, on average, on average, on average, on average, on average, on average, on average, on average, often, often, often, often, often, often, often, often, often, often, often, often, for the most part, for the most part, for the most part, for the most part, for the most part, for the most part, for the most part, somewhat, somewhat, somewhat, somewhat, somewhat, somewhat, somewhat, partly, partly, partly, partly, partly,

partly, partly, you could say, you could say, you could say, you could say, you could say, you could say, you could say, you could say, you could say, you could say, you could say, reasonably, reasonably, reasonably, reasonably, reasonably, reasonably, reasonably, reasonably, reasonably, reasonably, reasonably, sort of, sort of, sort of, sort of, sort of, sort of, sort of, sort of, sort of, sort of, sort of, partly, partly, partly, partly, partly, partly, partly, partly, partly, partly, I suspect that, I suspect that, I suspect that, I suspect that, I suspect that, I suspect that, I suspect that, I suspect that, I suspect that, I suspect that, seems like, seems like, seems like, seems like, seems like, seems like, seems like, seems like, seems like, seems like, seems like, apparently, apparently, apparently, apparently, apparently, apparently, apparently, possibly, possibly, possibly, possibly, possibly, possibly, possibly, possibly, possibly, possibly, possibly, possibly, could be, could be, could be, could be, could be, could be, could be, could be, could be, could be, could be, you could say, you could say, you could say, you could say, you could say, you could say, you could say, you could say, you could say, some would say, some would say, some would say, some would say, some would say, some would say, some would say, some would say, some would say, likely that, likely that, likely that, likely that, likely that, likely that, likely that, likely that, likely that, likely that, likely that, mostly, mostly, mostly, mostly, mostly, mostly, mostly, mostly, mostly, mostly, mostly, mostly, mostly, sometimes, sometimes, sometimes, sometimes, sometimes, sometimes, sometimes, sometimes, sometimes, could be, could be, could be, could be, could be, could be, could be, maybe, perhaps, to me.

Chapter 3

Dysfunctional Disagreement

We're all islands shouting lies to each other across seas of misunderstanding.

— Rudyard Kipling

Public discourse is how societies learn what they believe and what they want. I'm going to go out on a limb and say that it's therefore important that it works well. To work well is to lead us to a shared understanding of the world that is accurate, and that aggregates our individual values and wants into a similarly shared moral order where everyone's preferences are represented fairly. Too bad then, that public discourse is rife with dysfunction.

To disagree well, parties need a shared understanding of what the disagreement is about, what the positions are, and why. Vigorous, even heated, debate is healthy, but ideas must be accurately communicated and evaluated, or it becomes dysfunctional. Ever since I started writing about the issue in 2015, I've tried for a simple, clear definition of dysfunctional disagreement. Attempts include:

—The people involved are further apart from each other in the end than they were in the beginning.

—The nature of the disagreement, or the nature of either party's position, is itself part of the disagreement.

—The disagreement is at least in part an artifact of at least one party misinterpreting the other.

The best single sentence definition I've been able to find is that a disagreement is dysfunctional if it contains misrepresentation that at least one party is not trying to correct. This may be for many reasons, including but not limited to ignorance, laziness, or strategy.

Misrepresentation has this central role because collective reasoning is a system through which information and ideas are transmitted and in that process get evaluated according to shared values[12]. When ideas are distorted as they move from person to person, collective reasoning lacks a stable object and cannot work— it's like trying to cook with ingredients constantly transfigured.

"Misrepresentation" is to be interpreted broadly, covering anything that changes the meaning of an idea as it travels and gets expressed, re-expressed, and re-presented. It includes:

—paraphrasing others' beliefs in ways they don't agree with
—responding to something else than what was meant
—sowing confusion about what is being claimed and what isn't
—changing the subject or pretending it's something it's not
—giving different reasons for one's own beliefs that the real ones
—obfuscating one's own views to make them harder to criticize
—pretending things are clear-cut and obvious when they are not
—assuming agreement on beliefs that are not in fact agreed on

Just as it's damaging when ideas don't have stable enough meanings to be discussed effectively, it's further damaging when misrepresentation creates false, exaggerated, or distorted images of what others believe, fueling anger, anxiety, polarization and delegitimization, destroying the norms of peaceful exchange upon which liberal democracy is built.

I realize this list can be used to call almost anything dysfunctional, and I agree. Dysfunctional disagreement is the norm, the same way openly oppressive and corrupt government used to be the norm (and still is in many parts of the world). But that doesn't mean it always has to be.

It's not about abolishing conflict. People can be angry with each other and even hate each other without it being dysfunctional, as

[12] This set of shared values are at the same time constantly re-evaluated by the same process.

long as they are angry with accurate understandings of each other and recognize when their values and judgments are subjective. Straightforwardly fighting over valuable resources, like warlords or street gangs do, can be gruesome but is not dysfunctional in this specific sense, since the terms of the conflict are clear.

The private and social purposes of public discourse

I've been criticized for calling discourse dysfunctional (or a "failure") on the grounds that people have all kinds of goals they're trying to achieve by taking part, and they may be successful at those despite falling short of my ideal. You might just want to vent your frustrations, gain popularity among your friends, experience the joy of exercising power, silence others by making it unpleasant for them to express themselves, or make a quick buck from engagement. If you're getting what you want out of it, who am I to call it failure and dysfunction? It's true that "dysfunctional" is not a scientific term, what it's supposed to refer to isn't an objective fact, and there is considerable philosophical debate around what it means for something to have a *function*. But leaving that to one side in the interest of avoiding catastrophic derailment, let's start here: when we have a situation where one person says something and then another answers by addressing something different from what the first person meant, then it's reasonable to construe it as "something going wrong".

If I thought the problem was that people were trying their best to communicate in good faith but failing at it, I'd be significantly more clueless than I am. It's that the social purpose of public discourse is something over and above the private purposes people have when they engage in it. Saying that nothing's wrong because people aren't failing at what they're trying to do is like saying there's nothing wrong with there being trash everywhere on the street because people aren't trying to put their litter in the bin.

Think of the "marketplace of ideas" metaphor. The private purpose of a firm is to make a profit, while its social purpose—i.e. the reason the institution of the firm is good idea—is to create value for consumers. Markets work well when the pursuit of profit results in the creation of such value. This requires certain conditions: firms must obey the rules and not defraud their customers, consumers must have accurate information about what they're buying, they must be able to buy from someone else if they prefer it, and externalities—side effects on third parties such as environmental destruction—must be small enough to not offset the value created. The better these conditions hold, the better markets work.

The social purpose of public disagreement is to learn how the world works, create cultural self-knowledge, evaluate ideas, build trust and understanding, to enable what most people consider positive change and prevent what most people consider negative change. That is, *to build a shared, legitimate understanding of reality that combines accurate beliefs and agreed-upon goals.* This also requires certain conditions, such as ideas being represented and processed with stability and precision. When those conditions don't hold and the desired results can't be achieved, it counts as failure on a social level the same way corruption or anticompetitive practices in business do, even when they are successful at benefiting those who engage in them.

There are two contexts in which people work hard to have functional disagreements. *Scientists* share a goal to gain accurate, reliable knowledge, and clear and precise language is required for a scientific discipline to be able to specify its questions enough to resolve them with reference to evidence. A discipline that cannot do this is dysfunctional. When the goal of accurate knowledge is sacrificed for personal gain or political power it is a threat to the health of the discipline, and if the reliability of its results is compromised by widespread adherence to conflicting goals, and this isn't effectively policed by practitioners, then it is also dysfunctional. Secondly, *people in close personal relationships* also have habits that foster functional disagreement. Because they are personally intertwined they feel obligated to treat each other with respect and consideration, to listen and make an effort to understand where the other is coming from, and to treat the other's interests as legitimate. Relationships where people do not do this are dysfunctional.

While public discourse isn't an exact analogue to any of the two, I will say that insofar as it is missing *both* qualities that make scientific and personal disagreements work, it is dysfunctional.

Disagreement systems

By this standard it's easy to see how the "Science Wars" example in chapter one was a failure. Hostility was a factor, but it was the lack of a shared vocabulary, meaning the disagreement couldn't be pinned down, that allowed hostility to get the upper hand over academic norms. The issue couldn't be boiled down to a single, clearly defined proposition that we can put on a table between us and start listing arguments for and against.

Our working memory is famously limited to holding around 7 items at a time, and whatever the equivalent limit is for socially shared attention, it's clearly not higher. We can lock eyes on single pieces of the puzzle, but we are unlikely to understand them without considering how they relate to everything *not* currently under the spotlight. Maybe it gives us the wrong idea to call it a "disagreement", because it's not—not in the way the word is normally used. It's more like a "disagreement *system*", analogous to the distinction between "belief" and "belief system". We have a disagreement when we have different beliefs, and we have a disagreement system when we have different belief systems.

With them you have to do what I did in chapter one, but more thoroughly: work through the parts one by one, doing detective work to uncover and articulate the hidden structure of the internal belief systems and motivations that create our reactions of agreement or disagreement with individual claims, and then work out how those pieces interact to create those reactions.

We need to understand that a disagreement system is a *system* and make the necessary adjustments to our attitudes and habitual ways of interpreting what we see and hear. We cannot assume to know what each part means to the other until we know what they all mean. We need to keep pulling at threads, with curiosity, charity and care, until we've made sense of each part and how they relate to each other. Then we stand a chance of actually communicating meaning correctly—in other words, understanding what was said roughly how it was meant.

Theory escapes academia

The obvious question becomes: why? What good is it to acquire these habits and skills? Why is it worth doing all that work just to gain a better understanding of abstruse disagreement systems between practitioners of different academic schools and disciplines? Berger and Luckmann suggest it isn't:

> To exaggerate the importance of theoretical thought in society and history is a natural failing of theorizers. It is then all the more necessary to correct this intellectualistic misapprehension. The theoretical formulations of reality, whether they be scientific or philosophical or even mythological, do not exhaust what is "real" for the members of a society. Since this is so, the sociology of knowledge must first of all concern itself with what people 'know' as 'reality' in their everyday, non- or pre-theoretical lives. In other words, common sense 'knowledge' rather than 'ideas' must be the central focus for the sociology of knowledge. It is precisely this 'knowledge' that constitutes the fabric of meanings without which no society could exist.

To simplify their dense, 1960s academic prose: ordinary people do not look at the world the way academics do. Theorizers love abstract concepts and think a lot about how they relate to each other, while normal people have commonsensical, concrete beliefs. Thus, analyzing systems of abstractions is inappropriate for understanding how most people think. We could be wasting our time if features of academic disagreement systems—deep philosophical commitments that are difficult to articulate, separate communities with their own standards and priorities, temperamental differences in intellectual style, and fighting for the privilege of being able to assert your preferred account of the contested and have it be accepted—are not relevant to ordinary public conversation.

Berger and Luckmann were probably right at the time, but a lot has happened since 1966. For starters, more people are university educated and thus accustomed to abstraction and theory as the standard mode of comprehension. Schools emphasize abstract reasoning over rote learning more than they used to. Research and academic texts are, in general, even for non-students, far more accessible. The volume of books and other popular materials on science, philosophy, history, almost anything you can think of, aimed at the general public, has exploded. Non-academic works on business, self-help, politics—again, almost anything—use the trappings of academic research like jargon and abstract theoretical constructs.

Maybe, in the 1960s, we did get most of our worldview by directly experiencing reality, by interacting with people around us, and through limited media exposure. What Berger and Luckmann called "paramount reality" we call "IRL" or "meatspace" to separate it from the increasingly primary online world, and it's looking less and less paramount by the day.

There's now unfathomably more information coming at us in the form of second- or third-hand pre-interpreted abstractions and generalizations[13]. In a world of information overload, sensemaking is an industry by itself, creating stories, models and belief systems that lie right in between everyday common sense and the conceptual cathedrals of academia. As a consequence, belief systems that battle it out in today's arenas of public discourse are heavily influenced by academic-style complexity, and communication across them suffers from many of the same dysfunctions as interactions between academic disciplines.

---

[13] The philosopher Jean Baudrillard noted this back in 1981, in *Simulacra and Simulation*. He has *not* become wrong since then.

Ullica Segerstråle, a chemist turned sociologist of science, published *Defenders of the Truth: The Sociobiology Debate* in 2001, a book-length treatment of controversies around E.O. Wilson's *Sociobiology* from 1975. An omnibus on evolved animal behavior, it also speculated about applying the same evolutionary logic to humans, thus setting off a series of heated debates over the role of biology in social behavior that continue to this day. Segerstråle spends several hundred pages carefully working out what motivated the various players and factions: their assumptions, their beliefs, and their sometimes opposing but often merely independent moral concerns. Her exemplary approach serves as my model for how complex disagreements should be understood.

When explaining how a circus of misunderstanding, misrepresentation and bad faith could result, Segerstråle emphasizes that the parties involved agreed on so little that they could not communicate effectively, and both the drive towards internal consistency and the social dynamics of group conflict made the problem worse.

> [T]he two academic camps that had formed on the basis of the IQ and sociobiology controversies effectively came to live in two different worlds of factual knowledge, taken-for-granted assumptions, and attitudes towards such things as the media. Basic social psychological theory can make some predictions as to what will typically happen in a case of such pre-existing interpretive frameworks. Any incoming information will be accommodated in line with existing convictions; various well-known cognitive defense mechanisms will be operating to effectively protect the members of each camp from serious challenges to their existing 'knowledge'; and within each camp, members will reinforce one another's beliefs.

If this situation was ever peculiar to academia, it isn't any more. Our contact with the world was always mediated by other people, but it used to be limited by geography. This had a moderating effect, since such local communities had somewhat equal representation of different personalities, temperaments, and pathologies. Social media, with its algorithmic feeds and hyper-niche communities, reflect our own sense of reality back to us by connecting us with those who differ from the average in just the same ways we do. The resulting subcultures are full of unnaturally similar people, armed with abstraction and generalization powers far stronger and more habitual than in times past, and they have far larger repositories of facts, examples, and anecdotes at their command when building their shared belief systems.

Such ideological bubbles resemble academic fields in that people self-select into them based on interests, assumptions, skills, and priorities, peers validate and reinforce each other's ideas, build on what others have said, making ever higher towers of abstraction that make communication more efficient among the faithful but also more context-dependent and laden with assumptions. The mechanisms are the same whether it's neoliberals, furries, feminists, MAGA-ists, cryptocurrency evangelists, transgender activists, ethnonationalists, AI doomers, or almost any other group.

The internet is to ideology what the rainforest is to biology: a space so rich and nutritious that evolution, freed from constraints, goes crazy and creates bizarre, hyperspecialized creatures. It's why the phrase "very online" has come to mean ideologically unhinged. A classic 4chan post puts the difference crudely but succinctly:

Before internet

>i want to fuck toasters
>don't be a fucking retard
>grow up

After internet

>i want to fuck toasters
>google
>find a community with 1000+ members about people wanting to fuck toasters
>fuck up your life

As ideas and tropes coming through the porous borders of hyperniche communities play a growing role in public discourse, Segerstråle's approach to making sense of an academic controversy becomes more and more relevant to public discourse as a whole.

Conventional wisdom is out of date

When we think of disagreement in a "classical" sense, we think of two people talking to each other in a back-and-forth dialogue. They might be friendly, they might not, but at least there is the possibility of communication between actual people, putting forth claims that can be discussed. In the current environment, dialogue between coherent, well-defined subjects is less the norm than musing, yelling or venting straight into a shapeless, cacophonic whirlwind where you're at once addressing yourself, no-one in particular, and partially real, partially imagined versions of loosely defined groups of friends and enemies.

In the culture war trenches we don't engage with others as people per se, but them reduced to avatars of constructed factions: "you people are like this", "another one of 'you' said that", "this is what your side always say" and so forth. We cast the other as a representative without their consent or even knowledge, making them play bit parts in a story with us as the hero. And they do the same to us.

Drawing a parallel between individual and collective thinking, this shift is like going from the thought pattern of a healthy, rational person to one characteristic of a schizophrenic. Our common sense understanding of how disagreement works has not kept up. When our differences can be articulated in simple, common-sense terms, you don't need to be proficient in careful philosophical analysis just to understand them. Communicating with people with completely different belief systems, however, is an unnatural situation, meaning our intuitions will lead us to assume we can skip straight to the settling of a disagreement without doing careful work to set it up it first.

It's well understood that our era is ideologically polarized, that public debate leaves a lot to be desired, and that our disagreement skills need an upgrade. It's less commonly argued that this requires more than just good will and better schooling in "debate" in the traditional sense—putting a proposition on the table and discuss it using clearly defined arguments understood by both parties, drawing on a mostly shared set of background assumptions. The more the situation deviates from this norm, the less sufficient our standards are. They're fine for a room of Roman senators debating whether to attack Carthage, because they are all the same guy. At least they are when compared to an evangelical Christian prepping for the apocalypse coming to blows with a blue-haired postdoc in Queer Studies on Reddit. What they're doing is not a "debate" like what the senators had.

Well-known, well-worn core concepts like the difference between facts and values, and logical fallacies like *no true Scotsman, appeal to authority, ad hominem, slippery slope* etc. are valuable but fall short when applied to conversations very different from the one-to-one, back-and-forth argumentation for which they were formulated. It does more harm than good to view something as a debate when the complications you just assume are already solved and round down to nothing in a debate setting are big enough to dominate the situation.

Formal debate was always an artifice, but an artifice that worked. Now it's losing relevance when public conversation is more natural, without artificial specificity and logic, and with social and personal factors playing key roles. We usually have such casual conversations with people we're friendly with and share many experiences and beliefs with. When those conditions are not met, and we're speaking to a "hostile alien" in ideological terms, with neither shared vocabulary nor investment in good relations, such loose conversation leads to collapse. We *need* an artifice, but formal debate isn't it. It solves a different problem.

I don't know exactly what our new artifice should be like. We're getting closer as insights and tools evolve towards up-to-date collective self-knowledge, but it's slow. This book is an attempt to take some of the scattered understanding and sketch out one possibility.

Chapter 4

The Postmodern Condition

Irony's singularly unuseful when it comes to constructing anything to replace the hypocrisies it debunks.

— David Foster Wallace[14]

Disagreements growing into disagreement systems is a symptom of the postmodern condition. That may not tell you much, because "postmodern" and "postmodernism" are confusing words that get thrown around without much care. However, the confusion isn't entirely a product of abuse. They refer to a family of genuinely vague, difficult ideas that gained prominence in the decades following the Second World War, manifesting differently in philosophy, social science, art, and politics. The *postmodern condition* is the state of being in a period of time characterized by, described by, and influenced by, postmodernism. We have been in it for decades now and its characteristics are only getting more pronounced.

The key to understanding postmodernism is right there in the name: post–*modernism*. It comes after and contrasts with *modernism*. What's modernism, then? Oversimplified history is risky, and before I begin, I should warn you about *caibuses*. *Caibus* is Latin for a pebble that's been rounded and smoothed by being repeatedly washed over by waves on a beach. Later it's come to refer to accounts of reality so simplified as to misrepresent the complexity of their subjects, while nonetheless being true enough to be of value. What we think of as general knowledge (of history, science, etc.) consists largely of cai-

[14] If postmodernism was a person.

buses, from school or popular literature. This is healthy, as they tend to be at the level of sophistication where we get the most understanding per effort and headspace.

Just like other kinds of data compression, making caibuses lowers quality and creates artifacts. The distortions are much worse than with images or sound because of the astronomical levels of compression involved, and specialists sneer at them for understandable reasons: only they perceive how serious the losses are and how caibuses make non-specialists (infuriatingly) overestimate how well they understand something because they read about it once. Since we can't be experts on everything, however, we must be comfortable with caibuses and accept that most of what we know is hard compression that doesn't tell the whole story[15].

A caibus about postmodernism

With that out of the way, here comes one: *post*modernism comes after modernism and is an extension of and reaction to it. Modernism in turn came after something else, which we for this purpose can call "premodernism". In the broadest of terms, this trio of words concerns what is taken for true and good in society during different historical stages in the west. That is, ideas that describe, govern, and constitute social reality—roles, obligations, expectations, institutions, "knowledge", and power. Before modernity, the social order and the nature of reality were considered one and the same, largely taken for granted and essentially religious. These truths were handed down to us by tradition[16]. We learned what was true and how things were supposed to be done, and we kept doing them that way because that was the order of things. The "isses" of the true and the "oughts" of the good were not separate but wrapped up into a complete system of factual and moral truths. While this is a simplification and not

[15] Before I present my caibus about postmodernism I should come clean: it isn't really Latin. It's an acronym for *Compressed And Inaccurate But Useful Story* and I made it up, but old Latin terms get more respect.

[16] That's what *tradition* means: "handing over".

what everyone thought, fully and all the time, this view had *hegemony*, meaning it was the socially dominant story that made sense of the world and governed people's lives.

Modernity upended it. From the Renaissance on, a series of technological, economic, and intellectual changes dismantled the traditional system. The printing press, the birth of science, the Enlightenment, and the industrial revolution changed the world, and our ways of understanding it changed as well. In turned out that the natural world could be systematically studied, understood, and eventually controlled and put in the service of mankind. With that, the social order also became the object of reason, critique, analysis, and eventually systematization and engineering. This brought us *progress*. Or rather, Progress! with a capital P and obligatory exclamation. Scientific advancement and the power unleashed by industry will remake the world! We can apply scientific analysis to find out how everything works and organize it Rationally and Correctly! It's amazing! And make no mistake: it *really was amazing*. It still is. But success breeds hubris, and there were in fact limits. Mistakes were made. We couldn't just calculate how to solve any problem. People weren't as malleable nor as rational as they would've had to be, for starters. As enamored with systematic planning as the midcentury west was, it did not create a Utopia. At the same time, early twentieth century philosophical attempts to put knowledge on firm ground by formalizing language and turning reason into logic, and science to a reliable step-by-step-process, had failed.

Enter postmodernism: the disillusion with, and critique of, the modernist project. It was less an ideology, a framework, or a system of thought than it was the rejection of ideologies, frameworks, and systems of thought. The 2014 article *The Millennial's Guide to Philosophy: Postmodernism* in *Primer Magazine* puts it as:

> Postmodernism, you have to remember, didn't grow out of a need to make sense of the world but out of a failure of the world to make sense. That might

> sound infuriatingly vague, and again, you wouldn't be wrong.

If modernity took from us an absolute divine order and substituted the power of science and reason, postmodernity took *that* away and substituted nothing[17]. Progress is not a given. Society resists planning. Humanity resists perfection. We can't formalize the scientific process to yield predictable results. Logic cannot give us certainty. Objective truth is a myth. Postmodernism is the idea that there is no one true belief system with legitimacy to dominate society. Not Christianity, not Science, not Marxist historical determinism. Nothing.

Shared reality in pieces: the curious case of the war on Christmas

Postmodernity is the era that lacks a dominant shared understanding of the world and society. Its culture is marked by subversion, decontextualization, and recombination of signs and meaning, as first-hand experience is increasingly displaced by culturally generated images—Berger and Luckmann's paramount reality getting less paramount. In the arts it manifests as a playful yet nihilistic ("ironic") mixing of styles, self-referentiality, breaking the fourth wall, and taking ele-

---

[17] That's the zoomed-out view. On the ground, this all came about through many detailed and technical critiques of earlier detailed and technical modernist thought. A lot of it had to do with language. During the 20th century, philosophy took a turn away from thinking of words as referring to objective reality and towards thinking of them in terms of relationships to each other. Instead of trying to pin down correct meanings of words and arrange them into a correct description of reality, as was the standard before, thinkers broadly construed as postmodern thought of them as tokens in social games. Signs, concepts, and categories form structures out of air, referring to nothing but a constantly shifting set of shared associations. Many postmodern works aim to reveal this "truth" (since postmodernism questions everything there's a lot of scare quoting involved), and show us how we're victims of illusory objectivity, by destabilizing and "unsettling" the meaning of terms and symbols, often by making them feel confusing, contradictory, alien, and weird.

ments out of their original contexts. In social life it means more and more conflict around what norms there should be and what we can expect from each other.

Like icebergs breaking off a glacier to float freely, pieces of taken-for-granted social reality are coming loose. Modernity did some to dislodge what felt fixed and stable as it reconstructed social reality to be held in place by reason, agreement, and scientific authority rather than the word of God, but it was postmodernity that delivered the coup de grâce by showing the failures of reason, taking agreement apart, and cutting scientific authority down to size.

It can be upsetting when things you could just rely on to be a certain way are no longer, and you find yourself thrown out from a comfortable existence where you are one with the world into one where everything is called into question[18]. Reactions vary depending on how much you liked things before and how great your psychological need for stability is. We could feel liberated, completely unconcerned, or gripped by profound dread all waking hours. Needless to say, when we don't understand the underlying condition we have different feelings about, it's hard to communicate.

The "War on Christmas" has faded in prominence as a culture war front compared to the early-to-mid-2010s, but it remains instructive for how controversies tend to go when there are several layers of philosophy between what is going on, what people are reacting to, and what they're literally saying. The story was: symbols of Christmas are disappearing from the public arena in the United States, as both government entities and corporations shy away from them in an effort to be politically correct. If you put a conspiratorial spin on it, you could say that Christmas is *intentionally* being removed from public life.

---

[18] It's fitting that perhaps the most famous among directly and aggressively postmodern-in-style works of fiction, namely *The Hitchhiker's Guide to the Galaxy*, starts off with having the Earth, that solid ground beneath our feet, literally vaporized, throwing the protagonist into an absurd universe where eventually the plot is lost.

To many, this was hysterical in the extreme. How can people be so deluded as to think that Christmas, this behemoth of holidays, is in any way threatened just because service workers are told to say "Happy Holidays" instead of "Merry Christmas"? It's unhinged. A Reddit thread asked "How can American Christians truly think there is a war on Christmas?" and attached a picture of an empty parking lot on Christmas Day. The implication being that if Christmas has the power to keep the mighty retail stores closed, it's hardly threatened. And it's not. To suggest that it's disappearing because major institutions are making an effort to be more welcoming to non-Christians[19] seems obviously absurd. But let's assume those who claim it are serious, and ask what they really mean. It *is* ridiculous to think that anyone is trying to make Christmas disappear altogether, but can there be a kernel of truth around which hyperbole has congealed? Another Reddit commenter hit on something when criticizing complaints about Starbucks removing Christmas imagery from their cups in favor of plain red ones back in 2015:

> The author doesn't seem to understand that things like this are meant to make people of all cultures feel welcome, not to make Christians feel unwelcome. There is absolutely nothing about the "war on Christmas" that is actually anti-Christian. Really, it's just opposed to a Christian monopoly on the holiday season.

There you go. Complainers aren't worried that Christmas will disappear, only that it will be removed from its position as a cultural default. When public institutions and corporations stop using Christmas symbols it means they no longer assume everyone observes it. And of course, since not everyone does it's only fair and right to not make that assumption. If you did it would exclude a lot of people. While it's not strictly false that there is *something* that some call "a

---

[19] Or non-Christmas-celebrators, I hasten to say as a non-Christian Christmas celebrator.

war on Christmas" going on , it shouldn't be called a "war". Christmas is just being asked to move over a bit to make room for few more around the table, that's not an act of war because it's not illegitimate aggression.

Or is it? What's legitimate is a matter of opinion, and there's no unambiguous definition of "aggression". Any action that has a negative effect on anybody or anything, however indirect, can be cast as such. By this logic, taking away Christmas's status as *social norm* on purpose is an act of aggression and a longer campaign is a war, even if there's no existential threat. Christmas, as the piece of social reality it is, exists not the way material objects like a rock, a bridge or Neptune exist, but the way abstract social entities do: by virtue of their role in coordinating behavior.

Social reality has the strongest, most solid existence when it is the unquestioned norm. Some traditions, observances, rituals or scripts are the practical equivalent of *common knowledge*—the things we assume others know, and they know we know they know, and so on. We *know them together*. The equivalent common *practices* are things that "everyone" does and that everyone knows everyone does and everyone knows everyone knows everyone does. We *do them together*.

When something in social reality becomes assumed-to-be-universal it goes through a qualitative shift, like water freezing to ice. Knowledge becomes common knowledge and practice becomes common practice. Keeping it solid does require some measure of authoritarianism: making sure nonconformists don't exist, or at least don't count. Common practices are more real the more people practice them, and more solid the fewer people *don't* practice them (and the more powerless and invisible such non-practitioners are).

Marginalization of exceptions as a mechanism for building solid shared realities is no longer considered acceptable vis-a-vis a growing set of minorities. That's a moral advance, but it has real consequences for the solidity of common knowledge and practices. Not everyone deals with this dissolution of norms well. We have evolved to live in small, close-knit groups with unified cultures, traditions and practices, where all knowledge is common knowledge and all practices are common practices. In these conditions, social reality is as rock solid as the physical world. We don't even understand there's a difference. Today's large, pluralistic societies are dramatically different, and only a few such features are fully solid.

When particular social practices cease to be the norm, the *unquestioned* norm, they're no longer quite as real. They still *exist,* sure, but not as *the same type of thing*[20]. To go from consensus to majority view, from hegemon to *primus inter pares,* from immovable background to foreground player, is a demotion in metaphysical status.

This account of how Christmas *can* be considered destroyed by losing its status as unquestioned common practice is inspired by a story told by the philosopher Owen Flanagan in his book *The Problem of the Soul: Two Visions of Mind and How to Reconcile Them* from 2002. It's about how the mind is understood by science and scientists on the one hand, and the lay public on the other. He argues that the popular concept of free will is incoherent, unfit for its purpose, and must be replaced by a version compatible with science. Understanding that the transition will be difficult, he compares it to what happened to the concept of "the Earth" after the Copernican revolution:

> Now imagine a forlorn defender of the Ptolemaic view who has accepted defeat saying to his therapist, "We have lost the earth. There is no earth. Earth doesn't exist." Is this guy out of touch with reality? Maybe not. There is a sense in which Ptolemaic astronomy and Copernican astronomy can be said not to mean the same thing by the term "earth" since they assign it radically different, indeed mutually inconsistent properties. According to the first view, the earth is stationary and the center of the universe. According to the second view, the earth is in double rotation - first, on its own axis, second, around the sun - and is not even the center of the solar system,

[20] We discuss what it means to exist as different types of things in chapter 9.

> let alone the universe. The therapist, if she is wise, will see what it is that legitimately worries the Ptolemaic. She might try to relieve his despair by saying, and saying truly, that there is still a sense in which the two views do mean the same thing by "earth," namely, "this heavenly body we call home." But the Ptolemaic may rightly respond that he meant much more by "earth" than this thin idea, this primitive core sense. By "earth" he meant this heavenly body we call home and that is stationary and lies at the center of the universe. Earth, in his sense, no longer exists. He sees this and even accepts that it is true, but it sickens his soul.

The Earth being the at the center of everything was much more than an astronomical detail in medieval cosmology. It was key to the whole moral order of the universe. The axis from lower to higher went from Hell in the bowels of the Earth, past the surface where we live, and up into the superior Heavens. Nowadays the idea of moral ranking being built into the physical structure of the world is just weird, and thus the Ptolemaic was right: his Earth, and the entire conception of reality of which it was a part, was indeed destroyed. Could he have claimed there was a "war on Earth" going on at this time? Doing so would be hyperbolic and inscrutable to outsiders, but not wrong, necessarily. It should be acknowledged that he was losing something, however necessary the loss was. And just like thinking that being in the center of the universe is what makes Earth *Earth*, modern Christians could think that without "a monopoly on the holiday season", Christmas isn't *Christmas*[21].

As postmodernity grows older, similar dissolution of the formerly solid is happening faster and faster, as the maintenance of norms

---

[21] Note that I don't mean that this is the full explanation for why anyone complains about "the war on Christmas", only that it's one way pushing for pluralism can count as aggression.

has become, well, not the norm. The conflicts around same-sex marriage were of this kind, ultimately about the nature of marriage and how much it can change while retaining its essential nature (i.e. still existing). Traditionally, marriage was about the mutual dependence of husband and wife rearing children together as the basis of the continuation of society, and deviations from this like childless/childfree couples were tolerated because they were easier to view as just minor, incidental exceptions that could be rounded off to have no effect on the essence. Increasing wealth, effective contraception, and more women supporting themselves economically have eroded the practical necessity of marriage. This, same-sex marriage, divorce liberalization, have been parts of a process of changing the essence of marriage into "social recognition of a committed relationship". To some conservatives, this has meant destruction of an institution that used to exist.

The legitimation of knowledge

Postmodernity means a lack of stability and solidity when it comes to words and meaning, and social norms and expectations. Most dramatically, however, it means a lack of stability of *knowledge*—and here we mean "knowledge" in the sociological sense of "that which is treated as knowledge". We realized that it wasn't as simple as "things are either objectively true or false, and Science and Expertise effectively and reliably sort one from the other", and we are now dealing with the consequences. Everything is up for questioning as authorities and experts are no longer trusted (sometimes justifiably, sometimes not). When we can't count on agreement even on what food is good for you, how many genders there are, whether we should get vaccinated, or who wins elections, it's not clear that knowledge-in-the-sociological-sense even *exists* anymore. Our collective mind no longer has coherent beliefs.

The philosopher Jean-Francois Lyotard brought the term "postmodern" into the lexicon in his 1979 book *The Postmodern Condition: A Report on Knowledge*. He gives us this caibus:

> Simplifying to the extreme, I define postmodern as incredulity toward metanarratives. /---/ The narrative function is losing its functors, its great hero, its great dangers, its great voyages, its great goal. It is being dispersed in clouds of narrative language.

Seeing the germ of today's obliteration of consensus, Lyotard homes in on *legitimation*. What process turns claims into "knowledge"? It can't be just science, he says, because not everything we consider knowledge comes about through science. Outside science, claims are legitimized differently because we're playing different *language games*. The term comes from the philosopher Ludwig Wittgenstein, responsible for the idea that words get their meaning not from what they point to in reality but from the roles they play in conversations with certain rules. For example, the essential nature of the knight piece in chess isn't defined by reference to actual knights, but by its set of legal moves in the context of the game. The same is true for words, Wittgenstein says.

The language game of science requires claims to be legitimized with evidence, reproducibility, and measurability, but it is not the only one that pretends to knowledge-in-the-sociological-sense. Elsewhere in society, various things other than scientific evidence legitimizes claims, like tradition, financial and social success, confidence and charisma, victim status and sympathy, rhetorical convincingness, stories of miracles, political expediency, intuitive appeal ("truthiness"), and, not to forget, raw, naked *power*. We have systems of legitimation that mix all of them—or at least we used to. While authorities like clergy, academics, government bureaucrats, activists, and journalists have been able to function as legitimators, they find it difficult to retain that status as information flows have opened up.

Since knowledge cannot be reduced to logic (philosophers who've tried to do so have not succeeded), and we can't have that ironclad, assumption-free procedure of legitimation, and science is slow, impractical, and imperfect, judgment calls are going to be necessary[22]. Judgment calls necessitate judges, much like sports require a referee. There is a reality, sure, but someone has to make the call about how it is to be interpreted and codified. Is that a *foul*? Is that a *goal*? Was it *offside*? Those concepts refer to physical facts, but they are not identical to them—and the facts must be translated into social reality somehow.

To make direct reference to questions that were briefly in focus during the covid-19 pandemic: do masks work? Do vaccines work? Do lockdowns work? These are questions with a lot of careful interpretation and detail involved. What qualifies as "work" exactly? What kind of masks, worn exactly how? In what circumstances, and to achieve what result? At the level of abstraction where issues are debated and decisions made, the answers are not determined by physical facts. In the postmodern condition we recognize the consequence: legitimation is an irreducibly social question, and the authority to perform it is the grand prize in the culture war.

Postmodernity: the good, the bad, and the way forward

The greatest benefit from breaking up norms has come to those who didn't fit in. When we can sort ourselves based on psychological similarity, everyone has somewhere to feel at home. This is a beautiful thing, a godsend for everyone outside the mainstream. However, as we have discussed, cultures formed around real psychological differences are more like academic fields than local communities, which may have cultural peculiarities and variations but fundamentally similar human material to work with. They build upon and reinforce the very differences around which they form; a group of neurotic introverts is going to have other norms than a gang of gym bros or touchy-feely New-Agers. Thus, they grow more different and mutually incomprehensible than local cultures ever could. Whatever unusual quirk, obsession, fetish, or outright disorder you have, you have

---

[22] Philosophical critiques show that this applies even when we have exhaustive, high-quality scientific evidence available for every question we need to answer, which we of course do not. For more, see chapter 13.

a better chance today than ever to find a place where it's the norm. This is a good thing in moderation, but we still live in societies together. Somewhere to feel at home is good, expecting to feel completely at home everywhere in society is not, because it cannot be true for everyone at the same time. Democracy requires compromise, and that requires that we're on the same page enough to discuss our issues and make legitimate collective decisions. How can we do that without agreeing on what's legitimate knowledge and values? How is it possible to accept the pluralism and ambiguity inherent in the postmodern condition with the need for common ground inherent in democracy?

There's a range of possible responses. On the one hand you can try to force hegemony. When former arbiters of what-counts-as-truth-and-legitimacy are no longer trusted, they can reassert power more aggressively and try restore the situation where nonconformists are few, isolated, and powerless. This says nothing about which ideas the hegemony would consist of, only that there would be one. Attempts can come from either populist or establishment sides of the political landscape. Populists seek to restore the power of informal social norms like family, nation, local community, and common sense against weirdo degenerates, while the establishment side supports institutions like academia, journalism, and government agencies against deplorable peddlers of misinformation. They're opposites in many ways but both are looking to crowd out and delegitimize their opponents, pretending like the postmodern condition is nothing but a bad dream.

The other extreme is to take the po-mo pill and admit nothing can be justified over anything else. Anything goes, at all times. Like other brands of radical skepticism, it's easy to justify in principle since it follows from being unable to justify anything else, but impossible to live by. Scratch a professed relativist and you'll find a human being with beliefs and moral convictions. A *community* like it is hard to imagine; with no norms or beliefs taught as truth it's unlikely that any could exist, let alone an advanced economy. The closest would be a libertarian-ish fantasy of a patchwork of legal-moral systems sharing physical space but running on different assumptions about everything from how magnets work to whether it's acceptable to own pets. I'm not optimistic about that working out.

Bog-standard liberalism, or "the boring best"

Between the populist/establishment and anarchic/libertarian extremes lies boring, difficult, psychologically unsatisfying, standard liberalism. In renewed, reinvigorated form, it recognizes the valid points of postmodernist critique: existing authorities, whether traditional social norms or institutions who control information flow, have overstepped their boundaries and created more apparent homogeneity and certainty than is really there. It also has enough confidence to recognize the limits of that critique. Some claims are truer than others, and some norms more conducive to human flourishing. A kernel of shared social reality that we're expected to take for granted must exist (although perhaps smaller than we're used to). Its contents will be subject to constant renegotiation, and it's imperative that this legitimizing process is itself considered legitimate, not just by a slim majority but an overwhelming one. As informal modes of government, systems of legitimation[23] must have the consent of the governed.

When information flows cannot be controlled, morally or practically, and we clearly won't simply trust each other, transparency is the only way. Only a visibly open and unbiased process of argumentation and evidence can bestow legitimacy on truth claims. For questions of values and preferences it's more important to step back and accept that there's diversity of opinion and refuse to enforce conformity when possible, and when not, make sure that the process aggregating values and preferences into collective decisions is as fair and equal as possible.

Isn't this just sleight of hand? It sure looks like it doesn't accept the postmodern critiques at all and simply tries to reassert the hegemony of traditional Enlightenment values of objectivity, reason,

---

[23] They may be human organizations or processes, but also technological institutions like wikis or artificial intelligences.

and individual rights-based liberalism. Is it just the old boss with a fake moustache?[24] Yes and no. Like postmodernists pointed out, modernist reason and rationality thought too much of itself and aimed to control everything rather than self-consciously look for its own limits the way a version incorporating postmodernist critiques would. The core of the liberal worldview is still, I argue, the only workable basis for postmodern societies because it came about precisely as a way to deal with diversity without repression or violent conflict. It's just that the modernist revolution, like any other revolution, had a vanguard just a bit too oppressive themselves, once in power.

To dismiss a humble and minimal rational liberalism as "just another ideology" and its dominance as "just another hegemony" is to miss how it is different from what we typically think of as ideology. A "ground-level" ideology straight up tells us what is true and good; for every question it has an answer. A society dominated by a ground-level ideology is oppressive, and totalitarian when it recognizes no part of life as outside its scope. A "second-level" ideology is less direct and less intrusive, as it lacks fixed answers to everything. Instead, its dogma is about *how to answer questions*. Democracy, free markets, and rule of law are second-level notions because they're about how to make decisions instead of what decisions to make. Going further, we get that a third-level ideology is about how to work out mechanisms for how to determine how to make decisions, and a fourth-level ideology tells us under what conditions we best develop mechanisms to determine what to do. And so forth.

While you can always construe ideological dominance as oppressive if you like, regardless of which level the ideology operates on, it gets less defensible as we ascend the ladder. In the anarchic/libertarian camp you can find the view that laws are fundamentally violent and being subject to any enforcement at all is equivalent

---

[24] I have not and cannot justify this non-circularly, the criticism is right about that, and it's perfectly *logically* coherent to reject it. It's just that since we must make some assumptions, this is one of the most conducive to human flourishing.

to being held at gunpoint—a brand of argument that deliberately disregards that the big deal about being held at gunpoint is the visceral immediacy of it. Being shot dead then and there for parking in the disabled spot without a permit is far more oppressive than reality, even if it is strictly true that if you resist *every* attempt to enforce the law as fiercely as you can, it will eventually get you killed.

Moving up the steps of indirectness happens in tandem with societies becoming more free, more prosperous, and more accepting of diversity[25]. A dominant "ideology" distant and abstract enough to leave a lot of space for freedom and pluralism in everyday life, looks less like an ideology than an interface with which different ideologies can exist together. That is a big difference that should not be collapsed into nothing.

Liberalism in this sense is a political ideal, but this book is not primarily about politics proper. I want to expand the liberal framework to apply to all differences in beliefs and belief systems. We need intellectual infrastructure for this "interface", and I think incorporating the insights of postmodern and constructionist thought under a rational, pro-scientific umbrella can do it.

It requires broad acceptance of the second-level norm of *tolerance,* in the traditional sense not of approving of everything, but accepting that what we wish didn't exist nonetheless has a right to. That can be *hard* because most of us, in our heart of hearts, don't enjoy that and will only accept it if the alternative is worse. We may have to be convinced that seizing the means of legitimation for ourselves isn't going to happen. Maybe a recapitulation of the origin story of liberalism is necessary: we saw the value of agreed-upon rules of engagement because of how destructive wars and revolutions were in early modern Europe. Maybe things have to get ugly for a while and more of us, on all sides, must be seriously hurt by culture wars before the lesson can be learned again.

---

[25] Within certain boundaries, undeniably.

Interlude

Fantasia for Two

Andy (*puts down coffee*) You support X? Really? I never thought that about you. Why, oh God why?

Bella (*stares*) Eh, because of Y? The right to Y, remember? I take it very seriously, and X is yet another instance where it's threatened, and nobody seems to care.

Andy You've got to be kidding me. You too? Some people are freaking obsessed with Y, and, honestly, in my experience, everyone who won't shut up about it also supports Z.

Bella Well, I kind of understand that. What's so terribly wrong with Z? I mean I don't necessarily *support* it, I see the problems but I get it. It's a lot better than U and V, that's for sure, and they always get a pass.

Andy U and V are obviously true! You have to see that, right? How would you even get W without them?

Bella You... don't. There's not really any W, it's a myth. People just believe in it (or pretend to believe in it) because they don't want to accept P.

Andy P? P?! You've gone full crackpot now.

Bella Hardly. P is way less crackpottish than you think. You know Q and R have studied it extensively? I've read several of their books.

Some fascinating stuff there. It's just amazing that nobody seems to know or care. Or, I shouldn't say "amazing", because it makes sense, believing in W and all.

Andy You can't trust Q. Everybody knows that. I read he supports Z. And R works in S, which is total nonsense all the way through. Is this really the best you can do?

Bella Q is always taken out of context on Z. I assume you've never actually read his own writings on it? This happens all the time, which is why you and everybody else, it seems, misunderstand Z so much. I doubt you've ever heard about it from a non-idiot, whether supporter or detractor. And the whole of S is nonsense now? Who told you that? Let me guess: your T teacher?

Andy As a matter of fact, yes. So what? Are you going to tell me all of T is nonsense?

Bella Maybe. Let me guess: this person also tried to tell you that A and B are completely valid methods, and C is worthless armchair theorizing?

Andy She taught us about B, yeah. I don't know about A, but I do know that C rests on wrongly assuming D and just never questioning it.

Bella (*points to Andy's face)* Not wrongly! You gotta have D! Sure, it's not perfect, but you have to have it in there somewhere or you're off to cuckoo-land. A, on the other hand—which B completely relies on by the way but I'm not surprised your teacher glossed over that because it's such a big weak spot—is maybe true in a few isolated cases but so far from a general, reliable truth that everything that takes it for granted becomes a joke. Accepting it can be a fun exercise, no argument there, but it has nothing to do with reality.

Andy That's exactly what I would say about D. Why is it right about A? Plenty of bluster from you but no argument.

Bella Well, for one, if true it would imply N.

Andy Yeah, for sure. It does.

Bella (*holds cup in front of mouth)* You believe in N?

Andy Not in every case, but I can see the point. D is just so much worse though, with G and all.

Bella G? How on Earth do you get there from D?

Andy Well D is rooted in C, which is pretty much guaranteed to mean G.

Bella No it doesn't. It doesn't mean G at all, what are you talking about?

Andy In my experience if somebody supports C, they really mean G.

Bella Do people say that or do you just assume it?

Andy Most don't say it out loud, but I can read between the lines. I've been right so many times before.

Bella And every time you do "read between the lines" you assume you're correct, I'm sure, so you feel more and more confident each time you do it, based on your own circular positive feedback. Well, here's some contrary evidence for you: I accept C and don't support G at all.

Andy (*shrugs)* I guess you're an exception, if you're honest, which I doubt. But most aren't like you.

Bella To me anyone who equates C with G is an exception. I've literally never seen it.

Andy Depends on what you mean I guess, people usually say M rather than G, but everyone knows that's code.

Bella No, "everyone" doesn't at all. Except your friends the N-supporters, I guess. Is that where you got that idea?

Andy They're not my friends! I haven't even met any of them, we only hang out online. And I don't listen to them *because* of N, I just like their views on O.

Bella Oh O... Ok. Look, there's some value to O, no doubt, fine, yeah, sure, I wouldn't just dismiss it. But that's only if you understand it together with E, and everyone into O that I've met has no clue. If they did, they'd realize something like I is a much better interpretation.

Andy (*chuckles)* They *really* hate I, it's all a bunch of sellouts who've accepted the gutting and neutering of a truly transformative, revolutionary idea by watering it down with E.

Bella (*empties cup)* And you agree?

Andy I'm not sure. I feel like I've been fed E all my life but it certainly seems like bullshit when you learn to see through it.

Bella That doesn't justify O, not by a long shot. I'm card-carrying I supporter, which is—*repeatedly taps palm*—what you get when you understand the problems with E but also that you can't go all the way to crazy O without losing sight of K.

Andy (*rolls eyes)* Stop fetishizing K, that's another really unattractive thing those who harp on about C do all the time too, and I'm sick of it. They should learn to F.

Bella I don't give a shit if it's "annoying" and "unattractive". They're *right.* People are far too trigger happy in telling others to F. Like 95% of the time it's just an excuse to shut down H, supposedly to "protect V".

Andy Well... if H is threatening to V maybe it isn't such a good idea. Have you even thought about that?

Bella I have, and H is absolutely essential. I'm not going back on that.

Andy Not at the cost of V! Not categorically! Not to me, anyway. And I care, unlike you who don't really need V. I get why you don't give a shit. V means W, and that means J. I'm not losing J because a bunch of H-fundamentalists won't give in, and if you weren't so self-absorbed you'd acknowledge that!

Bella I already told you W is a myth. Things will clear up a lot for you if you just dissolve that concept altogether and let the rest of your brain rewire itself. I agree that J is paramount though.

Andy (*shakes head*) You do?

Bella Yes! But it happens because of L, not because of W.

Andy L? Lol. I've never heard of L. Is that even a thing?

Bella Sure it's a thing. But I'm not surprised you haven't heard of it, it's counterintuitive and just a little bit too difficult to be discussed in school as it is. So people don't know it. And, yeah, without it, P certainly seems even more counterintuitive.

Andy Again with the P-ism!

Bella It's not an -ism! It's a natural, inexorable consequence of D, C and I put together, but yeah, sure, you do need to understand L to see that. And P, together with H—that you also don't seem to get so no wonder you're so confused—is required to get M.

Andy That's-

Bella And no I don't mean M as code for anything!

Andy Of course you do! Everybody does! It's literally impossible! No one *really* believes in M!

Bella I assure you they do. We do. And yes, that's why we take Y very seriously. Not just when it helps us, but always.

Andy (*sighs)* So, in conclusion, I guess: you support X?

Bella Yeah.

Andy Well, I suppose I understand why now. You're not just wrong about X, you're wrong about *everything*.

Bella No *you're* wrong about every-

Andy Save it. I get that it all makes sense to you. I even see *how* it makes sense. It's like looking in a funhouse mirror: everything's wrong, but wrong in a predictable way that you can understand if you try, with superhuman fucking patience, and manage to avoid vomiting in the process.

Bella Right, except that it's you who are wrong about everything, and I'm the one struggling to keep my muffin down. (*smiles and plays with crumbles)*

Andy (*leans back*) You know, I'm glad we had this conversation. Hell, I'm glad it was even possible. We might disagree about everything but at least we both know what all the letters refer to, and we know that the other knows this, and so forth. It'd be a complete nightmare to talk if we couldn't rely on that.

Bella Oof yeah, can you imagine?

PART II

Ambiguity for Fun and Profit

Chapter 5

Kuhn Distortions

Translation is the art of failure.

— Umberto Eco

Berger and Luckmann said that ideas and experiences far away from everyday concrete reality get distorted when expressed in ordinary vocabulary.

> I 'translate' the non-everyday experiences back into the paramount reality of everyday life. This may readily be seen in terms of dreams, but is also typical of those trying to report about theoretical, aesthetic or religious worlds of meaning. The theoretical physicist tells us that his concept of space cannot be conveyed linguistically, just as the artist does with regard to the meaning of his creations and the mystic with regard to his encounters with the divine. Yet all these—dreamer, physicist, artist and mystic—*also* live in the reality of everyday life. Indeed, one of their important problems is to interpret the coexistence of this reality with the reality enclaves into which they have ventured.

To them, these other worlds away from the concrete and shared were religious experience or esoteric physics, but to us, in the current year, it may be frog-Twitter, fan fiction, keto blogs, furry fandom, incel forums, lizard person conspiracies, 4chan culture, or whatever it's called when you design separate pride flags for 72 genders.

In postmodernity, direct experience of everyday life is replaced by consumption of second-hand accounts and the abstractions of which they consist. Our daily hours of direct interaction with reality haven't increased in the decades hence—more likely they have become fewer—while for many, and disproportionally those most engaged in public discourse, other people's interpretations of reality ("takes") is increasingly the bulk of experience. That might even be understating it, since what we're getting is often takes on other people's takes, on yet other takes, on an increasingly buried and irrelevant reality.

Thomas Kuhn's incommensurability

At this point, another classic from the 1960s becomes relevant outside its original scope. In *The Structure of Scientific Revolutions* from 1962, the philosopher Thomas Kuhn claimed that science progresses not by continuous accumulation of facts but by occasional revolutions that replace one grand model with another, turning everything on its head. During such revolutions, scientists switch allegiance from one set of assumptions, methodologies and interpretational habits (called a paradigm) to another, this as a result of anomalous observations piling up, making the old paradigm untenable. Popular examples include the Copernican revolution replacing an Earth-centered solar system with a Sun-centered one, and the switch from Newtonian to relativistic physics in the early 20th century, where basic terms like "mass", "time", "velocity", and "force" would get new meanings.

Most controversially, Kuhn argued that "conversion" between paradigms couldn't be a rational process but more like a literal, religious conversion. Since each paradigm can't be expressed in the terms of the other, no formal procedure can compare them. They are, in his words, *incommensurable*. This can be hard to see because often a new paradigm retains terms from its predecessor, but with meanings subtly altered to work in the new system. The *Stanford Encyclopedia of Philosophy*[26] gives some examples:

> [T]he meanings of the terms 'temperature', 'mass', 'chemical element' and 'chemical compound' depend on which theories are used to interpret them. Conceptual changes also result in the exclusion of some old elements of the extension of a concept, while new elements come to be subsumed by it, so that the same term comes to refer to different things. For example, the term 'Planet' referred to the sun but not the earth in the Ptolemaic theory, whereas it refers to the earth and not the sun in the Copernican theory.[27] Incommensurable theories use some of the same terms, but with different meanings, to refer to different sets of things. Two scientists who perceive the same situation differently, but nevertheless use the same vocabulary to describe it, speak from incommensurable viewpoints.

Kuhn's experiences made him realize that you can't expect to understand another when their worldview is so different from your own that the meaning even of individual words become unreliable.

> According to Kuhn, he discovered incommensurability as a graduate student in the mid to late 1940s while struggling with what appeared to be nonsensical passages in Aristotelian physics. He could not believe that someone as extraordinary as Aristotle could have written them. Eventually patterns in the disconcerting passages began to emerge, and then all at once, the text made sense to him: a Gestalt

[26] From its article on "Incommensurability of scientific theories".

[27] Cf. "we have lost the Earth" from last chapter.

> switch that resulted when he changed the meanings of some of the central terms. He saw this process of meaning changing as a method of historical recovery. He realized that in his earlier encounters, he had been projecting contemporary meanings back into his historical sources (Whiggish history), and that he would need to peel them away in order to remove the distortion and understand the Aristotelian system in its own right (hermeneutic history).
>
> For instance, when he encountered the word 'motion' in Aristotle (the standard translation of the Greek "kinesis"), he was thinking in terms of the change of position of objects in space (as we do today). But to get more closely at Aristotle's original usage, he had to expand the meaning of motion to cover a much broader range of phenomena that include various other sorts of change, such as growth and diminution, alternation, and generation and corruption, making an objects motion in space (displacement or 'locomotion') just a special case of motion.

"Gestalt switch" is the key phrase. From the German for "form" or "shape", *gestalt* in English means *wholeness*, and a gestalt *switch* is when our perception of which whole arises from the parts suddenly changes. It happens on both levels at once: the meaning of the whole, and what role each part is playing. One of the most famous examples are the *Old woman/Young woman* illusion, a drawing that depicts either a young woman looking away, or an old woman looking down, but not at the same time. As you switch from one to the other, individual elements change referents: the young woman's ear, cheek, and necklace become the old woman's left eye, nose, and mouth, respectively.

As Kuhn saw it, paradigm shifts were gestalt switches writ large, where instead of suddenly seeing a drawing as picturing something different, you'd see your object of study as working according to different principles.

Figure 3, the famous Old woman/Young woman illusion

Having different conversations

In our own time, Kuhn's insights apply to more than just arcane scientific and philosophical problems. Successful communication requires a shared paradigm, and when we don't have that—like say, scientists talking to social constructionists, neoliberals to climate doomers, or therapy enthusiasts to gym bros—it breaks down. Best case, the conversation falls apart cleanly and immediately, but often it doesn't because the gulf is just small enough to maintain the illusion that we understand each other. We're having different conversations, like in an old sitcom, except hilarity fails to ensue.

This sort of thing got me into erisology in the first place. Back in 2009 I wrote a bachelor's thesis in philosophy about how scientific claims about the human self and will in biology/neuroscience are reinterpreted when they escape academia and enter public discourse. To summarize my 18,000-word paper: there are two implicit and incompatible conceptions of what the self is and how our will operates. There is one traditional, intuitive, and quasi-mystical, and there is one scientific and materialist. The two assign different meanings to words like "self" and "free", and "cause". They have different meanings because they are embedded in entirely different conceptual systems, and you can't express a concept's meaning in one system using the terms of the other.

Scientific claims about the self and the operation of the will originate in a context where these things are understood as features of the material world, and *freedom* as the absence of constraints outside the self. They are then transplanted into a popular understanding where the self is assumed to operate outside physical causation, and thus the will is unconstrained not just by factors outside what counts as the self in the materialist view (like the brain or personal experience and history), but by *any* feature of material causation whatsoever. Scientific claims about *how* the self operates, *how* our wills work, and *how* we make choices, will by necessity be in terms of physical mechanisms, and thus, claims in such physical terms will, when filtered through the popular view[28], come across as *denying* rather than *explaining* the self, freedom, and choice.

Other examples are more politically charged. In radical contexts, for example, "racism" is used, as part of an elaborate belief system, to mean something like (taking part in and benefiting from) a social system that produces unequal outcomes between races. Given that, the claim "everybody is racist" or "society is racist" cashes out a certain way. Looking at it through a liberal lens, however, where the meaning of "racism" is closer to the moral conviction that people of some races ought to be the social inferiors of others, it cashes out differently. When that claim jumps contexts, therefore, it also changes from true to false[29].

The consequence in both cases is that one paradigm develops an incorrect representation of the contents of the other, as in "*they* believe *this*". It sounds esoteric but it's not a rare occurrence. In her treatment of the sociobiology controversy, Segerstråle says it was partly driven by the camps casting its central claims as playing roles

---

[28] The *manifest image,* as Flanagan calls it in *The Problem of the Soul.*

[29] Something similar occurs when labels like "Black" or "Queer" are used as political identities in some contexts, and plain descriptors of objective attributes in others.

in two different larger discussions, making each side mischaracterize what the other was about. E.O. Wilson and Richard Dawkins saw the evolutionary basis of behavior in light of the relationship between science and religion, and thus their focus was on natural selection's general capacity to create complexity and order so it could account for what was previously thought to require divine intervention. The specific details and the particular histories of species were less important. For Richard Lewontin and Stephen Jay Gould on the other side, however, particularity was key because they thought of evolutionary theory in terms of left- vs. right-wing economic politics. To them, evolution being an optimization process rewarding an inherent "fitness" property with survival and reproduction implied a hierarchy of more and less fit, which could be transferred to society to justify inequality. Emphasizing the *contingent, random,* and *collective* aspects of the evolutionary process would undermine any notion of individual "just desserts" that could be misused to defend the status quo. Focusing on the specific histories of species rather than general abstractions like fitness would also draw attention away from similar, politically relevant abstractions like IQ, which they also opposed.

It's not the position, it's the shape of the field

Even when we understand that our own opinion is not synonymous with the truth, we still tend to think that our paradigm is correct, meaning that we assume our conception of *the space in which opinions exist* is, in fact, the true space in which opinions exist. We assume that someone who disagrees with us simply occupies a different *position* in a given space of possible views (the common word "position" for opinion itself betrays the ubiquity of that assumption). But this is not true. Disagreement is *not* just taking different positions inside a common, agreed-upon space; we often disagree on the *shape* of the space. Which views are near each other, and which are far apart? What counts as effectively the same? Which differences define essential fault lines, and which ones can be rounded down to irrelevance?

For a toy model, consider three groups of positions, all equally distant from each other on a flat 2D surface. If we by force collapse them onto a linear political spectrum, two of them will look indistinguishable if the dimension they differ on is irrelevant to the chosen main dimension. In the figure below, from the point of view of the grey dots, the black and white ones look the same, despite the difference between them being as large as between them and the greys.

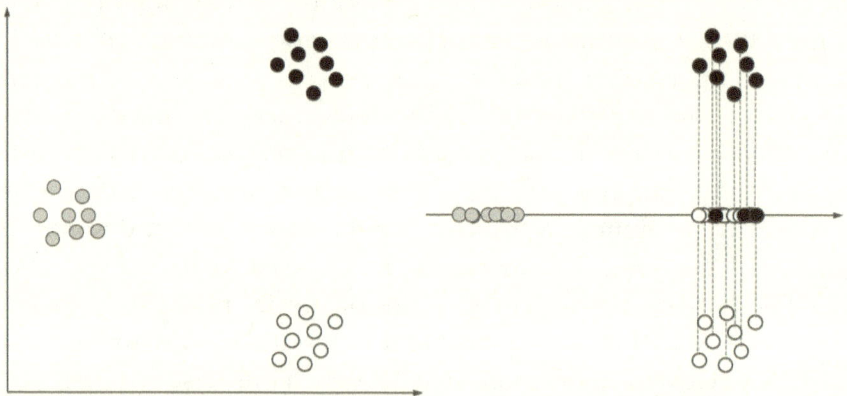

Figure 4, three opinions, equidistant (left), where two of them look identical when reduced to a single spectrum (right).

This is the mechanism through which socialists and liberals look the same to conservatives, and fascists and libertarians look the same to socialists. The economist Arnold Kling's model of political divides relies on this principle. In his book *The Three Languages of Politics* from 2013, he argues that progressives, conservatives, and libertarians ("liberals" outside the US) are tribes speaking different languages. Their arguments don't land outside their own group because each interprets what it hears in terms of their own belief system rather than the one it originates from. According to Kling, progressives think in terms of an oppressor vs. oppressed distinction, and everything they say is to be interpreted as staking positions on a field characterized by it. Since what *others* say will also be, disagreement with a pro-oppressed stance will be taken as a pro-oppressor stance. Once on X/Twitter I saw this exact point made by a leftist joking about how all criticism of social justice ideology from the right comes down to the idea that "maybe the oppressors are right". Of course, it says more about his own beliefs than those he was criticizing; if everything in the world is about group-based oppression, disagreement with that view is *also* going to be about that.

In reality, those critics do not think of themselves as staking out a position on an oppressed vs. oppressor playing field. Rather, other dimensions define the space. For conservatives, Kling says, the main dimension is *civilization* vs. *barbarism*, and to them, political positions are thus not defined in terms of more or less powerful groups. What matters is whether it supports (with carrot or stick) long-term responsible and productive behavior that supports civilization. Naturally, then, progressives and conservatives come down with opposite attitudes to e.g. crime, and general unruly, crime-adjacent behavior among the lower classes. This isn't because progressives are "pro-crime" and conservatives "anti-poor", but because they are both willing to sacrifice the other's primary value in service of their own—and the values are on different axes, not simple opposites. This is also why the Israel/Palestine conflict inflames passions between leftists and conservatives like almost nothing else, even though distant from their everyday life[30].

For libertarians/liberals, the main axis is respect for individual rights and agency vs. reasons to infringe on them (order and traditional social norms for conservatives, compassion and equality between groups for progressives). Every group feels morally superior to the others, and they're all correct. On the field as understood by each, the others *are* occupying the "bad guy" areas. The far left has few qualms about calling libertarians fascists because the emergent economic inequality they accept is to the leftist no different from politically enforced hierarchy, while the distinction is essential to the libertarians themselves. In the same way liberals have a habit of call-

30 Which side represents "civilization" vs. "the oppressed" in the eyes of their respective supporters is left as an exercise.

ing socialists fascists because of their shared disregard for individual rights, ignoring how they think of strong vs. weak and powerful vs. oppressed in opposite ways, which is central to them but of lesser importance to liberals[31].

The "playing field" issue is bigger than Kling. It lies behind "outgroup homogeneity bias", the cognitive bias that makes us think everyone who disagrees with us are the same. E.g. hardcore Christians might consider any non-Christians to be "heathens" or in league with the devil; Marxists call everyone else "capitalists"; anarcho-capitalists talk about everyone else as "statists", nationalists call everyone else "globalists", and I myself once had a habit of insisting that anyone who hadn't worked out an entirely materialist worldview like me was "religious"[32].

The nasty part of all this is that mere communication does nothing to help if we can't perform the appropriate gestalt shifts. On the contrary, interaction actually makes polarization *worse,* since anything coming from the other side sounds like villainous screeching when translated into our own language, confirming that they're just as horrible as we thought.

---

[31] Liberals/libertarians agree with leftists that discrimination is wrong, but with different justifications. Treating people worse for their race or sex is wrong because it's a breach of a symmetric social contract "we agree not to do this to each other". They therefore think leftists are hypocrites when they don't mind discrimination against white people or hateful comments against men etc. However, to leftists, this misses the point entirely since morality is all about supporting the weaker groups. They then assume the pushback is (laughably) trying to paint men/white people as the ones who are "really oppressed", because they take for granted that *only the oppressed* are entitled to complain about bad treatment.

[32] Stephen Hicks, author of the polemic *Postmodernism Explained* from 2011 paints with a similarly broad-to-the-point-of-uselessness brush when he calls everything in opposition to his own rationalistic individualism "postmodernism".

Chapter 6

Cat Couplings

Magic is the most philosophical performing art, because—like philosophy—it replaces the illusion of knowledge with the knowledge of illusion.

— Nikolas Jintri

Years ago a colleague and I had a mild disagreement play out over an internal mailing list. While I defended the idea of societal progress, he, the more cynical of us, brought up a quote from Fenno-Swedish philosopher Georg Henry von Wright, author of the book *Myten om framsteget* ("The Myth of Progress"):

> Pessimism has its downsides, but is still preferable to naive optimism.

We kept talking about progress and I didn't until later explore my intuition that there was something off about that sentence. What is it really saying? Specifically, what role is "naive" playing? Is it only picking out the subset of optimism that's naive—i.e. in this context *mistaken*—and saying pessimism is better than that? In that case, granted, but it's not much of an argument if we don't know *how big* that subset is. Or is it saying that *all* optimism is naive simply by virtue of being optimism, and therefore pessimism is preferable? Can't be, that just assumes its own conclusion...

None of the two interpretations make much sense as an argument, and yet it's rhetorically effective. I struggled with countering it even though it did nothing to convince me and falls apart on inspection. But why? What's going on?

It's the *ambiguity*; once that is removed it stops working. There's a broad interpretation that says what you want (optimism is worse than pessimism *because* it is naive), and a narrow interpretation that's easily defensible (optimism is worse than pessimism *when* it is naive). The first isn't uncontroversial enough to be asserted without support, and if it was unambiguously stated it could easily be countered. It's effective only because it can hide behind the second interpretation. As long as both are possible, the weaknesses cancel each other out.

To use a slightly worn metaphor: the claim exists in an interpretive "superposition" between two states like the famous Schrödinger's Cat—hence I call it a "cat coupling". In the original thought experiment illustrating a phenomenon in quantum mechanics where things are undetermined until they are measured, a cat in a box is in a state of both living and dead at the same time until we decide to open the box and look. In the same way, a cat coupling is in a state of two combined interpretations until clarified (which it almost never is).

I started seeing this everywhere. I found this one in a Reddit discussion about a possible six-hour workday reform:

> the only ones that will lose out are rich bosses

Who are the rich bosses? The bosses who happen to be rich, or all bosses, who, as we know, must all be rich? Both versions have weaknesses, but the opposite ones: too narrow to be of consequence vs. too broad to be true, and like an alloy, mixing them is key for strength. Furthermore, by saying this we end up with the association between "bosses" and "rich" strengthened, which I'm certain is in line with the speaker's worldview.

The observation isn't original. The standup comedian Sara Pascoe once went off on Pret-a-Manger bragging about their food being free from "unnecessary preservatives". She noted, correctly, that this doesn't mean much. Are all preservatives unnecessary? That can't be true. So, they're only abstaining from the unnecessary ones? That's not saying a lot. How many is that, and why wouldn't everyone?

Novel or not, it helps to give something a name. I'm proud that I've managed to get other people to notice cat couplings since I first introduced it in an essay in 2019. The science journalist Tom Chivers pointed out one on X/Twitter (from an article in *The Telegraph* about Brexit):

> EU nationals will still be free to work in Britain – though he will make it easier to deport unsavoury foreigners and will also clean up the benefits.

"Unsavoury foreigners" is a perfect example. There's "foreigners that also happen to be unsavoury" on the one hand, and "foreigners, who are unsavoury by virtue of being foreigners" on the other.

Competitive sensemaking through implicit rhetoric

Cat couplings are possible because language is ambiguous, and we exploit this to manipulate others' understanding of reality. Talking about "naive optimism" or "unsavoury foreigners" strengthens the connection between a *kind* and an *attribute* (optimism and naivety, foreigners and unsavouriness), not by stating it directly but by putting a different claim at the center of attention, allowing the association to sneak by. You could make the same literal point by, for example, saying "naivety" instead of "naive optimism", but no, both words must be there. That's the important part—that indirect effect—not the literal (undefined) truth value of what's being said.

By making sure to allow both interpretations you imply that there's no significant difference between them—between bosses who are rich and bosses in general, or preservatives that are unnecessary and preservatives in general. This is *implicit rhetoric,* distinct from *explicit* rhetoric. Explicit rhetoric argues for something, stating a point to be accepted at face value: optimism about the future shouldn't be trusted, or a six-hour workday wouldn't hurt anyone who can't afford it, so we should do it, etc. Implicit rhetoric doesn't make its point directly but instead builds and shapes concepts by pointing to things and sets of things, grouping them into categories, and pinning attributes on them. All this to make the library of generally recognized and referable-to concepts more favorable to you and your political and social goals.

So far, all examples involve attaching some negative characteristic to somebody or something. Are there positive examples? There are! I found this in a discussion of medicine:

> Internet research isn't really a substitute for a professional who's not only directly keeping up with the latest science in their field, but also has practical experience from seeing people come in and observing directly what works and what doesn't.

It's longer than a two-word phrase, but it's a perfect structural match for "naive optimism". The kind is "a professional" (i.e., a doctor) and the attribute is "keeps up with the latest science and has direct experience with what works and doesn't". Sure enough, advice from a doctor that does indeed do those things and does them well is a lot better than doing your own research as a nonspecialist, but the argument elides that you can't actually rely on doctors to be that perfect. It's impossible for a GP to keep up with *all* the relevant science, and "knowing what works and what doesn't" implies both a lot of experience with the specific condition in question, and having access to, and soberly evaluating, accurate and exhaustive feedback on the full range of possible treatments. It's a high bar.

The explicit argument is a *comparison* between two constructs, but the real payload is getting to take that second construct (doctors can be relied on to do these things) for granted. Just like when a magician fools us with a sleight of hand, the real action is somewhere other than where our attention is focused. The result is, as always, to connect the kind and the attribute—the argument claims, indirectly and surreptitiously, that doctors are better than they are.

Types and their far sides

By making a "type" of person (like doctors-who-fulfill-ideal-criteria) and at once using it for a comparison, you're assuming it's a valid construct, and by doing that you're treating the group of doctors-who-don't-fulfill-these-criteria as if they don't exist. You don't outright deny their existence, but you present reality from an angle where they can't be seen, like the far side of the moon.

In fact, every kind-with-attribute construct, every *type*, has this quality of there being a hidden far side of kind-*without*-attribute that's rounded off to nothing and forgotten. Another group-who-do-certain-things coupling comes to you translated from Swedish Reddit. This one is again negative:

> The Left Party has been clear in their criticism of neoliberalism and this has had an effect on the regional government's handling of the crisis. Generally, they're the only party who've come out and said they want to get rid of venture capitalists who hollow out our public systems, whether in schools or in elderly care.

The kind is "venture capitalist" and the attribute is "hollows out our public systems" (you're now capable of finding the interpretations, the ambiguity, and the far side on your own). And then there's this quote from a blog post about status-seeking on social media:

> most investors are middle-aged white men who are already so high status they haven't the first idea why people would seek virtual status

With the kind being "middle-aged white men" and the attribute "already very high status", I don't need to spell out the interpretations nor the (absolutely gigantic) far side. Nor do I need to point out that if you just wanted to say what you're supposedly saying—that most investors don't understand striving for status because they're high-status already—you could've just said that. But no, there's something extra, a little concept-building going on there on the side, making the drive-by implication that middle-aged white men, across the board, are swimming in social status.

On that note, I can't help but look at the phrase "toxic masculinity" through the same lens. *It's just a particular and bad kind of masculinity!* Yeah, ok that makes sense... but one gets suspicious, because if you didn't want to take a swipe at masculinity as a whole (*it's impossible to avoid, you understand...*) you could phrase it differently. If you *cared at all* to not do that... if you thought there was anything on the far side that shouldn't be ignored. Alas.

It sounds paranoid to bring it up, but this sort of ambiguity sure as hell often feels like a feature and not a bug. It's as if we do know how this works, even before it's been pointed out to us, and, mostly unconsciously, just let it happen when we speak. For some more examples I've noted, how about a description of a house party as full of "introverted weirdos", a gaming club of "rude nerds" or a workplace of "hysterical women"? Or a forum "infested with argumentative libertarians"? Nothing incorrect about those phrases per se, but it gives off just a little whiff of *intent,* doesn't it? *Disregard* at the very least. It could have been just "weirdos", "assholes" or "hysterical (or argumentative) people" or some other formulation, *if you'd had the slightest desire to avoid tarring certain groups of people in the process.* Here, take some more spotted items as exercises: "socialist hellhole", "creepy middle-aged men", "out-of-touch elites", "contrarian bullshit", "90 percent male cesspool", "dumb jocks", and "the shrieking harpy Left".

There's a reasonable objection to be made at this point. Do these last cases really qualify as making digs at some group or concept through an ambiguous statement either picking out a subset or describing a whole? Sometimes both parts of the expression are necessary for accurately describing what you mean. "Introverted weirdos" is not the same thing as just "weirdos". It's a particular kind of weirdo. Similarly: What kind of nerds? The rude kind. And what kind of rude people? The nerd kind. What kind of elites? The out-of-touch kind. What kind of out-of-touch people? The elite kind. What kind of cesspool? The 90 percent male kind. What kind of 90 percent male space? The cesspool kind. And so forth.

Most often this is just a result of people having certain existing types in their head which they think others will be familiar with and they don't mind perpetuating. Back when I worked as a consultant a client once praised my report for *not* being "a consultant's report packed with jargon to impress and intimidate". She could have just said that it was good that it was clearly written but no, a consultant report like that is a *type*. She referenced the type because she knew it, expected me to know it, and didn't mind perpetuating it, even if only to say it didn't apply to my work.

I complain about them, but types are *great*. They're an indispensable tool of both thought and communication, and we're right to greedily acquire and use them. We do so not only through our own experience but by learning from others, which is what makes us such a powerful species. We can pick them up on nothing but indirect social cues, based on no knowledge of the subject at all. If an alien spaceship appeared in orbit and the captain beamed down to have a drink with you and proceeded to complain that "asteroid mining is hard work and all I've got is a crew of pampered Zorblaxians" then you'd know right away that 1) Zorblaxians are considered soft (and hard-working Zorblaxians are far-sided), and 2) that the captain doesn't mind reinforcing that (stereo)type[33].

Types and sets are different things

Types arise through cat coupling-like mechanisms because they're so easy to make and comprehend. It's a lot harder and less intuitive to pick them apart and spell out the shoddy logic. This is because logical analysis in terms of sets and subsets ("all of", "most of", or "some of" etc.) isn't how language normally works, and that's because it's not how *thinking* normally works. It runs on types, not set logic. Remem-

[33] A word on prefixes: when we disapprove of a type being articulated or referenced we put "stereo-" in front of it. When we approve we go without prefix or try "arche-".

ber, logical terminology and procedure had to be invented by Aristotle. It doesn't come preinstalled on brains.

Notably, types and sets are very different things. In our heads, types get represented by a single example item. The type "German", for instance, is mentally represented as an example person, with the same kind of characteristics a person has (appearance, personality traits, behaviors, clothes etc.) This is because our brains are pattern recognition machines and not logical reasoners (they can work as such but have to be trained to and even then it's iffy). *Sets* however, like the set of all Germans, have *entirely different attributes than the items they consist of.* Sets have properties like *counts* (how many are there), *averages* and *distributions* of attributes, and *correlations* between them. There's an average height for the set of Germans, a proportion with blue eyes, and a correlation between, say, intelligence and income, but no plain height or eye color the way there is for a single person, and there's no fixed rule that tells you the relationship between intelligence and income for any individual German.

Why is this pedantry important?

Confusing correlations in a set (intelligence is positively correlated with income) with rule-like associations in a type (intelligent implies rich, and vice versa) is the result of miscasting set attributes as type attributes. I can only speculate and infer because I work with statistics professionally, have practiced it in some form since I was 12, and thus it is second nature to me, but it seems that people do not automatically interpret set attributes as such when talking about sets. For example, many try to disprove set claims (the Dutch are very tall) with single exceptions: "I know a short Dutch person". In statistical terms ("set talk"), that's just nonsense, making the objector sound like an idiot, because since we're talking sets we're *obviously* referring to averages (or similar summary statistics). Objecting makes perfect sense in "type talk" however, because then you're trying to draw attention to an unfairly ignored far side: "this is not a hard rule of the kind that's implied in a type, there are exceptions that you should not make invisible".

Set attributes like averages, proportions and correlations aren't understood correctly when we use type talk to process them, because they have no true counterpart there. Proficiency in set talk has to be acquired through education in statistics and probability, and then it has to be intentionally used. I would go as far as saying that type talk and set talk are two *different paradigms* as discussed in the last chapter, and claims get mangled and misinterpreted when transplanted from one to the other.

Disagreements over the legitimacy of making generalizations is made messier by having these two incommensurable systems. The seemingly stupid objections are so common because type talk and set talk interpretations exist, unrealized, together in conversation, and we flip back and forth on how to treat what is said based on what is more important to us. We may understand that "the Dutch are taller than the Spanish" is correct and harmless in set talk, but potentially offensive in type talk if we're Spanish and don't want to be stereotyped as short[34]. We notice this subconsciously, and then type talk takes over as our interpretive frame so we can object and prevent others hearing the claim go unchallenged. It's quite sophisticated, and notable that we do this without being conscious of how it works.

Cat couplings make sense in type talk

In summary, our intuitive ways to think about categories clash horribly with the newly (relative to the whole of human existence) invented logical-statistical terminology that is set talk. This mismatch causes an absolutely gigantic amount of dysfunctional disagreement.

Treating cat couplings as set talk makes them look incoherent, but as type talk they make perfect sense. They're not making logically interpretable claims about sets, they're evoking, constructing, and

[34] Confusing the rules of type talk for laws of nature gets us *essentialism*, the belief that all examples of a category somehow contains the essence of that category. E.g., if you're a tall Spaniard there's still some "essential shortness" in you that you get from being Spanish (and your tallness is somehow "less real"). This is, of course, nonsense.

articulating types, thus taking place in the abstract domain of concepts and their relationships, which obeys different mechanics than the physical, logical, and statistical. "Naive optimism" is a type, a piece of mental and social equipment used for both thinking and communicating. So are "rich bosses" and "unsavory foreigners". "Doctors who keep up with the latest science and know what works" and "venture capitalists who hollow out our public systems" are arguably types as well, if less neatly packaged (and some certainly want to rearticulate and reinforce them). Cat couplings that look fiendishly complex in set talk become dead simple when translated into type talk. Think of this sentence (from the 2020 article *David Shor's Unified Theory of American Politics* in *The Intelligencer*):

> The Senate was always a really fucked-up anti-majoritarian institution.

There are institutions that are anti-majoritarian and fucked-up, and highlighting both these properties suggests, but doesn't assert, that anti-majoritarian-ness implies fucked-upness. Ambiguity goes further than that, because even if we agree that anti-majoritarianness implies fucked-upness it's still not clear if anti-majoritarianess *causes* the separate property of fucked-upness or if it itself *constitutes* fucked-upness. Do you think the author worked this implied philosophical insanity out in advance, to make a coherent logical-causal claim? Of course not. That's not the kind of claim it is and if it's interpreted as such, it breaks down into incoherent mush. It's just ordinary type talk.

Chapter 7

Load-bearing Ambiguities

We were on a break!

— Ross Geller, *Friends*

We've learned that cat couplings are best understood as an exercise in constructing and rearticulating types, but can also be a way to say two things at once and exploit the ambiguity between them: one ironclad but trivial, and one impactful but indefensible (if made explicit). The latter is a nutshell version of the idea first put forth by the philosopher Nicholas Shackel in his 2005 article *The Vacuity of Postmodernist Methodology*, and then catapulted to internet fame in the mid-2010s: *motte-and-bailey doctrines*.

A motte-and-bailey is a two-part medieval castle structure with a cramped fortification (the motte) surrounded by a village with fertile, valuable land (the bailey). The bailey is difficult to defend, so when attackers show up, the villagers retreat to the motte and shoot arrows at them until they go away. Then they come back out to work the land again.

Shackel suggests some philosophical positions work the same way. His example is relativist and anti-rational views in postmodernism, whose proponents like to make bold, radical claims but back down to assert only mild, common-sense versions when challenged. Left alone again, they revert to acting like the radical versions are true. "Reality is socially constructed" lends itself to this, as we've seen. So do "sex is not binary" and "there's a war on Christmas".

Unfortunately, "motte-and-bailey doctrine" is not a catchy name. I've seen so many point out that they always forget which is which (there is not sufficiently widespread knowledge about medieval warfare to support the metaphor). It's a testament to its value that it has caught on anyway. Most is due not to Schackel himself but star blogger Scott Alexander, who's done more than anyone to popularize it. He has some examples (from his article *All in All, Another Brick in the Motte*):

> 1. The religious group that acts for all the world like God is a supernatural creator who builds universes, creates people out of other people's ribs, parts seas, and heals the sick (bailey). Then when atheists come around and say maybe there's no God, the religious group objects "But God is just another name for the beauty and order in the Universe! You're not denying that there's beauty and order in the Universe, are you?" (motte). Then when the atheists go away they get back to making people out of other people's ribs and stuff.
>
> 2. Or... "If you don't accept Jesus, you will burn in Hell forever." (bailey) But isn't that horrible and inhuman? "Well, Hell is just another word for being without God, and if you choose to be without God, God will be nice and let you make that choice." (motte) Oh, well that doesn't sound so bad, I'm going to keep rejecting Jesus. "But if you reject Jesus, you will BURN in HELL FOREVER and your body will be GNAWED BY WORMS." But didn't you just... "Metaphorical worms of godlessness!"
>
> 3. The feminists who say you can't be a real feminist unless you believe in specific commitments in X, Y and Z (bailey). Then when someone objects to "feminism", they argue you can't object to feminism because it's "just the belief that women are people!"

> (motte). Then once the person hastily retreats and promises he definitely didn't mean women aren't people, the feminists get back to demanding everyone support affirmative action because feminism, or arguing about whether you can be a feminist and wear lipstick.
>
> 4. Proponents of pseudoscience sometimes argue that their particular form of quackery will cure cancer or take away your pains or heal your crippling injuries (bailey). When confronted with evidence that it doesn't work, they might argue that people need hope, and even a placebo solution will often relieve stress and help people feel cared for (motte). In fact, some have argued that quackery may be better than real medicine for certain untreatable diseases, because neither real nor fake medicine will help, but fake medicine tends to be more calming and has fewer side effects. But then once you leave the quacks in peace, they will go back to telling less knowledgeable patients that their treatments will cure cancer.

Cat couplings are easy to pick apart once you know what to look for, because they have two easily identifiable interpretations. Motte-and-bailey doctrines are the grown-up version (the Pokémon evolution, if you will). They're bigger and more complex, making the issues with them all the more difficult to articulate.

Motte-and-bailey with division of labor

One complicating factor is their *distributed* nature. When we're discussing a widespread idea, doctrine, or ideology instead of a specific claim, we're "talking to" a loosely defined group who don't all believe the same things. Instead of a single person changing their position when challenged, every individual may stay consistent but the whole group appears to equivocate "strategically" because we come across different members at different times. We can be diligent in not assuming a conversation partner believes something they didn't say, but this is an impractical and unattractive option since, when in the trenches of X/Twitter, Reddit, Tumblr, or the New York Times comment section, you don't want to argue with some single rando but with "libertarians", "multiculturalists", "Musk stans", or "anti-vaxxers" as a whole. That's the level on which we have opinions, and a stranger on the internet is little more than an avatar of whatever group we think they represent. Thus, when some of them refuse to conform to our prejudices, it looks like the group is doing a motte-and-bailey: "*you people* always say this wild thing X but here you come only saying mild thing Y, *how dishonest*."

This is obviously unfair to those who don't agree with everything everyone else "on their team" says. At the same time, limitless charity will cost us, because whether they intentionally coordinate or not, there is a symbiotic relationship between radical and moderate supporters of an ideology—between the respectable political movement and its street thug enforcers, so to speak. For every sophisticated theologian who thinks of God as the conceptual foundation for existence or something, there's a fundamentalist who literally believes in heaven, hell, the great flood, and creation in six days—and whether they like it or not, the former provides cover for the latter. Every nuanced and sophisticated evolutionary psychologist provides cover for the crudest of redpillers, sensible liberal feminists provide cover for the most unhinged manhaters, and social democrats with reasonable concerns about inequality provide cover for communists who want to abolish private property and send anyone who objects to a labor camp (or worse). If you're genuinely worried about economic dependence and high crime rates among some ethnic minorities you are granting some legitimacy to foaming-at-the-mouth racists. Are you a quantum physicist discussing the counterintuitive aspects of your field? Congrats, what you say lends support to hippies droning on about "vibrations". And those who express unease about the impact of climate change do help activists who insist that humanity is going extinct within a decade unless their preferred brand of misanthropic degrowth is adopted. Conversely, if you express any doubts about the seriousness of the crisis, or the viability/desirability of radical economic self-restraint as a solution, you're legitimizing those who think it's all a hoax.

This is *not* a good thing. I'm *not* saying that people with nuanced, moderate views that function as mottes to crude, extreme ones should be held at all responsible for what someone else says and does. I honestly think this state of affairs qualifies as an ongoing disaster. I'm describing an unfortunate fact of life.

Given this, everyone would do well to keep in mind that while you shouldn't have to, it *is* wise to take care to separate yourself from the radical fringes (e.g. avoid their terminology), even if it is tedious, and puts you on the defensive. At the same time, we should make an effort to not be part of the problem ourselves, by assuming less about what others think.

Multipart mottes: an economic example

Another complicating factor is that equivocation isn't always along a single dimension. There may be more than one ambiguity in play, as, for example, with the idea that "free trade benefits everyone".

I've had some education in economics. I've also had experience with people disagreeing about the merits of free trade in the context of globalization, and there's a lot of talking past each other. Resistance to free markets, global trade, outsourcing etc. from people who've lost their jobs or face a less generous job market as a result, is, by the economically literate, often dismissed as not just selfish but *irrational*. Free trade benefits everyone, you know. Economists have shown this, so only an ignorant rube would disagree.

This is actually a two-dimensional motte-and-bailey. We can see how by listing the interpretations of each ambiguity on a different axis, which results in a 2-by-2 matrix. Look at the phrase again: *free trade benefits everyone*. I'm not even going to touch the complexities of what exactly "free trade" means, but you know—free movement of goods, money, and labor, that kind of thing. I'll just look at the meaning of "benefit" and "everyone". Simple, right?

When we say something benefits someone, do we mean that the something makes the someone better off *on net*, counting total gains minus total costs? Or does it mean that it produces *some* identifiable benefit for them, that may or may not be greater than the costs? In international free trade terms, if you lose your job because your widget factory closes and moves to China where they can operate at a lower cost, it "benefits" you in that you get your widgets cheaper like everyone else. But it's unlikely to be a *net* benefit, considering that you lost your job and all[35].

That's two meanings of "benefit"[36]. What about "everyone"? When we say "everyone" we might mean every single person, individually: "tomorrow I'll give everyone an apple" means every person gets an apple of their own. But it can also mean the group "everyone", *in total*: "tomorrow I'll give everyone a cake" probably means I'll bring one to share. The case for free trade in Economics 101 relies on the second meaning, and I think back to the way one of my course mates summarized it in an introductory macroeconomics class (paraphrased):

> the sum of the benefits from trade is greater than the losses, meaning that in theory the winners could compensate the losers in full and still be better off than before (that this never actually happens is of course another matter).

---

[35] That's at least true in the short term. Economists might say it forces you to upskill, which makes you better off in the long term. However, this isn't certain for you individually, and not critical to the argument here.

[36] This is the same ambiguity that fuels the "privilege" discussion trainwreck: does "being privileged" mean having some advantage that counts in your favor at some time, or does it mean ending up advantaged overall? A lot of its rhetorical power comes from combining the broadness of the first with the implications of the second.

With two options for each word, we can put together our 2-by-2 *interpretation matrix*:

		"Everyone" means...	
		The group "everyone"	Every single person
"Benefit" means...	Net benefit	*Free trade brings a total benefit greater than the total costs*	*Free trade improves life for every single person*
	Some benefit	*Free trade brings something of value to someone*	*Free trade brings something of value to every single person*

Figure 5, different interpretations of "free trade benefits everyone".

Each quadrant has its own distinct meaning. The bottom left is weak enough to be irrelevant; all it says is that free trade does have *some* positive consequence. The top left is the textbook line: the total gain is greater than the total cost. This is true, at least in a narrow economic sense, but not strong enough justification. It's easy to think "oh jeez, you mean to tell me that me losing my job is worth it because my boss and the shareholders gained more than I lost? Imagine my joy". Here's where the bottom right comes in: it says that every single person gets some benefit (e.g. can buy widgets at a lower price).

Top left and bottom right are true but entirely disjunct, which has an interesting effect: since *one* claim where "benefit" means "net benefit" and *one* claim where "everyone" means "every single person" are true, it's easy to get the impression that the one that combines both, i.e. "every single person gets a net benefit", is true as well. But the top right one is *not necessarily true,* at the very least it's a lot more questionable than its neighbors to the left and down. For the phrase to come out true, "benefit" can only mean "net benefit" if "everyone" *doesn't* at the same time mean "every single person", and vice versa.

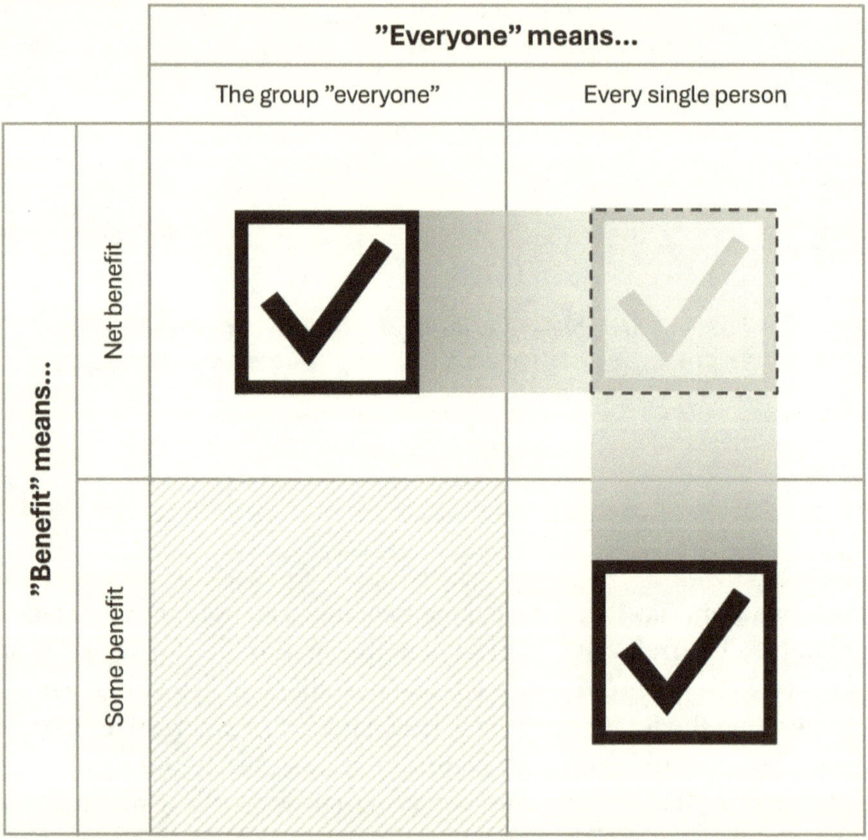

Figure 6, top left and bottom right being true makes top right feel true, even when it isn't.

If top right *was* necessarily true, it would indeed mean that opposing free trade is irrational[37]. As it happens it isn't, but still difficult to argue against since it requires pinning down the meaning of two slippery terms at once, and that's beyond the capacity of shared attention in most non-academic contexts. Thus, the top left and bottom right act as a two-part *distributed motte* to the bailey on the top right.

The ambiguities of collective action

The possibility of jumping between interpretations is used in rhetoric all the time, partly on purpose but also partly not, because we genuinely and honestly underestimate how ambiguous words can be. This is even true for everyday, straightforward words we don't expect problematic behavior from (like "everybody"). This issue lies behind a whole class of dysfunctional disagreements, for example a few enabled by ambiguity of the word "we" and the concept of an action. For example, in this tweet I once saw:

> Should we treat all people equally?
>
> Should we value everyone (e.g. parents, children, friends, strangers) equally?

Most of us would answer the two questions differently, and the implication is that this makes us inconsistent. But the context makes us interpret "we" as "society as a whole" the first time, and "each individual" in the second, and recognizing this dissolves the apparent contradiction. It's perfectly consistent to believe both that society should treat people according to equal rules, and that individuals have special relationships and special duties toward specific people.

---

[37] None of this is meant as an argument against free trade. It, and the general advancement of the great techno-institutional-economic machine of which it is part, has produced vast riches. It has lifted much of the world out of poverty and continues to do so as we speak. But the process does create losers along the way, and they are not irrational for complaining, nor is their dissatisfaction simply ignorance.

Only by referring to two different things by the same word does it appear contradictory.

Then there is the idea of an action. On the one hand there is *individual action* by specific people, and on the other there's *collective action* by a group. They are very different things. A person can simply take an individual action, because a person is an agent[38]. Groups of people *aren't* naturally agents and can't act because they don't have selves[39]. We can simulate selves and agency collectively by setting up structures that enable us to make decisions together semi-coherently (e.g. corporations, clubs, armies, governments), but this does not happen spontaneously.

Equivocating between individual and collective action allows confused propositions, leading to dysfunctional discourse. I remember a survey where I was asked to agree or disagree with this:

> We can save the planet by exercising our consumer choice.

It looks like a single claim, but it's really two, spliced together:

Claim 1: we can make consumer choices

Claim 2: consumer choices can save the planet

Let's not dig into what "save the planet" means right now, because that's not the point. It's this: both are true, but only when "consumer choices" refer to different things in each claim. To show how, let's generalize the logic: "[action] is available for us to take" and "[action] is effective in solving the problem" combine into "the available [action] solves the problem" only when [action] refers to the same thing. We can easily *take* individual action (e.g. I can buy locally grown tomatoes) but it doesn't solve the problem (one person's consumption

---

[38] This mostly holds, although there are cases (e.g. addiction, procrastination) where a person doesn't act with coherent agency. This will be discussed later in the chapter.

[39] Just as agency and free will disappears at a certain high resolution — when we look at brain cells and neurotransmitters (more on this in chapter 13) — it disappears again when we zoom out from the individual to large groups of people.

is negligible). Coordinating most of the world to act together could solve the problem but isn't available to us the way individual action is, because no mechanism for collective decision-making and enforcement is in place. By interpreting the action as individual in the first sense and collective in the second, both claims can be true, giving us the impression that effective action for solving the problem is available for us to take. But when true they are no longer equal and can't be combined, so it's an illusion.

You could argue that this is intentional obfuscation for the purpose of making people take personally costly but ineffective individual action by pretending it's equal to effective collective action[40]. In any case, it's strong rhetoric because the logical error makes it hard to articulate the real reason most of us aren't acting more environmentally friendly: we don't want to make major sacrifices unless it actually solves the problem. For example, whenever it's said that you should go vegetarian for the sake of the climate (as one of my friends likes doing), you're asked two questions at the same time, to which I, and I suspect many others, have opposite responses:

> "Would you stop eating meat to stop climate change?"

Yes I would.

> "Would you stop eating meat as a symbolic act, counting infinitesimally towards stopping climate change?"

No I would not.

I reject the implication that I'm some brute who says no to the first because I say no to the second, and that's what this rhetoric is saying. The same disconnect between sacrifice and solution applies to going

---

[40] In the hope that enough will eventually be convinced to actually make it effective.

vegan to stop factory farming, or not drive a car, and a host of similar choices. The main/only effect of making such unilateral sacrifices would be to make me feel better about myself for not being a part of the problem. And while I would enjoy that, I would enjoy it much less than I enjoy eating meat and driving a car.

Paying taxes is a notable counterexample. It works because there actually is a coordination and enforcement mechanism, and it's worth it for me to have to pay because me having to means others have to as well, bringing in a lot of money. If it didn't, it wouldn't be worth it (which is why arguments like "if you like taxes so much why don't you just pay more yourself" are disingenuous).

A cynic would say it's all purposeful, but it is at least partly a genuine confusion. The name for the gulf between individual and collective action is called *collective action problems*, and despite being standard fare for economists, it's not as well understood and appreciated by the general public as it ought to be. The Canadian philosopher Joseph Heath writes in a blog post called *Ricardo's Difficult Idea*:

> [S]eeing the world in terms of collective action problems has become such second nature to me that I have increasing difficulty imagining what it would look like in any other terms, and thus, I have difficulty believing that anyone still fails to see it in those terms. I teach the Prisoner's Dilemma, the Tragedy of the Commons, and all the basic stuff about collective action problems, every year in my classes. And yet I feel intensely self-conscious every time I do, figuring that what I'm saying is so obvious that I'm boring most of the students. (I usually preface my little lecture with an apology to all those who have heard the basic line before.)
>
> And yet, the other day I was reading this little book by Naomi Oreskes and Erik M. Conway, The Collapse of Western Civilization, and they totally don't

> get it. The book is all about climate change, and yet the concept of it being a "collective action problem" just doesn't show up. Thus they express complete bewilderment over the fact that we might all know that outcome x is undesirable, and yet fail to act to avoid outcome x. So they wind up getting stuck on the dilemma that so many environmentalists wind up stuck on, when it comes to explaining our inaction: either 1. it must be the fault of scientists, for somehow failing to communicate effectively how bad x is going to be, or 2. there must be some "ideology" that holds us prisoner, preventing us from acting. In the end they go with both, but leaning more towards 2—they wind up positing an ideology, called "market fundamentalism", which is somehow supposed to explain our inaction[41].

In a comment on the same post he also says:

> When I first taught the Prisoner's Dilemma, I told the class that I had graded their midterm papers too harshly, so I intended to raise their grades. Some of them already did quite well though, so I gave them the option of either having their own grade raised by 5%, or else giving everyone in the class an extra

[41] I think there's a deep disconnect that might make writers like them call collective action problems "ideology". Many on the hard left don't take it as a given that people act in broad self-interest the way economists model, and which is required for collective action problems to make sense. They genuinely believe it to be natural for people to act "for the common good" as a core motivation that is just as strong as the one to provide for yourself and your family, and that people are "trained" out of this by ideology ("capitalism", "market fundamentalism" etc.). The assumption could be that people simply wouldn't be self-interested at all if it weren't for capitalism making us so, and therefore that collective action problems don't naturally exist.

> 1%. I handed out index cards, for them to write their preferences down and return the cards to me. I also had about 80 students, only 3 chose to give everyone the 1%. I then took great pleasure in pointing out that the class had just collectively passed up the opportunity to have their grades raised by 80%. Then I told them that I wasn't actually going to raise their grades, and that it was all to prove a philosophical point. They all hated me, but I proved my point!

Without a coordination mechanism, i.e. a way to artificially create a collective agent capable of taking actions, the students could not do what was in their own shared interest.

Coordinating with yourself

This hidden equivocation applies beyond coordination problems as traditionally understood. Consider this advice: "you can lose weight simply by eating less." It's the same trick! It's easy to eat less *on any given occasion,* but it's not effective. It's effective to eat less *on ~every* occasion, but it's not easy because it's not a singular action available to take. It's not one action but many, and this phrasing pretends the distinction doesn't exist[42]. Losing weight is a coordination problem in a half-metaphorical sense: you're trying to get many agents to all give up something in service of a common good that's only achieved if everyone cooperates. It's just that in this case it's not different people having to coordinate, but the same person at different times. Your future selves must all agree to eat less, and they must be able to trust each other to follow through. It's not worth it for me to have steamed cauliflower instead of cake *now* unless I can count on my future selves to make the same decision. Same with other exercises in self-control like quitting smoking: it's worth it to not have this cigarette

[42] Sometimes this is meant to communicate that there's no "trick" or no way to make it easier and you just have to hunker down and do it. I think that's not entirely right, but that's a different issue.

now if it means I never smoke, but if my future selves are going to puff away anyway I might as well light one up now. Self-control problems are coordination problems across time instead of across people. And they are similarly misrepresented, using ambiguous words to hide the difference between two kinds of "action", and thus make the real issue disappear through sleight of hand.

Chapter 8

Think About Polysemy All the Time

—What's so unpleasant about being drunk?
—Ask a glass of water!

— Douglas Adams, *The Hitchhiker's Guide to the Galaxy*

My apologies, but we're not done with ambiguity. I will beat this dead horse until even the most hardened of slasher film enthusiasts have to look away.

By now it's clear how normal it is for words to really be multiple words in a trenchcoat. To make things even worse, it's not always a set of discrete, well-defined meanings, but sometimes continuous spectra of meaning, along several dimensions. This can mean, as we shall see, that a claim can contradict itself, depending on how a word is interpreted. Multiple related meanings, called *polysemy,* is not corruption or mistake but a natural, essential part of language. The *Oxford Research Encyclopedia* says:

> Virtually every word is polysemous to some extent. Still, the phenomenon has been largely ignored in the mainstream linguistics literature and in related disciplines such as philosophy of language.

The same article says that it "rarely seems to cause any difficulty for speakers of a language", and I hope to convince everyone reading this that they are hilariously wrong about that.

Consider a simple word like *fruit.* The height of midwittery is to point out that the tomato "is a fruit, not a vegetable", implying that this means something important, instead of just stemming from "fruit" having more than one meaning. There's a botanical meaning and a culinary/cultural meaning, and they happen to be referred to by the same string of sounds and letters (or *signifier,* as it's called). But we could just as well, if we were aiming for clarity, use two different terms for what are two different concepts (or *signifieds*).

The word "animal" has gone through similar process as "fruit". In ordinary language[43] it means "non-human creature", but as biological knowledge advanced, the word was repurposed to fit into a scientifically informed system, now *including* humans. However, the word, just like "fruit", is still used in its traditional, non-scientific sense. Note the implication: "humans are animals" is true for one common, correct meaning of the word, and false for another. The statement itself, sans context, is neither true nor false.

But what's the *real* definition of "animal"?

Stop it. *Stop it right now*[44].

I once asked in an X/Twitter poll if snow is ice. Of course, since ice is water in solid form and snowflakes are water in solid form snow "is" ice. However, our everyday understanding of ice is as a hard, transparent, slippery substance, and this can directly contradict the scientific meaning. If my wife asks me if there's ice on the driveway, I would be *wrong* to say yes if it's covered only in soft powder snow, because that's not what she asked. "Is snow ice" has no correct answer without an interpretation that makes it commensurable with concrete facts. We could have had a similar confusion with "air" if scientists had continued doing what they did in centuries past and refer to different gases as "airs", but we were spared that.

We're not idiots. We do understand that words can mean different things since we're adept at using metaphors (and frequently used

---

[43] I'd like to import the Swedish expression "i folkmun" to cover a lack in English: literally "in common-people's-mouths", it refers to the way normal nonspecialists use words.

[44] Not to say that all potential meanings are equal, but there is not one real meaning by some metaphysical necessity.

metaphors become established alternate meanings). We understand that the "head" of a department is different from the "head" on a person, or that an explosive news story is not explosive like dynamite is. But that's because such alternate meanings are clearly separate from each other. There's no continuity of meaning between those senses of "explosive", and only a tenuous one between, for example, "dream" as "something I wish for" and as "a hallucination I experienced in my sleep" (the link is daydreaming, being adjacent to both). They're sufficiently separated for it to be obvious that they're different, and which is meant. For many words, however, meanings are not as clearly separable, and the intention is not as obvious.

"Does a straw have one or two holes?" is an effective piece of engagement bait. It gets people debating the question, staking out positions and defending them, despite it appearing meaningful only because the multiplicity in the meaning of "hole" is *just about* non-obvious enough to mess with our heads. A hole can be an opening *into* an inner space, or an opening *through* an object, and a straw has two openings into its internal space but only one opening through itself. The correct answer therefore is "it depends on which meaning of 'hole' we're using". That's it. There's no single correct answer because there is no single correct meaning of "hole" that makes the question well-posed. However, it feels like a "hole" is *one* thing, so when we subconsciously grab on to a meaning we think it's *the* right one, and we start arguing about it.

That we think this riddle is novel or interesting instead of obvious and boring suggests that we're not familiar enough with polysemy, and I'm going to keep nagging until we are.

It is at this point I feel compelled to point at that I, indeed, can be fun at parties.

Word decomposition: a how-to

These partially separate meanings arise by semi-metaphorical extension, or *metonymy*. It works like this: words referring to types implicitly assume some attributes occur together. For example, *art* traditionally means both "is beautiful" and "requires impressive skill to make". Since we're good with metaphors we can extend the word and call something beautiful "art" even if it's mass-produced and doesn't require impressive skill, or be so impressed by a skill that we'll call something "art" even if it isn't beautiful. As a result, "art" can refer to things that have *nothing* in common. However, since the core meaning is still there, acting as a bridge, those extended meanings don't come apart fully.

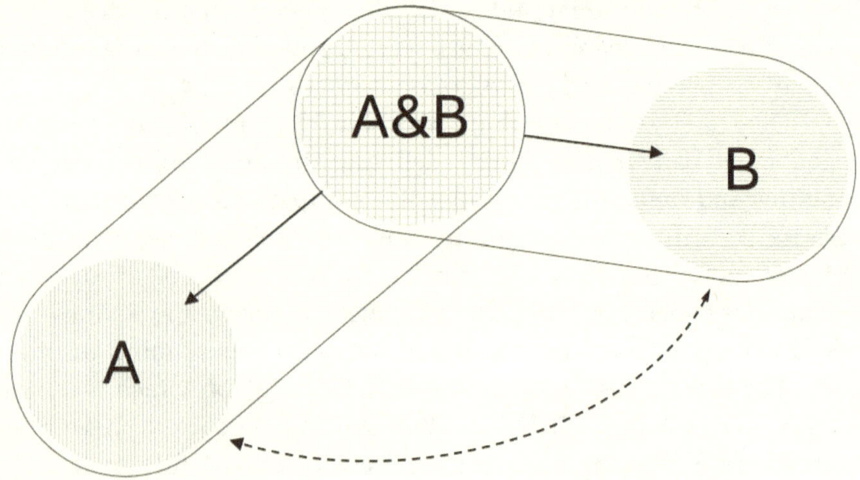

Figure 7, a word with multiple facets can be extended semi-metaphorically in different directions using only one facet each, and come to describe things with nothing in common.

We can go back to chapter 1 and take apart "reality" this way. If the core meaning of "reality" is "the world we experience, as it really is" we're talking about two things: what we experience (what philosophers call *phenomena*), and what really exists outside us (what they call *noumena*). The word itself does not make a distinction, and if different people focus on each of the two components, their idea of "reality" will drift apart in opposite directions. Science focused on the "how things really are" part (and was so successful that we now need to build stupidly expensive particle accelerators to expand our knowledge into the nature of physical matter any further), while parts of the humanities focused on the "what we experience" component, making their use of "reality" drift in another direction, sometimes even writing off the "how things really are" aspect altogether.

"Understanding" is similar. Back when I studied history of science, my professor, knowing that he was addressing engineering students, wanted to point out a difference between the sciences and the humanities. "The sciences seek to *explain*", he said, "while the humanities aim for *understanding*". It's stuck with me because it felt sneaky. "Understanding" something can mean you have correct knowledge about its nature and how it works, which is nearly identical to "explanation" in the scientific sense, but it can also refer to a subjective "experience of understanding", i.e. an intuitive sense that you've got the hang of something.

Construing "understanding" as a single thing suggests that the subjective experience of understanding goes together with genuine explanation-through-knowledge understanding. But it doesn't necessarily. I couldn't help but think, if *explanation* is off the table in the humanities, by what standard do we know that the experience of understanding reflects real knowledge and isn't just an illusion? Pre-scientific peoples may very well have got the experience of understanding from stories telling them that the sun is a god, the stars are tiny holes in the dome that is the sky, allowing the light of heaven to shine through, or that thunder and lightning results from Thor dashing across the sky, pulled by his eight-legged horse and throwing a magical hammer at his enemies. How is such illusory yet genuine-feeling "understanding" separated from real understanding, if not by explanation in the scientific sense?[45]

[45] There's of course plenty of literature on the validity of knowledge in the humanities, but as far as I know there's not a clear, canonical answer. On the lowest level, such knowledge has to relate to historical facts and sources, but as we get more abstract, when it comes to what general, theoretical patterns to construct from the facts, it gets dicier. In practice, what matters is what the experts in the field find convincing. Nonetheless, you run into problems when you theorize over things that are both *abstract* and *vague*, i.e. not constrained by anything other than the intersubjectivity of practitioners (neither by physical reality like the

The distinction is subtle enough to fuel confusion and disagreement, and to be leveraged in rhetoric. Consider another example: "myth". Its core meaning is "a non-factual story that people treat as true and which acts as a source of common values". It comes apart into:

1) things people commonly believe but aren't true

2) a story that establishes common values

Those two have no direct relationship. However, because the core concept is there, satisfying both criteria, it creates a continuity between the two—a bridge—that can be used to equate them in a motte-and-bailey-like manner. You can, by describing something as a myth in the second sense, imply that it also fills the first (is false and shouldn't be believed). I'm thinking of books with titles like (all real): *The Beauty Myth, The Deficit Myth, The Porn Myth, The Abstinence Myth, The Myth of Mental Illness, The Ethnic Myth, The Myth of American Meritocracy, The Myth of American Inequality, The Myth of Left and Right* and *The Myth of Continents*.[46]

The author of the blog *Applied Divinity Studies* once accused the CEO of the coding academy Lambda School of lying because he had publicized a number of examples of its alumni landing lucrative software engineering jobs. Not that this is dishonest per se, but since the example salaries were all higher than what the average alumnus took home, it did seem dishonest to claim it was a *random* sample, which the CEO had done in a tweet:

---

technology-adjacent hard sciences, nor by the strict formalism of mathematics). If you at the same time lack the ideological and temperamental diversity required to prevent the inevitable assumptions, simplifications, priorities, and generalizations from consistently drifting in a specific direction, the field will confuse their produced results with true conclusions about the world. The more that happens, the less their expertise is worth.

[46] I haven't read them all so I can't say whether they all rely on this trick, but it is potential tool in their arsenal and every time I've heard someone use "myth" about a broad concept there has been references to its role in establishing values, not just as a factual belief.

> Honestly I'm just looking at our offers database pulling out random names at this point, this isn't even hard.

He may not have meant that he was taking a random sample in the statistical sense. "Random" has a formal mathematical meaning but is also commonly used to mean not following a rule or procedure ("lol I'm so random") or not being exceptional or standing out, or being just one among many ("I'm just a random blogger"). This relaxed sense may have been how he meant it. Not that it makes everything alright, but an understandable slip.

"Normal" means both "average/typical/unremarkable" and "ideal/proper", and when the two diverge we get contradictions. Is it *normal* to be obese, or depressed? In many societies today the answer is "yes", in the sense of them being common and unexceptional, but "no" in the sense of being ideal and healthy. There are other times where "normal" refers to something being acceptable, even if *not* typical[47]. Exclusive homosexuality, for example, is uncommon as in being a small share of the population, but is normal as in being socially accepted as not a pathology (at least in public life in the west).

The word "opinion" is an interesting case. An opinion is the opposite of a fact in the sense of depending on personal judgment, but we don't make a distinction based on the *way* an opinion is not a fact. It can be either through uncertainty ("in my opinion, Argentina are going to win the World Cup") or through subjective preference ("in

---

[47] In my 2017 article *The Nerd as the Norm* I pointed out that what we consider "normal healthy social skills" are perhaps good and ideal but not normal in a statistical sense. Historically it's not been the standard to interact socially with people we don't already know, and when we did there were scripts for how to behave (formal greetings, titles, introductions etc.) and a certain stiffness was expected. Today we're supposed to be natural and at ease with strangers right off the bat. There's no script, all improv, requiring historically unprecedented levels of social fluency to be considered normal. I argued that this is because people with strong social skills have disproportionate influence over social norms, exactly because of those skills.

my opinion, pineapple is good on a pizza"). This lack of distinction allows us to use the properties on one side ("everyone is entitled to their own subjective preferences") on opinions that differ from facts along the *other* axis ("you can't criticize another's judgment on factual questions"), as if they weren't different things.

"Objective" is a sneaky word too. Discussion around *technocracy*, in the sense of making important judgments (hiring people, allocating university spots, determining punishments, etc.) using algorithms or other formal decision procedures without human judgment involved, suffers a lot from the polysemy of "objective". These systems are good, argue proponents, because they are objective and thus less vulnerable to biases. Wrong, say the detractors, they aren't objective at all because there are biases built into the ways they are set up and what properties are measured and how.

The solution is to articulate their differing meanings of "objective". A system that ranks job applicants by, for example, their height, would be objective *in execution* because once the rule had been set up there would be no room for anyone's subjective judgment in applying it. But it wouldn't be objective *in design* because subjective judgment decided what the rule was going to be. It's true, at the same time, that such a system *is* objective, and that it *is not* objective. Confusion over words does in fact obscure the substantive disagreements people have on the issue, preventing them from being properly discussed.

I once got into an argument with a friend about the logic of time travel after watching the 1999 movie *Thrill Seekers*. To me, the ending didn't make sense because the story didn't obey the rules it had set up for itself. He thought it did because to him it was more important that nothing counterintuitive happened than that implied rules were followed. "It's about logic," he said, "as in, what is easiest for the human mind to comprehend". I balked at his notion of what "logical" meant, because as far I was concerned, it means to obey a formal reasoning procedure, regardless of intuition. I'd missed that, in common parlance, "logical" gets used as a synonym for "makes sense" (which implies "intuitively"). So, when rules clash with intuition, something can be both "logical" and "not logical" at the same time.[48]

To "compromise" means "giving up something you want and meeting another party halfway", which can be split into "giving up something you want" and "meeting another halfway". I noticed this in an article describing parents who want to retain some of their pre-parenthood lifestyle as "refusing to compromise". Paradoxically, it was exactly wanting to meet in the middle regarding the lifestyle demands of parenthood that was deemed a *refusal* to compromise, while other parents who went all-in on parenthood (and therefore didn't compromise but rather gave in completely) were not described this way. In this case, "compromise" meant only the "giving up what you want (entirely)" part. Had only the other facet been used, the judgement on who were doing the compromising would've been the reverse.

Strategic use of polysemy is common across the political spectrum. It became popular on the right in the 2020s to accuse LGBTQ activists of "grooming" children, where the creepy connotation of pedophiles grooming children for sexual exploitation is applied to the normalization of LGBTQ lifestyles by using the general meaning of "grooming" as purposeful preparation for a future role (e.g. grooming someone for leadership) as a bridge.

Then there's this tweet by pundit Matt Yglesias, showing how polysemy of "homeless" enables misrepresentation and obfuscation:

> Researchers, HUD, and the journalists who rely on their data use "homelessness" to mean the situation when a person does not have a home.
>
> But people complaining about "homelessness" usually mean something like "people acting out on the street."

[48] Compare with the two meanings of "understand" from before.

I could go on and on[49]. There is almost no end to it, or to disagreements that go off the rails because of it. I've seen people absolutely flummoxed by how anyone could refer to habitual liar and braggart Donald Trump as "honest". But it makes perfect sense: while "honest" has the meaning "saying only true things", which does not describe him, it also means "saying what you really think instead of being tactful", which does.

I hope the onslaught of examples has convinced you that, despite what the Oxford Research Encyclopedia says, polysemy does cause plenty of problems. And they *should* know, since Ludwig Wittgenstein complained about it in *Philosophical Investigations* (published posthumously in 1953). Progress in philosophy, he claimed, was hampered by a misunderstanding of language. Instead of words having clear, unambiguous definitions suitable for logical operations, like philosophers like to assume, he claimed that concepts (like "game", his favorite example) describe clusters of members that share overlapping features, like a family shares traits without having any single one in common.

The problems in philosophy he complained about are also problems in public discourse, and increasingly so as it becomes further abstracted, ideologized, and academicized—and without importing corresponding academic norms. The situation can, however, be improved with more awareness and prudent practices. For example, I like to use the tilde ("~") in front of words or phrases. It serves to remind the reader that a word has multiple interpretations and not all of them apply. It's my way to say that one does not exactly and completely mean a word, and that it cannot be joined with other instances of the same word as if they were equal (its use by others looks similar, even if they might not articulate in in the same way). I recommend it.

[49] Originally I did, there are many examples I decided to cut, and perhaps some more I should have.

PART III

Bids for Social Reality

Chapter 9

The Big List of Existing Things

Before 1802, cirrus, cumulus, and altostratus clouds hadn't been given names. Untitled before 1802, the shapes were present in the sky, ethereal or ephemeral, presumably since the big bang, but undesignated, until they needed to be. Why then? The world hasn't been fully seen, until it is named.

— Lynne Tillman, *Men and Apparitions*

After dissecting so many words in the last chapter, we're ready to take on the big boss. I've been in a few philosophical discussions over whether this or that "exists", and by extension what it means for something to exist. It turns out that "exist" (or "real", which serves the same purpose) is one of those words that fight back and get more confusing the harder you work to make sense of them. It's not as simple as them having two or a few related meanings. Rather, "X exists" and "X is real" are shorthand for a bewilderingly diverse array of claims. Before we can even begin to think about whether they're true, we need to work out what they're shorthand *for*.

To start with an easy one, what does it mean that some *person* exists? An obvious example, a real person whose existence everybody knows about, is Prince William, future King of England. He is real, obviously. No issue there. What about Napoleon? He died over 200 years ago. Does he exist? Not *now*, not in the same sense Prince William does. But we wouldn't say that he's not a real person. He isn't *made up*, like, say, Sherlock Holmes is. Just like it makes sense to say that Prince William exists in a way Napoleon doesn't, it makes sense to say that Napoleon exists (or "is real") in a way Sherlock Holmes doesn't. Sherlock Holmes clearly doesn't exist, though. He's fictional. That means "doesn't exist", right? Not so fast. If someone asked if there is an *existing* character we can use for a detective story set in 19th century London, you'd say: "yes, what about Sherlock Holmes?". Fictional characters do exist, as in, there's a commonly used sense of "exist" that applies to fictional characters. It's used to differentiate between those that have been created and used in fiction and those that haven't. Sherlock Holmes is a *real* fictional character, unlike Archibald Dundermunch, the abrasive crime fighter with a drinking problem and complicated relationship to his ex-wife, that I just made up. And Dundermunch has actually been made up *as an idea,* so he exists in a way purely hypothetical characters that nobody's made up as examples of made-up characters do not. Holmes exists in a way Dundermunch doesn't, and Dundermunch exists in a way countless hypothetical characters don't.

However, regardless of whether historical figures, fictional characters, or imagined fictional characters exist in some sense, we feel that Prince William *really* exists. He exists not in some extended or metaphorical in-a-sense way, but *literally.* He belongs in the Big List of Things That Currently Actually-Truly-No-Shit Exists For Real. It feels as if there should be something like that list. Simple: things come into existence, exist, and then stop existing. At any point in time there is therefore a complete list of existing things, in theory. This is the same as saying that "X exists" is either true or false for anything in place of X. Prince William is such an existing thing. He does change a little bit all the time as the atoms in his body move around and get gradually replaced, but that doesn't mean he disappears and comes back as somebody else. He has an identity that persists from the moment he starts existing to the moment he's taken off the list.

People are the easy cases. They have concrete physical boundaries and change gradually enough for us to comfortably model them as a single, cohesive entity. The same can't be said for other entities, where we're more likely to be, and feel, confused about what existence means.

A good old philosophical classic is *heaps*. Do heaps exist? If you take a fistful of candies and arrange them into a heap, has a *new thing* come into existence? Does the Big List have a new entry, just like the list of people is updated when a baby is born? What if you define a new *kind* of object? I arrange exactly 13 candies in a row and proclaim that this is called a "threap" from now on. Does it earn a place on the list when I arrange them, or when I declare the definition? Or never, because it's not a "real" kind of thing? What if we also define "tweap" as "heap with an even number of items", and keep adding? Does it blink in and out of existence each time we add another piece? Is it the same tweap coming and going, or a new one every time? What's the total number of tweaps existing throughout history?

While the idea of a big list of existing things *feels* true, it gets weirder and weirder as we keep thinking about the implications of that intuition. Can we really increase or decrease the number of objects in the universe just by rearranging stuff or making up definitions of new kinds of things? It's at odds with what it feels like for a thing to exist. The part of my mind that says there should be a Big List also thinks that the list should have a set number of entities and only change when things *actually* come into existence or are destroyed. But what's "actually"? Kinds and things are partially or wholly overlapping in complicated ways. Tweap is a kind of heap, and pine is a kind of tree; a steering wheel is part of a car, a finger is part of a hand, but the Big List is supposed to only have one entry for each object! It leads to some strange consequences: a thing can only be on the list once, as a member of a single category, while other categories it's also a member of are abstracted and constructed—not real. "Human" feels like a real category while "tweap" doesn't, so humans have unified, persistent identities and tweaps don't, and inbetweeners like regular heaps, fictional characters, and countries, are confusing.

Following naive list-intuitions to their logical endpoint gets us to a place where things only really, truly exist if they are indivisible and fundamental—if they do not consist of smaller parts and they are not generalized forms of more narrow categories. In this strict sense,

Prince William, an abstraction of an ever-changing composite structure, does not exist[50]. The only way out of this contradiction is to admit that there is no Big List, no indivisible and fundamental "things" in the ordinary sense, and thus no essences. They are artifacts of how we represent reality, not the real nature of that reality. It's not that our model is *wrong* (and could be made right), it's that our model is a completely different kind of thing from what it's representing.

The many maps of recognized concepts

In real life we don't use one big list but many smaller lists, and which list is relevant depends on the context. An object being on a list (i.e. "existing") means something different depending on the list: Sherlock Holmes is in the list of fictional character but not in the list of living persons. His list membership (existence) depends on which list we're talking about.

Maybe lists aren't the best metaphor. Our models of reality are more complicated; things just don't hang around all alone and unstructured in lists, they have relationships to each other, consist of each other and are abstractions of each other. What we have in our heads are more like maps, of objects (and types of objects) with properties (and types of properties) and relationships (and types of relationships) to other objects, and the relationships are themselves objects with properties, and so on—maybe the relationships can have relationships to other relationships, and structures of relationships can be objects, and there can be types of such objects?

Everything under the sun can be represented by a token in our hodgepodge of maps: objects, sure, and their properties; categories, yes; relationships, too; and higher-level stuff like processes, structures, patterns and agents, including multilevel abstractions like the properties of the processes by which a type of pattern of relationships between structures change. If that sounds impossible, think of words

[50] Unless of course he has an immaterial, immortal, (indivisible and fundamental) *soul* to serve as his persistent essence. What an intuitive and convenient concept that "solves" a lot of difficulties.

like *democratization, credentials, professionalism, usefulness, civility, centralization, treaty, polarization* or *finance,* and what it would take to define them in concrete, physical terms. They're shorthand to an extreme degree. Or, they would be, if we if actually thought in material terms and then created shorthand for those thoughts to communicate them. But we don't. We don't use them as a summary of something whose full complexity we work out and understand internally but don't specify to others. We pack these philosophical nightmares into neat-looking chunks, slap labels onto them and treat them like they're "things" in the way a rock or an apple is a thing. It's an extraordinarily powerful system.

We pay for that power in clarity. We pay for it by giving up the possibility of matching our words with reality and cleanly distinguishing existence from nonexistence. Does it even make sense to say that such entities represent a "real" object in the world? Looking at what we got when we looked at people and fictional characters, we realize that it really depends on interpretation. In other words: existence depends on context. That phrase is destined to be misunderstood. After saying something like it I was once told in response:

> What exists or not is dependent on context? What kind of relativist bullshit is that? This is what makes people look down on philosophy. No, there is an objective reality.

Yes, there is an objective reality. It's just not made of words and not at all structured the way our linguistic representation of it is, and the relationship between the two is far less straightforward than we tend to think it is. Whether something exists depends on context not because objective physical reality changes with context but because the exact meaning of "exist" does, and therefore the truth of the *verbal claim* that the thing exists. Consider what we mean, in concrete, physical terms, when we say that these things do/don't exist or are/aren't real:

global warming
a solution to global warming
magic
numbers
negative numbers
infinitely many prime numbers
circles
the Patriarchy
Belgium
Kurdistan
devil worshippers
free will
quiet quitting
cancel culture
ADHD
Black English/Ebonics/AAVE
white privilege
the Friendzone
the Wall
violence against women
violence against men
meritocracy
fate
luck
existence
seasons
possibilities
probabilities
personality types
learning styles
genders other than male and female
the color blue
the color "tongue flesh"
the word "irregardless"
the War on Christmas

human rights
money
a chance of rain
a meaning of life
the meaning of life
moral truth
God

When any entity, no matter if concrete or abstract, simple or complex, physical, structural, or conceptual, can be represented as a "thing", that may or may not "exist", relationships between model and reality can be unfathomably diverse. With language, we can use a single phrase format to say completely different sorts of things while having it sound and feel like we're saying the same sort of thing.

We're blind to shorthand because we can be

We don't think of "grass is green" as shorthand for a complex physical state of affairs involving chlorophyll, light frequencies, and photoreceptors in our retinas. We just think that grass is green, period, as a brute fact. And we think of it as *knowledge*, even though the vast majority of us wouldn't be able to explain what it means materially.

The same goes for other beliefs that are simple to state but complex or impossible to concretize, including social and political ones we often disagree about. Yale researchers Leonid Rozenblit and Frank Keil coined the term *illusion of explanatory depth* in 2002, after noticing an effect where people believe they understand things in much greater detail than they really do. From Wikipedia:

> In the experiment they conducted with 16 Yale undergraduate students, they asked them to rate their understanding of devices and simple items. They were then asked to generate a detailed explanation of how they worked and then rerate their understanding of their understanding of that item. Consistently, ratings were lower after generating an explanation, suggesting they then began to understand

> that they lacked understanding of that item after attempting to explain. Rozenblit and Keil concluded that having to explain basic concepts or mechanisms, confronts people with the reality that they may not understand the subject as much as they think they do.

There's hilarious research showing that people, when asked to sketch familiar items like bicycles, often draw them with obvious errors that make them nonfunctional. We don't need to represent bicycles in great detail to be able to operate them, so we don't. This wouldn't be a problem if we knew enough about our own limitations to be humble about it, but Rozenblit and Keil's research suggests we don't. According to them, the effect shows up in domains as wide-ranging as "mental disorders, natural phenomena, folk theories, and politics". Specifically, such unjustified confidence in the domain of politics has been said to contribute to polarization.

Our capacity to learn from experience is not set up to arrive at perfect truth. We've evolved to be ruthlessly pragmatic, wanting to know just enough to navigate the world, but without being aware of the difference. Experiencing regularities (things fall down, fire burns you, sharp rocks can cut things) makes us form an internal representation of rules, and of types that behave in particular ways. It matters to us that blueberries are predictably sweet, which gets mentally modeled as an essence and rule: "it's sweet *because* it's a blueberry". This rule summarizes a dizzying structure of physical facts: in the genetic code that produces a certain set of plants there are sequences that, when translated into proteins, sets up a molecular machinery that produces sugar, given certain conditions, and that sugar plays a role in our own physiology that involves causing, among other things, a chemical chain reaction involving the taste buds and the nervous system, that we describe as sweet taste. The sensation, the pleasure that accompanies it, and the system that produces it, all came into existence because of the role sugar plays as an energy source for our bodies and the role seeds play in plant reproduction.

Through experience we learn that we can rely on a set of characteristics (the shape, color, and positioning typical of blueberries) to infer that pleasure will result if we put one in our mouth. We misconstrue this observed association between two pieces of constructed shorthand as a law of nature. Such rules *explain* nothing but are good enough because we need to predict, not explain.

Systematizing this intuitive tendency to form types with essences was the basis of philosophy descending from Plato. Inspired by advances in mathematics, where the Greeks had found out that you could generalize from the existence of round and triangular things to circles and triangles as abstract objects and get valuable knowledge from reasoning about them as such, he reasoned about abstractions in general. Types and properties were real—more real than their particular instances, in fact—and their nature could be apprehended by pure thought, meaning we can arrive at knowledge about the fundamental nature of reality by thinking carefully about concepts.

Centuries hence, one branch of this truth-seeking enterprise birthed the scientific revolution. Progress in science eventually suggested that Plato got things upside down, and another school of ancient Greek philosophers had been closer to the truth. The *atomists* thought that matter rather than concepts was fundamental, and that events in the world wasn't the result of ideas and purposes but the macroscopic manifestation of tiny particles they called "atoms" (meaning "indivisible", and a word we adopted in their honor) mixing and sticking to each other in various ways due to their different shapes.

Fooled by fiction

It's a sign that our intuitions are badly aligned with reality that while some things feel confusing and some don't, this does not at all match what does and doesn't make sense physically and scientifically. E.g. the durability of material objects makes us think they have essences that persist over time, and when this is problematized through thought experiments like the Ship of Theseus (a ship whose parts all get gradually replaced until nothing of the original remains) or *Star Trek*-style teleportation/duplication of people, it feels confusing. Is it still the same ship? Is the copy still "you"? Can you meet "yourself" from a different time? From the perspective of scientific materialism, these "mindfucks" are complete non-issues.

Conversely, there are things we should find weird but don't. The magic of fantasy fiction is effortlessly comprehended even when it makes no physical sense, because the nonsense corresponds perfectly to our blind spots. A wizard may transfigure something into another form but it's still somehow the same object (and can be transformed back again, which raises the question of where the information about its real form was stored in the meantime). It's physical nonsense because its arrangement of atoms is the *only* property an object ~really has and all attributes we assign to it are derived from that. Most of us learn through experience and education that such transfiguration is impossible, but we have no intuition that forbids it. While impossible, it's not at all incomprehensible, and even little kids accept it without issue.

Wizards can also violate the conservation of matter by making things bigger or smaller, conjuring or vanishing objects, or project arbitrary amounts of energy, and none of it is perplexing. Neither are tropes like stopping time, where a protagonist can still see, breathe, and move instead of instantly freezing to death or being stuck in place by immovable air molecules. It's also, as far as I know, a near human universal to believe that the mind can be separated from the body (and put into another body!). Given a scientific understanding of the mind as the physical information processing going on among the neurons of the brain and nervous system, it's an absurdly convoluted thought that makes no sense, yet confuses absolutely no one. Am I being pedantic? Yes! That's the point! These objections feel like minor technicalities despite being violations of the core principles of the physical universe.

We started this chapter by picking apart what it means for something to exist. In doing so, we saw how loose the connection between words and physical reality is, and by extension how hard it is to bring down an abstraction to prepare it for concrete evaluation. So hard in fact, that we don't do it unless forced. We treat our shorthand as fundamental.

Chapter 10

Facts, Slogans, and Compounds

It depends on what the meaning of the word "is" is.

— Bill Clinton

When we use abstractions we don't engage with the vast complexity that would result if we tried to map them onto concrete, material reality. What we are doing is evoking concepts from a shared library, and once we look at "exist" from that angle, all the difficulty evaporates: "[thing] exists" means "this concept ought to be a part of our shared library". It's phrased as a factual claim—an in theory highly complex one—but can be rephrased as a normative one, and turn dead simple in an instant.

Casting to the social makes it all so simple

In the rhetorical war over the status of transgender people, the side in favor of upholding the importance of biological sex sometimes assert that "biology is real". It's opaque as a truth claim but straightforward as a normative claim about shared social reality: "biology *ought to be represented* in our notion of gender". On the other side, affirmation of transgender identity is often phrased as a "right to exist", a claim whose wild hyperbole when taken literally vanishes if you take it to mean a right to be represented in social reality. Accusations of "erasing" people or perspectives must be understood the same way—not as removing someone or something from actual reality but removing their representation from social reality. To *exist,* in the sociological sense, is to be *collectively acknowledged*. The parallel with the social constructionist meaning of "reality" is obvious.

Arguments about which abstraction may or may not exist, whether we're taking about "cancel culture", "pretty privilege", or "the deep state", are mostly *not* over specific facts. The disagreements are on a higher level of abstraction, where there's enough flexibility for social and political concerns to become more straightforward than factual accuracy. In that situation, the social constructionist frame, counterintuitive as it may be, simplifies things: unimaginably complex *is*-claim vs. dead simple *ought*-claim.

That apparent simplicity can be seductive, since it allows us to push all the difficulty of referring to the real world out of sight. It might even seduce us into forgetting reality. It's true that we're not *only* talking about physical facts, but neither are we so independent of the material that they become irrelevant. Constructionism pays a price for defining away the philosophical complexities, namely losing the ability to separate between different *reasons* an idea is collectively endorsed. It could be the truth, a merely useful model, a collective delusion, or a lie enforced through propaganda, but without reference to reality there's no basis for a distinction[51].

Their temptingly simple frame must be moderated, since existence claims run the gamut from being purely about matter to being purely about concepts, and most of the time their position on that axis is genuinely ambiguous. It's possible, and I think preferable, to look at them in a way that combines its materialist and constructionist interpretations and focuses on *fit*. Think of it like this: "this concept ought to be in our map" can be rephrased as "a map with this concept *fits* reality better than a map without it". It's still an ought-claim, but with reference to reality.

It's a claim of fit between two things (reality and a verbal description), and it has two degrees of freedom, two movable parts. Now, see what happens when we hold one part fixed at a time. Holding the map constant, we say something about reality. In the Kurdistan example from the last chapter, we can take a definition of existence/list membership as a given ("is an internationally recognized

---

[51] It's easy, and tempting, at this point, to make your politics the basis.

state with functional sovereignty") and say that Kurdistan is not in the list of such things, and therefore "doesn't exist". In this case we're *giving information.* If we on the other hand hold reality constant, that is, take the facts about Kurdistan as a known given and claim that it is real, then we're saying that "real" in this context *should mean* something that *includes* Kurdistan—something like "being a geographical area dominated by an ethnic group with common history, language, and identity and that deserves self-determination". In this case we're talking about *how we want words to be used.*

In normal conversation we don't specify which end we're holding fixed. If you say "Kurdistan doesn't exist" you are saying (potentially) both something objective about Kurdistan's lack of sovereignty *and* what you think it should mean for something to be considered a "real country", in this case some way that doesn't include Kurdistan.

"Free will exists" sounds like it's saying something about how our wills work, but it's also, maybe most of the time, actually an endorsement of a particular idea of what "free will" *should mean* (i.e. something we actually have). And finally, saying other genders than male and female do or do not exist is partly about how people's psychologies actually operate, but mostly it's about how the concept of gender ought to be defined and used.

"Label fits thing" is a two-way relationship

This applies almost every time we stick a label to something. If I say "that guy is tall" I'm not merely informing you about his height, I'm also saying something about how I think "tall" should be defined (in a way includes him). And if that wasn't enough, I also indicate that "tall" is a valid concept that can and should be used (tallness is *real*). How much of each I'm doing is delicately dependent on context, like how controversial or borderline my judgment is ("you think 5'10" is tall?"). Factor in that we may disagree on what counts as controversial or borderline, and watch the layered complexity spiral out of control. It sounds hyperbolic for an example chosen for being simple and anodyne like "tall", but try and substitute "exploited", "selfish", "mid", "lazy", "hateful", "indigenous", or "abusive" and it's clear how it fuels plenty of serious disagreement.

Note that this muddies the old philosophical distinction between is and ought. I don't mean that you can derive an "ought" from an "is" through logic alone, I mean that normal claims in natural language have elements of both, in differing proportions. Plain facts occur when there is no significant disagreement about a word's meaning. This applies to most technical and scientific terms, and to many clear-cut social facts like the names of countries, companies, and currencies, or the winners of competitions. Note that in sports there are procedures in place, like precise boundaries and referee calls, specifically designed to eliminate ambiguity and make reality fit into rigid categories. In those cases, applying a label is so close to a pure statement of fact that the "ought" element is negligible. For illustration, here are a few facts:

Dolphins are mammals
Spain is a monarchy
Ganymede is Jupiter's largest moon
The Toronto Maple Leafs are an ice hockey team
Proteins are chains of amino acids
A hexagon is a six-edged shape
There is a cup on the table in front of me

Trouble is, we feel like we can rely on words having correct, uncontested meanings more often than we actually can. There's an expectation that definitions of words are objective facts, and therefore that every claim phrased like a fact is factual. The other side of the fit, the ought, is implicit. In other words, there's a pervasive bias about which side of the fit we assume is held fixed, and we default to thinking of words as tools for communicating information. But words are more than tools, they are also *art supplies*, with which we express and induce feelings and impressions, and they are *weapons*. They cast judgment, invite sentiments, and shape the way we see the world;

what seems real and what doesn't, what we notice and what we don't, what we celebrate and what we condemn.

The tools and weapons available in a society determine quite a lot about that society, so we fight to influence the set of communal equipment in the direction we prefer (implicit rhetoric). We want there to be equipment that makes it easy to do what we want done, and we don't want there to be equipment that makes it easy to do what we don't want done. There should be weapons that can harm our enemies, but there should not be weapons that can harm us.

It bothers me when people act as if Orwell's *1984* is all about surveillance. It isn't any more than *Chernobyl* is about nuclear power; both of them show the horrors of manipulating our sense of reality, and what happens to societies that corrupt and destroy their own ability to make sense of the world.

> Don't you see the whole aim of Newspeak is to narrow the range of thought? In the end we shall make thought-crime literally impossible, because there will be no words in which to express it. Every concept can ever be needed will be expressed by exactly one word, with its meaning rigidly defined and all its subsidiary meanings rubbed out and forgotten... The process will still be continuing long after you and I are dead. Every year fewer and fewer words, and the range of consciousness always a little smaller. Even now, of course, there's no reason or excuse for committing thought-crime. It's merely a question of self-discipline, reality-control. But in the end there won't be any need even for that... Has it ever occurred to you, Winston, by the year 2050, at the very latest, not a single human being will be alive who could understand such a conversation as we are having now?

In a *Black Mirror*-like manner long before *Black Mirror* existed, *1984* scares us by taking a real issue and turning up the volume to "deafening". Newspeak is not wholly different from real language, and it matters a great deal to us what words are adopted and what they're set up to mean. This is especially true for powerful, strategically important Stalingrad-grade words like "free speech", "democracy", "disease", "bigotry", or "misinformation".

To agree that a label applies to something is to agree that a whole set of attitudes and associated actions should be applied to it. What is and what isn't "theft", "hate speech", "genocide", "torture", "terrorism", or "eugenics" is one of substance and fact, sure, but perhaps more importantly one of *consequences*. If accused of a crime there may or may not be something I have in fact done, but in the end it's the label that sticks—guilty or not guilty—that determines what happens to me. Other labels come with less stark consequences, but with consequences they come. Medical diagnosis is an obvious example of how labels operate with reference to physical and social reality in delicate balance. On the one hand it describes physical facts about a person, but how to conceptualize and label this set of physical facts depends on the social consequences of the diagnosis: you might get treatment, or other entitlements or duties.

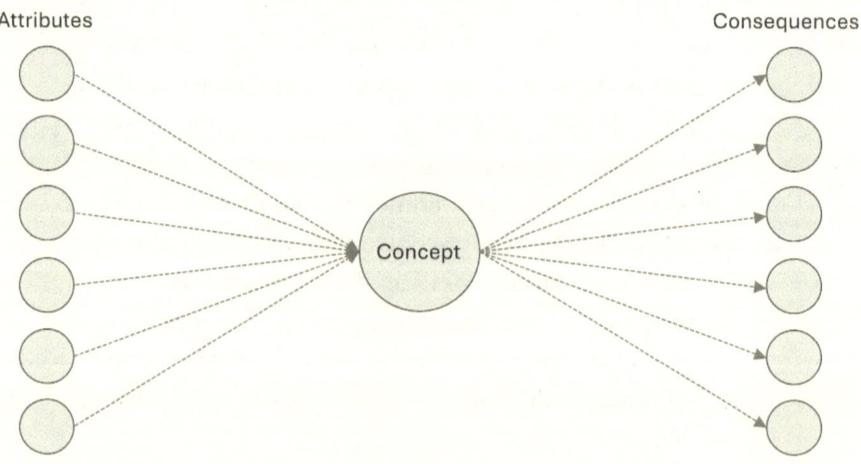

Figure 8, a concept is a label for connecting a set of attributes to a set of consequences.

The *meaning* of the diagnosis is defined both in terms of facts and of its role in regulating social behavior. In technical terms it's a node connecting a set of attributes to a set of consequences. And this is how concepts work a lot of the time.

Searle's social reality and the "counts as" substitution

President Clinton was mocked for getting philosophical over what "is" means, but it's a valid question. The philosopher John Searle got into it in his book on the construction of social reality, which, in an admirable effort at straightforwardness, he decided to call *The Construction of Social Reality.* It should not be confused with Berger and Luckmann's *The Social Construction of Reality,* which is an entirely different book; while B&L were sociologists finding social behavior interesting, Searle, being a philosopher, preferred the company of meticulously defined concepts. His book is an account of what social reality really is, and that account is grounded in the physical and concrete. He says it's an agreed-upon system of abstract entities and relationships, each with associated behaviors. Despite the abstractness of the system itself, we use physical objects and concrete events to represent components within it. Chess is an example: the game defines a set of abstract entities, but they are represented by physical pieces on the board. The rules, while also purely abstract, control the physical movement of the pieces by regulating players' actions. This shared representation works by collective agreement on statements of the form:

X counts as Y in C

A concrete object or event (X) is agreed to stand in for an abstract entity (Y) in a particular context (C). You get things like "this piece of wood counts as a pawn in this chess game" or "this piece of rubber counts as the puck in this ice hockey game". We do the same thing with people: this person counts as the goalkeeper for this team in this game. This person counts as the toastmaster for this dinner. This person counts as a guest. One counts as an intruder, another as your date. Different appropriate behaviors are implied.

Of course, we don't say "counts as". We say "is".

It's easy to see an object as representing an abstraction in the context of a game like chess, but more difficult in situations that aren't as cleanly disconnected from the rest of reality and as artificially formalized. How about:

This person counts as (is) the CEO of this company.
This person counts as (is) a police officer.
This person counts as (is) an adult.
This person counts as (is) guilty of theft.
This person counts as (is) a fascist.
This fetus counts as (is) a person.

While "the company" is a context, even for society in general the CEO is "a CEO" all the time. An adult is always an adult (we feel, if we don't have experience from different countries with different ages of majority). A court is a context where particular people play certain roles, and objects and events are mapped onto a system of concepts (this person counts as the judge, this person counts as the defendant, and this event counts as an opening statement, this as the verdict, etc.), but the system leaks from its immediate context and has consequences outside it; if convicted you're guilty, even outside the courtroom.

If the necessary context—the C term in Searle's formula—is implicit, without clear borders, and we rarely or never move outside it, or need to think about it, or treat something according to the rules of a different context, it easily defaults to just "in general", or independently of context. This unexamined, undelineated "general is" is subjectively indistinguishable from an essential property. It's at this point it becomes difficult to separate the *role* something is assigned in a system of rules from its inherent attributes. Searle is aware of this, of course. After laying out his account of "institutional facts", he says:

> It might seem there are obvious counterexamples to the claim that the features of the X term are insufficient to guarantee the function named by the Y term. For example, when the president or a state governor declares an earthquake or a major fire to be a "disaster", surely, one might say, the brute facts about the earthquake or fire are sufficient to qualify them as disasters in virtue of their physical features. There is nothing conventional about being an earthquake or a holocaust. But if one looks closely at these cases, even they illustrate the point. The function of a declared disaster is that the local victims qualify for such things as financial aid and low-interest loans, whereas fires and earthquakes by themselves do not generate money in virtue of their brute physical features and consequences.

And later:

> It should be clear from these examples that there is a gradual transition and not a sharp dividing line between social facts in general and the special subclass of institutional facts. In my society "going for a walk with someone" names a social fact but not an institutional fact, because the label assigns no new status functions. /---/ The criterion is always this: Does the assignment of the label carry with it the assignment of some new functions, for example, in the form of rights and responsibilities, which can be performed only if there is collective acceptance of the function? By this criterion, "husband", "leader", and "teacher" all name status-functions; but "drunk", "nerd", "intellectual", and "celebrity" do not.

If we relax Searle's distinction between social and institutional facts, which he agrees is gradual, we can say that any successful application of a label comes with some sort of status, even if not formally codified. Someone who is generally agreed to count as an "intellectual" gets treated differently than someone who isn't, same with "nerd", "drunk", and "celebrity". To repeat: the meanings of these concepts are as nodes between the concrete facts that justify their application, and the consequences the application justify in turn.

By applying labels, we sort individual cases into buckets for easy comprehension and communication. "This behavior counts as (is) an addiction", "this remark counts as (is) sexual harassment", "this act counts as (is) a threat". This is how minds work. This is efficient. This is a good thing, and a necessary thing. We save effort when we think and bandwidth when we speak by using stock concepts instead of preserving full complexity, detail, and nuance for every single case. We don't have the time, not the inclination, and not the processing power to do so. Given that this happens, that it has to happen, of course we want to control what labels are in use, what they cover, and what connotations and associated actions they have. We'd be stupid not to try.

Discourse 101: Lead by example

We learn new words by hearing others use them more than having definitions recited at us. We all know this, so when we want to modify language to serve our interests, an obvious tactic is to use terms the way we want them to be used, and hope others go along with it. A few examples:

> Meat is murder!
> Taxation is slavery!
> Silence is violence!
> Property is theft!
> The personal is political!
> Abortion is murder!

Abortion is healthcare!
Marriage is between a man and a woman!
You can't be racist against white people!
Trans women are women!
AI art is art!

They're *phrased* just like the facts from before, but notice the difference. None of them *communicate information* about their subject. They're not informing us what things count as, by uncontroversial definition, they're saying what they *ought to* count as. They're phrased like facts but are the opposite if facts: they're *slogans*. They're all the way over at the end of holding reality fixed and talking only about the map end of the fit. Whether AI art is "art" or not has virtually nothing do to with its concrete properties and everything to do with what status it deserves.

These particular examples are so obvious that no one is fooled. We know they're 100% slogans. Impure mixtures are much messier and nastier. Think about claims like:

alcoholism is a disease
alcohol is a drug
social media is a drug
socialists don't understand economics
listening to audiobooks is not reading
women are oppressed
Israel is committing genocide
the newest Star Trek series is not Star Trek
the unemployed are lazy
IQ tests are racist
math is racist
pasta is healthy
meat is healthy
masks work
it's selfish to want to have children
it's selfish to not want to have children

progress is stagnating
consciousness is an illusion
automation threatens jobs
someone is a climate change denier
something is rigged
something isn't proven
something is ruined
something is a nothingburger
something is determinist
something is unfair

...and so on. These cause the most dysfunctional shitstorms because of how difficult it becomes to understand what the hell we're even talking about. In each of them, ambiguity about which end we're holding fixed plays a key role in the disagreement[52].

Matters of model

We get that many disagreements have both fact-based and values-based facets, but we don't sufficiently appreciate that these "compounds" of facts and values have properties of their own that don't simply reduce to properties of the parts. Table salt consists of sodium, a dangerously reactive metal in its pure form, and chlorine, a toxic gas, but is itself none of those things. We're better off thinking of salt as its own substance, even though it's literally a combination of two elements.

Compounds of "matters of fact" and "matters of value" become "matters of model", irreducibly over *how to represent* reality. For example, there are many valid ways to make a map of the London Underground, but none of them have Waterloo and Westminster on the

---

[52] This fact-slogan mixture is the form survey questions often take, which is why I hate them and they hate me back. I once worked with interpreting survey data and complained offhandedly to my boss that the questions could be interpreted wildly differently. He just smiled a little out of the corner of his mouth and said "well, you're not the target audience".

same side of the river. "What's the best tube map?" is a matter of model, answered both in relation to reality and to certain goals and priorities[53].

We should invert our understanding of "is vs. ought". Instead of considering the endpoints fundamental and the region in the middle as a mix, we should consider the "is-ought compound" the default state (and "matters of model" the default type of disagreement), with pure "is" and pure "ought" as the degenerate extremes of a spectrum. To express it visually: if white and gray are the endpoints, we might naively picture a spectrum running from 100% grey to 100% white, with 50-50 in the middle, like this:

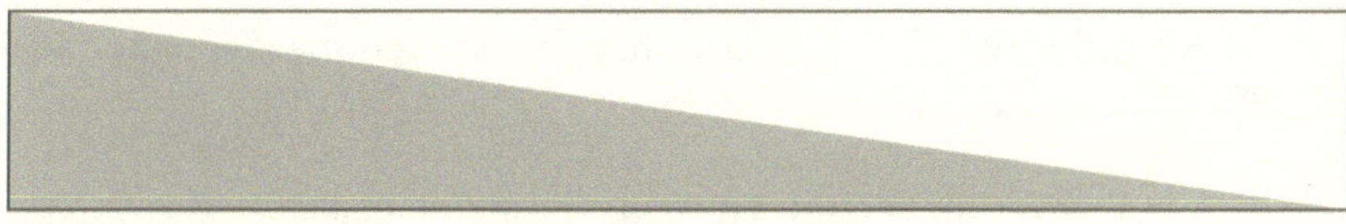

Figure 9, distinguishable proportions of "is" and "ought".

But the components don't neatly separate! It's more like a gradual change in nature from one end to another, is it not?

Figure 10, gradual qualitative change from pure "is" to pure "ought".

It's better, but note how the middle is still defined as a mix of what's at each end. What I have in mind is something where the normal, the standard, is in the middle and the ends are the weird outliers. Con-

[53] Annoyingly, that the map should correspond to reality is, strictly speaking, itself a value judgment, and this trips up a lot of discussions about objectivity and truth. What's objective vs. subjective is judged on two levels at once: there's plain objectivity and subjectivity, but *which one of them to prioritize* is a *subjective* decision. Think back to the distinction between objective-in-execution and objective-in-design, or to Lyotard's point that science cannot justify itself according to its own norms in the eyes of a society that doesn't assume those same norms (just like you can't justify empathy to a psychopath that simply doesn't care).

sider a pattern of white dots on a grey background. *That's* the normal case, and as the dots get bigger or smaller—the pattern gets weirder and more extreme—it becomes pure grey or pure white.

Figure 11, a pattern of "is-ought" that simplifies to pure is/ought at the extremes.

Our understanding of "matters of model"-type disagreement is severely underdeveloped compared to the classic matters of fact and matters of values. That, somehow, gives us the impression that they're not quite real. The philosopher David Chalmers's paper *Verbal Disputes* from 2011 begins like this:

> Is there a distinction between questions of fact and questions of language? Many philosophers have said no. But a version of the distinction is ubiquitous, in philosophy and elsewhere, in the notion of a verbal dispute. Intuitively, a dispute between two parties is verbal when the two parties agree on the relevant facts about a domain of concern, and just disagree about the language used to describe that domain. In such a case, one has the sense that the two parties are "not really disagreeing": that is, they are not really disagreeing about the domain of concern, and are only disagreeing over linguistic matters.

Chalmers discusses verbal disputes lucidly and in detail, so it's not like this is *news* or anything, but when you must turn to a philosophy paper to read about what should be a household insight, something's wrong. Clearly this isn't, even among philosophers, old hat enough to have been condensed into wisdom digestible by popular consciousness.

The classic "if a tree falls in the forest and no one hears it, does it make a sound?" is an entry point into philosophy because it gets people thinking about how words are not identical to the reality they describe. That it *works,* as in, it disrupts our habitual thinking patterns enough to confuse us and notice that confusion, represents a failure. In a well-functioning discourse culture we would find it obvious and boring. When we're not even comfortable handling such playthings, how can we be trusted with the grown-up stuff?

Towards defensive weaponry

Lacking a shared understanding of matters of model is dysfunctional by my earlier definition because it means there is no agreed-upon articulation of what is in dispute. There's also a moral problem with manipulating people's minds by affecting their maps of the world without them consciously aware of what's happening. We cannot easily pick apart and evaluate compounds of fact and slogan in unclear, complicated configurations before we take them on board, and this gets exploited. We can vaguely sense that we're being played, but like when a cat coupling comes our way, we don't have the tools to articulate how, so we can't disarm the aggressor. If there existed a shared, reasonably intuitive and consciously accessible understanding of how this works, a lot of such rhetoric could be defanged.

However, we're quite far from there. It's often derided to argue semantics because we, like Chalmers says, think such disagreements are not "real" and therefore that such objections are pedantic and inconsequential. But they are real, they are of consequence, and we need to come further in understanding how. When I was in the middle of writing this chapter I came upon a tweet by Sean Ono Lennon, son of the famous couple:

> I think a lot of our problems today are fundamentally semantical. People mean very different things when they say words like woman, or capitalism. If we could agree on our terminology I think there would be a lot less fighting.

He's a grown man and found this to be a new insight. I'm not dunking on him for it, mind you, he's come further than discourse as a whole. I just mean that this shows how we are, in terms of shared, taken-for-granted understanding, three steps behind where we need to be. The first step is what he said: what looks like factual disagreements on the surface are often about semantics. The second is to understand that this isn't some minor bug but a central feature. Today, the creation, shaping, and application of labels is the *primary activity* in public debate. It's always been there, but it has become more important as the speed of conversation increases and "dialogue", in the traditional sense of repeated interaction between two well-defined parties, is replaced by the pouring of rhetoric into a sea of disembodied voices, constantly grouped, ungrouped, and regrouped into ephemeral coalitions in an ever-shifting constellation of beefs.

Telling someone to not argue semantics is to imply they should accept whatever vocabulary is given to them. But that would be to give up and give in, since the object of the game is to get labels to stick, and to resist and disrupt your enemies' efforts to do the same. That's PR. That's rhetoric—but not the classical kind where a man in a toga tries to convince the court to execute Socrates. Implicit rhetoric isn't about some specific decision but about influencing shared vocabulary to be more favorable to you and your friends.

In late 2022, when Elon Musk bought Twitter, the arguments over what "shadowbanning" means and whether the former Twitter administration had engaged in it, erupted right on schedule, moving through the groove that "grooming", "white supremacy", "censorship", "ableism", "critical race theory", "incel", various kinds of "denialism" and anything ending in "-phobic" had traced out before. I had a conversation with a user claiming that arguing over the definition was just a distraction, and that we really should focus on whether what had been done was or wasn't justified. My answer was that fighting over application of labels is the way we do that, in practice. It's not so much a distraction as it's an obfuscating layer of indirectness that 1) is due to our need for simplicity and expediency, and 2) whose engineering acquires a great deal of significance.

It's all predictable: some word *W* ("misinformation", "censorship", or "conspiracy theory") comes with such strong negative implications that if something counts as *W* then it's always wrong and no one will try to argue that *W* can be right. Thus, getting *W* to stick is an automatic win. Because of that, if W has a narrow, specific meaning then it represents an untapped valuable resource. If we can expand it to cover more stuff we can use it to defeat our enemies!

In friendly, low stakes circumstances we deal with dynamic growing and shrinking of buckets just fine: the "fruits of your labor" are not literally fruits, nor are you talking about a literal purchase when you skeptically exclaim that you're "not buying it". Nobody cares to complain about this, nor to point out that someone who "watches football religiously" is not engaged in worship of the divine. However, when getting away with using a word means an auto-win, there are *stakes*. What's normal and fine in kind, collaborative communication becomes controversial in combative rhetoric, and fights over where lines are drawn result in trench warfare:

Is it only racist to think worse of people because of their race, or does it go all the way to just participating in a society where different groups have different aggregate outcomes?

Is "climate denialism" only the belief that the world is not warming, or does it go all the way to political disagreement with certain means of addressing the problem?

Is only hatred of all Jews "antisemitism", or does opposing Israel also count?

Is it only "censorship" when the government prevents someone from speaking, or does it go all the way to anyone doing anything to stop someone else from being heard?

It is only "misinformation" if it's outright false, or does it go all the way past misleading into not necessarily false or misleading at all, but going against officially sanctioned information?

Does "socialism" only refer to an economic arrangement where the workers own the means of production, or does it go all the way to "any restraint of self-interest"?

Is "white supremacy" only the conviction that "whites" ought to be legally and socially above others, or does it go all the way to support of industrial, enlightenment modernity and its associated norms, which originated in Europe and now dominates the world?

Is "wokeism" only the most radical of revanchist illiberal collectivism or does it include milquetoast liberal equality that everyone but a few hardline reactionaries are on board with?

Are "conspiracy theories" only stuff like "space lizards built the pyramids, faked the moon, and killed robo-JFK" or does it go all the way to thinking that some powerful institution is less than perfectly honest and unbiased?

Labels that automatically imply illegitimacy are so valuable that we fight for control over them like we do over oil wells and gold mines. We egg on the proliferation of verbal weapons to invalidate the beliefs and behaviors of our enemies ("sealioning", "victim blaming", "virtue signaling", "NIMBY-ism", "mansplaining", "suicidal empathy", "gatekeeping", "cultural appropriation"[54]).

Try "counts as"

We should be able to get this generally and explicitly understood. A hypothetical final, third step to deal with it more constructively and address our differences directly is a bigger challenge. The best tip I've got for now is to substitute "counts as" for "is" as often as you can and see how that changes things. It's been my habit for some time, and it has turned out to be surprisingly powerful. It steers your mind away from abstruse philosophical mudding about essences and towards what the issue is really about: *how we're going to treat something*. And as part of that, it invites the question of which specific context we're discussing, which can help to dislodge mistaken essentialism.

[54] The last two are especially funny to put next to each other since they are mirror images.

Chapter 11

The Room: Reading and Writing

Language is the foundation of civilization. It is the glue that holds a people together. It is the first weapon drawn in a conflict.

— Ian Donnelly, *Arrival*

The Australian standup Tom Gleeson once did a bit about a new Code of Conduct being sent around an office. The code contained a rule: "no body policing". Whoever wrote it knew that not everyone would understand what this meant, because it came with a clarification: "no commenting on people's appearance". But why, you could ask, would you even use the term "body policing" if you knew that it might not be understood, enough to include a clarification, and one that's not much longer? Why not just tell people not to comment on others' appearance?

Gleeson turned it into a joke, but it is a seriously interesting question. My suspicion is that establishing that specific language as policy is the point, because words are, after all, gang signs. That is, we use them to signal who we are and whose side we are on. And just like you can infer people's allegiance from the words they use, you can infer who has power from whose language is used in policy. Furthermore, once the language is installed, it's a source of even more power[55].

---

[55] In this case, as often, it's also that terminology itself comes in gangs. Certain terms, like "sin", "male gaze", "hypergamy", or "QALY:s" don't exist in a vacuum. They are part of systems of mutually reinforcing beliefs, and having them accepted as default language creates a way in for the rest of the group.

Beliefs are endorsements

Social reality is a non-codified kind of "policy" that we renegotiate all the time. We jockey to get concepts recognized (or dismantled), and labels applied (or removed). Our personal sense of reality, local in our head and in constant interaction with the shared one in the cloud, we call our *beliefs*.

We've already seen how social reality is not optimized for accuracy, and neither are personal beliefs. For me, it took a long time for this to fully sink in. I used to take it for granted that to *believe* something had a straightforward meaning: to think it is true. "Technically" true. Not good, beautiful, moral, desirable or fashionable. Just true, plain and simple. Quite far into adulthood, anything that wasn't clearly a matter of plain objective fact, was, as far as I was concerned, an opinion, sentiment, or attitude—not a belief.

I did notice that people just happened to miss this distinction an awful lot, but didn't pay much attention to it. I considered it a curious but insignificant slip. But it's not, and in the process of demonstrating this to myself I put together a collection of quotes from around the web:

> "I believe taxation is a literal instance of theft."
>
> "What if you just damned believed other people were worth less than you?"
>
> "I, personally believe now vegetarianism is a personal thing."
>
> "Do you believe it is the duty and obligation of other people, through the government, to support the poor through welfare payments?"
>
> "Because libertarians believe any compulsion is slavery."

"The reason I'm so curious is because I genuinely believe all human beings, irrespective of talent, wealth, etc., are equal."

"Religions promote a lot of mundane beliefs as well (about how to treat others, how to live virtuously, etc.)."

"He sincerely believes journalism is a noble duty to seek truth and uphold freedom of speech."

"If one person believes abortion is murder, then they are likely correct to vote for the one who will limit its scope."

"If you don't believe the lower classes are exploited, then I don't know what to tell you."

"I believe I have zero duty to follow the law.

"If you believe a sub is a sandwich, you must believe a hot dog is a sandwich."

"But Jesus did believe you had to pay taxes."

"A quiz administered, with questions such as 'Do you believe men and women should be equal?'"

"A huge proportion of ethicists believe eating animals is wrong."

"Do you really believe a man doesn't have the right to know if he is the father of a child?"

"I believe most, if not all, such regulations should be abolished."

These aren't truth claims! They don't refer to any facts; they're either moral claims or opinions about how to apply labels[56]. In my old headcanon, this use of "believe" was just a mistake, little more than a cognitive bias, and I assumed people would immediately recognize it as such if it was pointed out to them. When they didn't, it confused the hell out of me. I remember reading a Christian complain about atheists being "obsessed with having technically correct beliefs" and I wanted to ask: "Wait... do you mean to say that you *don't* think your own beliefs are technically correct? What does that even mean? Do you believe them or not?"

It was a conversation at age 30 with an anthropologist coworker who didn't see any problem with his field being an uneasy mix of science and political advocacy that finally triggered the gestalt shift: for most people, even well-educated, intelligent ones, what is true vs. what is good is not a salient, let alone fundamental, distinction. Thinking you can "believe" *moral* propositions like "you should pay your taxes" is not just a metaphor, nor a slip or bug, it is normal and functional[57]. Good heavens.

In other words, "x should count as y" (because it represents an actual truth) or "x should count as y" (because this is desirable), or even "x should count as y" (because that's what good, cool people think) are not obviously, intuitively separate things in the eyes of most people. The lack of distinction between them *in language* was not the meaningless quirk I had thought, but evidence of something I should have paid better attention to.

---

[56] I realize that this is controversial. I realize that most people, even many philosophers and scientists, believe there is some outside-of-us "moral reality" or "conceptual reality" just like there is material reality, and which we can depict perfectly accurately, without all the problems I discuss. If you do, I honestly don't know what to tell you. Our disagreement is simply too deep to address, and this would have to be an entirely different book if I were to try.

[57] It was around this time I started to feel alienated from society.

Fact costumes

Beliefs are just as social as they are epistemic, but we still pretend they aren't. Most people aren't as forthright as the Christian that confused me. We're coy about evaluating claims on other than epistemic grounds, partly because we don't know the difference, but also because we realize that it's problematic to treat our subjective judgments as objective facts. Even though we use "believe" about subjective things all the time, there's still the assumption that beliefs are supposed to be true or false. When there is such murkiness, we should be suspicious that it's for the standard reason: to let us get away with shit.

"Believe" implies objectivity that alternatives like "think" don't. "I *think* chocolate is the best ice cream flavor" makes perfect sense because we understand it as personal preference. "I *believe* chocolate is the best ice cream flavor", however, implies there's an underlying truth that holds generally, not just for me. Try it out. Substitute "think" for "believe" in the "believe"-examples from earlier. I don't know about you, but to me they no longer carry that smell of someone trying to get away with something. "I think I have zero duty to follow the law" is an honest phrase, not trying to hide its subjectivity.

If "think" is introverted, "believe" is extraverted. Beliefs are not just what you personally think, but what you think should count as correct *socially,* for everyone[58]. And what's correct for everyone? Truths. *Facts.* So, when we want to dress our preferences in fact cos-

---

[58] We use "believe" to mean "support" even when it's totally transparent. With "I believe in you!" we express personal support and loyalty, not a factual belief in someone's capability to succeed. Indeed, to "believe in" means to pledge loyalty to something the way you do to a person — or a god, a group, a nation, an enterprise, etc. We ask "do you believe in God?" not "do you believe God exists?", because the function of religious belief is the shared commitment to a symbol standing in for a community. It's the use of "believe" in the factual sense that's *newer.* According to *Etymonline,* "belief" originally meant "confidence reposed in a person or thing; faith in a religion" in Middle English. "Conviction of the truth of a proposition or alleged fact without certain knowledge" arose in the 16th century.

tumes we say we "believe" them, to make them compelling to others—literally compelling, as in something that compels.

Moral reasoning: making bids for social reality

Philosophers have long debated what moral statements mean. Is "murder is wrong" a fact? Is it an expression of personal preference? Or isn't it *claiming* anything at all, and is just the verbal equivalent of cheering or booing ("boo murder!")? Is it a meaningless statement?

They're none of those. They are *endorsements* of positive or negative judgments as part of collectively held social reality. "Murder is wrong" means that we *ought* to have a commonly accepted concept, "murder", that refers to certain actions, and which we consider to be *wrong*. The label "wrong" means that certain responses, like prevention, punishment, or ostracism, are appropriate towards it.

Just saying I personally want this policy isn't as convincing as pretending there exists a *fact* of its correctness, simply because people are obligated to accept objective facts but not obligated to accept my subjective opinions. The psychologist Jonathan Haidt, in his influential 2012 book *The Righteous Mind,* says:

> [M]oral judgments are not subjective statements; they are claims that somebody did something wrong. I can't call for the community to punish you simply because I don't like what you're doing. I have to point to something outside of my own preferences, and that pointing is our moral reasoning.

Although the material world doesn't contain any such thing as moral rightness or wrongness, social reality does. We're effectively saying "I want it to be standard practice in our community to punish those who do what that person did", but to make ourselves more persuasive, to suggest this is more than a preference, we *phrase* it like a fact, and this means positing a hypothetical "objective wrongness" property.

This is a case where the social constructionist critique is 100% right: "moral wrongness" does not refer to any feature of the physical universe. It is defined purely in terms of how it regulates social behavior, and its position in social reality is justified by pretending there's a direct representation of an objective truth.

Professing beliefs makes a lot of sense when understood as an attempt, a "bid", at influencing social reality[59]. They are little *sermons* like Kevin Simler (in an article titled *Here Be Sermons*) explains:

> [A] sermon is any message designed to change or reinforce what a group of people value. It might take the form of explicit exhortation, full of shoulds and shouldn'ts, oughts and mustn'ts. Or it may be entirely implicit, like the story of a selfless act that saves the day, huzzah! Commencement speeches, TED talks, presidential inaugurations—whatever else they may be, all of these are at least part sermon because they attempt to change or reinforce our values en masse.
>
> Moving beyond speeches, we also find "sermons" in such unconventional forms as movies, charity balls, national monuments, and corporate mission statements. A sermon can be as elaborate as a parade or

[59] The psychologist Susan Blackmore goes as far as arguing that this "bidding" practice is why we have selves at all. Her theory is based on *memes* in the traditional sense of cultural units that get copied from person to person and evolve, like genes, to get themselves copied more. In her view, "*I believe* grass is green" is a more fit meme (more likely to get expressed and copied) than just "grass is green", because piggybacking on our relationships and personal status makes it more likely to be professed and championed. Thus, memes evolve to include a reference to a hypothetical central entity—a self—which is then assumed to exist. She favors Zen Buddhist meditation as a way to deconstruct and minimize this illusory self, which she believes is unnecessary and pernicious. The full argument is in her book *The Meme Machine* from 1999.

> as straightforward as stating, "I believe in diversity" to a small roomful of people. Even ads can function as sermons. When Apple says, "Think different," it's urging us to celebrate iconoclasm not unlike how a priest might ask us to celebrate chastity or compassion.

Simler goes on to contrast sermons with *lectures*. Lectures, which just impart knowledge, treat their audience as a bag of individuals. The collective experience is not essential. Sermons, however, depend on the audience being a whole that forms shared beliefs. The difference between the two is the difference between facts and slogans: while lectures deliver information, sermons typically don't. They establish shared endorsement of ideas within a group of people.

The making of the room is in the reading

The above is half the story. Our socially shared, dominant belief system is something we try to affect and "write to", but also something we read from. "Reading the room" is what we call sussing out what the standard is around here. Tom Chivers described how this worked during the covid pandemic in his article *Can Dominic Cummings Read the Room?* in 2021:

> Back in March 2020, there was an elite consensus on certain things. Masks don't work. We shouldn't panic (37 days before lockdown, UK newspapers were mocking people who were scared of Covid and telling you you were more likely to be killed by a cow). Travel bans don't work. (I got that one wrong.) If you locked down early, the population would get "behavioural fatigue" after a few weeks.
>
> And if you had read the room, you would have agreed with all of it. I know I often did. That's what the experts are telling us! It's only Silicon Valley tech

> bros who want us to stop shaking hands, and Donald Trump who wants us to close our borders. The trouble is, the room was wrong, and reading it correctly didn't help. /---/
>
> These days, it's wrong not to like masks, and we're criticising the Government for not shutting borders quickly enough to counter the Indian variant. Behavioural fatigue turned out not to be a thing. I haven't shaken hands in 14 months. But we're still reading the room when we agree with those things. It's just that the room's opinion has changed.

To read the room is to perceive social reality. Not to think things through on your own, not to reason, but to navigate beliefs socially. "Accept the standard and stop making trouble" is not a rare sentiment, and that implies that ideas in that position as standard, i.e. with "a spot in the room" are at an advantage.

With that, we can reframe discourse as various actors trying to put stuff in the room or take them out. The nice thing about getting your beliefs into the room is that you don't have to argue for them. In science there's the *null hypothesis*, which is what we consider true in the absence of evidence to the contrary. E.g. we only get to believe our drug is effective if we have strong evidence for it, and failure to demonstrate effectiveness means that "not effective" is assumed. If you believe the null hypothesis, you don't have to do anything, because those disagreeing have the burden of proof. Public discourse is a struggle to acquire that default status for our own beliefs, because once we get it, it's like we've conquered territory. We can sit back and play defense, or use it as a base for further advances[60].

---

[60] This is, by the way, why people get upset by trivial, purely symbolic culture war controversies. Even if inconsequential on its own, a symbolic victory by our enemies is a display of power, demonstrating that they have the capability to dictate standards. We correctly perceive it as a threat.

The honest way to furnish the room is to diligently and openly argue that something is a good idea and deserves to be commonly endorsed. But there's an exploit: the room only exists in our heads. It is only made real by us reading it. If we can manipulate how others read, we can change the room. Indeed, it's often easier to hack the reading process to make people think something's already in there. This is what slogans and sermons do: use our ability to read the room and put things in it by acting as if they're already there.

The use of certain language in conversation is often such an attempt to assert dominance on behalf of beliefs. You'll let it drop how this politician is obviously an idiot, how that group is obviously good, or how happy/unhappy we all obviously are over this or that outcome. You plant your flag and look around to see if anyone wants to challenge. Unless you've drastically misjudged the situation and it's obvious to everyone that you're in the minority, it's costly for anyone to push back because it makes them the one that destroys rapport and makes things awkward. A successful such gambit means others will hear "hm nobody challenged that, that must be the standard here". Congratulations, you've done some furnishing.

A subtler practice, common in journalism and academia, is to describe ideas without direct judgment but in an "exoticizing" way, suggesting they're a curiosity that the reader is not expected to share, understand, or know of. That way you establish it as nonstandard, making the competent room-reader hear "this idea is not in the room, and if you're a competent reader you'll reject it". Once I was assigned an excerpt from Sharon Traweek's *Beamtimes and Lifetimes: The World of High Energy Physicists* for a seminar, and I remember balking at her implication that physicists considering elementary particles more fundamental than everyday macroscopic objects was somehow peculiar and dubious. Her description was not hostile, per se, but it made you feel excluded if you think the physicists are obviously right about that, and it felt like it was on purpose.

Scare quoting is a small version of the same tactic, where you need to discuss a concept that other people use, while signaling to your audience that it's not in the room and should not be taken seriously.

Sometimes disliked ideas are so well established that you can't pretend they're not in the room. Then, if you want to suggest they should justly be removed, you can engineer the implication that they have been actively placed there instead of being "naturally" present. Some words' entire function is to suggest that some part of shared social reality is an illegitimate artifice, like a usurper to the throne. Compare *marginalized, normalized, sexualized, othered,* and *glorified,* with *marginal, normal, sexual, other,* and *glorious* (and the interesting *minoritized* I've occasionally come across). The former suggest that something's current status has been imposed on it and is not its natural, proper condition. This *isn't* like this, it's been *made* to appear like this.

Like cat couplings, this is something you notice a lot once you've started to think about it, and sometimes it gets funny. An article about construction of a new, artificial island described it as "privatized" instead of "private", even though it, being artificial and all, had never existed in a natural state of non-privateness. A similarly eyebrow-raising example I've seen is calling our notion of sex (i.e. male and female) "binarized".

What does this tell us about "politicized"? It implies that something is made out as political when it "naturally" isn't. There was a time at work a few years ago, when some of my colleagues wrote a report about the discourse around Greta Thunberg and her climate activism. They summarized a group of critical articles as "politicizing" her and her message, and I thought… hang on a bit here... activism that calls for big social change is obviously *political* in the plain sense of the word, whether you agree with it or not. The sense meant, I inferred, was "political" as "is the object of legitimate public debate". "Politicized" then, means falsely presented as such, revealing that they (I think implicitly) viewed her message as simply settled truth and goodness, no matter how literally political, against which criticism or reservation constitutes "getting political"[61].

It's a pattern to look out for, all across the political spectrum: pushing for or enacting changes to policy or social norms and then accusing others of politicizing when they push back[62]. The idea is that if an idea is clearly right, settled, and not under legitimate, live debate, then expressing it doesn't count as making a political statement. Thus, when controversies arise, people disagreeing on what is settled will also disagree on who started it—who "got political". I've had people tell me that acknowledging Israel as a country is inherently political and objecting to it isn't *politicizing* anything. Other times people say that drag acts as entertainment is inherently political and objecting to it isn't *politicizing* either. Regardless of what you think about either, both sides, on both issues, think the other started it.

This is another entry on the list of social dynamics that ~worked when we had more coherent public discourse and were on the same page about what was and wasn't on the table, but causes dysfunction when combined with subcultural fragmentation.

Coalitions form in rooms

Jacob Falkovich, in his essay *Monastery and Throne,* condenses the idea of the Room. He says that the naive view I used to hold, and which still dominates as the *explicit* story we tell ourselves and each other, is upside down. Social coordination, not truth-seeking, is the *primary* function of professing beliefs, and of listening to others profess theirs.

> [S]o many people don't seem to notice or care that even institutions they consider to be "on their side",

---

[61] This is all perfectly normal human behavior. It just bothers me when it comes from intelligent, reasonable people who consider themselves enlightened and are eager to point out bias in others' understanding of reality, and thus should be held to a higher standard.

[62] "Culture war" is sometimes used like this as well, as in "the *others* are engaging in culture warring when they oppose the implementation of my side's obviously correct beliefs".

> like the CDC and the New York Times for the educated progressive tribe, are wrong or lying all the time. People look to those sources not for "truth" about physical reality but for coordination of social reality. The CDC's job is to tell other institutions which policies they can implement and not get blamed for, not which policies will keep their clients healthy. People read the Times not to find out what happened where and when, but to find out who is to be comforted and who afflicted. People just want to be on the same page as their peers. /---/
>
> If I had to summarize it in one sentence: being correct is not the same as being good at coordinating social reality, and what those "in charge" really do is the latter.

I may suggest that these rhetorical techniques are manipulative and deceitful, but I recognize that this stems from my particular values and personality. I understand that beliefs don't function the way I used to think, but I remain morally convinced that they ought to. That is, I feel that the subordination of truth-seeking to socially enforced group beliefs is morally oppressive and epistemically corrupt. To me, sermons in Simler's sense are a little icky, a little coercive, a mere inch away from sinister.

It's no surprise that things meant to establish specific shared realities by which I feel threatened and excluded, like group prayer or the ritual sharing of preferred pronouns, creep me out. Even what I broadly agree with feels unsettling when the vibe suggests dissent is unwelcome—when the room sternly demands to be read. I've been to one protest rally in my life, for something I strongly supported (opposition to mass surveillance), but even then, chanted slogans made me uncomfortable. The same happens in social situations where people throw out opinions expecting affirmation rather than evaluation, and others join in, using condemnation of something other as a bonding mechanism. Even when I'm broadly sympathetic, my insides scream in protest against the mood itself and I, in deep discomfort, make a choice between the mildest of possible to-be-fairs and awkward silence[63].

However, I can only conclude, by looking at others, that my categorical antipathy isn't the norm. Most of us *don't* get the ick from sermons, and *don't* feel in our bones that social influence on beliefs is evil. Many are willing participants, eagerly soaking up the convictions that will let us bask in the glow of being one with the group[64]. This is human behavior, and being able to read a room this way without it feeling like an alien imposition is a human faculty (although I resist calling it a skill).

"The Science" and epistemic closure

What about science? We have this institution that's supposed to be different; we have a domain of discourse where beliefs and arguments over them are supposed to be about uncovering truths, not negotiating alliances. Science doesn't close its cases by social pressure, but through evidence, logic, and reason! It's edifying that science has so many defenders today: "trust the science" we hear, so obviously we live in the Age of Reason.

Well... while it is true that science has norms that push it in that direction, the existing institution of Science is still infested with human beings. The ideal of objectivity is just that, an ideal, not always reality. Sociologists of science talk about "epistemic closure", which means that, at a certain point, it ceases to be socially acceptable to hold nonstandard views on an issue. The sociologist Trevor Pinch writes, in the *Encyclopedia of the Social & Behavioral Sciences*:

---

[63] I suppose I feel that moderating and breaking up groupthink is itself a moral imperative. You may read this entire book in the light of that.

[64] I can enjoy this too when it's 100% larping and completely inconsequential, like sports, but never about real beliefs.

> Generalizing from several case studies of controversies, Collins (1981) argued that during controversies scientific findings exhibited 'interpretative flexibility', with the facts at stake being debated and interpreted in radically different ways by the parties in the controversy. This interpretative flexibility did not last forever. By following a controversy over time researchers could delineate the process of 'closure' by which controversy vanished and consensus emerged. /---/
>
> Controversies when seen through the sociological lens turned out to be messy things and were very rarely resolved by experiments alone. /---/
>
> Often the losing side in a scientific controversy continues to fight for its position long after the consensus has turned against it. Those who continue to fight the good fight meet increasing disapprobation from their colleagues and may be forced to leave science altogether.

Pinch states the prevailing view in his field that the establishment and enforcement of a scientific consensus is a social process that cannot be understood as a result of evidence alone. Interpretation is required, which introduces subjectivity and thus social factors. At the same time, most nonscientists think of "science" as a set of facts we learn in school, and that all science is like that: proving facts, once and for all[65]. But science is a lot like public discourse: it produces a model of the world, with significant elements of choice, even some moral values. Just like we underestimate the difference between actual reality and our shared model of it, we underestimate the differ-

[65] Look out for the phrase "scientifically proven".

ence between actual scientific research and the interpretation of it that becomes part of social reality in the role of Scientific Consensus.

To return to picking apart words: "consensus" has multiple meanings, one being "this is what everyone agrees on", which looks pretty solid. But if we equivocate on "everyone" between "every single person" and "the group as a whole" like we did in the free trade example in chapter 7, it can mean "this is what the group as a whole has endorsed". The process to get there from individual beliefs is not specified, and it can in practice mean "this is what the most powerful coalition believes" or "this is what those who speak publicly on behalf of the group think"[66]. "Consensus building" sounds nice; it sounds like we're trying to come to an agreement everyone accepts. That is, however, impossible a lot of the time, so what it does tend to mean is enforcing a dominant view by silencing or pushing out dissenters.

I hasten to add that plenty of genuine scientific consensus of course exists. But this is true less often than most people believe, and when it is you rarely have to assert it. There's typically vivid debate both within fields and between disciplines with the same objects of study. Think back to Segerstråle telling us that on the issue of biology and human nature, different scientific communities had produced closure in different directions, making them unable to interact with each other constructively[67]. When there is consensus within fields but not between them, there's an even greater risk of things appearing

[66] One corrupting influence on consensus production is what the economist Timur Kuran calls "preference falsification", i.e. lying about your beliefs to look good and fit in. Because of it, beliefs that make people who profess them look good will be systematically overrepresented in social reality compared to the actual distribution of personal beliefs.

[67] Today, ideological subcultures similarly produce local closures that they think are general, making them misperceive outsiders as successfully marginalized and dismissible, or even legitimate targets of bullying. We wind up having tiny minorities acting as if they're in a position to enforce orthodoxy.

more certain and unambiguous than they really are whenever an expert (representing a single field) speaks[68].

If we're going to take sociologists of science seriously, we have to be wary of slogans like "Trust the Science" and "the Science is settled". Trusting well-established concrete facts is one thing, but we should not mistake it for trusting pronouncements of scientists (or even less, bureaucratic organizations with authority over science-related issues) on questions too vague, uncertain, or value-laden to be settled by evidence.

The case for manufacturing consensus

There's so much in human social dynamics that produce false certainty and simplicity. Consensus formation favors conquest over coexistence, where the minority (in terms of either pure numbers or power) is shoved aside instead of convinced or respected. The condition has not been cured; symptoms have merely been suppressed.

Sounds evil, doesn't it? *Oh, the brave, put-upon nonconformists!* I'm not mocking the sentiment, I feel it myself, but what happens after a paragraph like this is what always happens when my own rhetoric gets the better of me: I worry that I can be credibly accused of being an ideologue. This tendency to adopt beliefs as a social behavior isn't just a corruption infecting us from nowhere. It serves a purpose, and while it *could* hypothetically be a 100% nefarious purpose we could condemn, get rid of, and be better off for it, it isn't.

Calls must in fact be made. Debates must come to an end, and the short reason why is that we need to do things together. It can be as a country, wherein a lack of shared reality is a problem for democracy as it makes constructive political conversation impossible. It can

---

[68] Remember that an expert is an expert on a body of knowledge and not automatically on the thing itself that the body of knowledge is supposed to concern. For an extreme example: an astrologer is an expert on what astrologers say about star signs and personality, not the actual (non)relationship between star signs and personality. Milder cases also exist.

also be a smaller unit like a corporation; even a plucky startup or a family needs to be on the same page to coordinate their activities.

"Doing things together" sounds simple but is genuinely hard, and as organizations get bigger it gets harder exponentially. Management literature is all about how to get large groups of people to accomplish complex tasks together over time. A lot of it sounds vapid because most people don't engage with this task themselves (in our private lives we typically do things alone or in family-sized groups) and thus underappreciate how hard it is ("if you're someone's boss just tell them what to do??"). In chapter 7 I discussed how coordination problems become invisible when we equate collective action with individual action, or sustained action over time with action at a particular moment. Successful management involves both: making collective action work over time. It's staggeringly complex, and building a shared social reality as a background against which to communicate and align on goals is essential for making it possible. Growing dysfunctional due to failure to align internal beliefs and incentives with long-term company success is a specter haunting every large enterprise.

Writer and management consultant Venkatesh Rao argues that CEOs serve such a coordinating, rather than decision-making, function for large firms. From his essay *CEOs Don't Steer*:

> When I read or listen to exemplars of other categories of leaders, I am often impressed by the subtlety, nuance, agility, and complexity of their thinking.
>
> This is not true of most things CEOs say or write.
>
> Public displays of CEO thinking are impressive primarily for their sheer banality, far above and beyond the needs of non-offensiveness, political correctness and perception management. You can tell it's coming from deep down. It's not an act. I've seen it on display in candid, private settings as well, where

> there's no particular reason to keep things simple. CEO world views really are that simple.

If they don't excel at navigating complex circumstances and making informed, dynamic decisions, then what do CEOs do? Rao:

> CEOs are orientation locks. The opposite of steering is orientation locking. To enforce Newton's first law, the inertia one, on dancing human systems inclined to violate it. Contrary to popular belief, it isn't inertia that's the problem for most companies, it is lack of sufficient inertia in the right direction. Enough to punch through any resistance that might be encountered. And the reason they lack the inertia is that CEOs aren't steady enough in their jobs as orientation locks, providing a steady True North signal to everybody else doing more local kinds of steering work.
>
> The primary CEO function, and the trait the good ones are selected for, is to provide the gyroscopic stability required to keep a company vectored in the chosen direction. They end up in the jobs they do because they counterbalance an organization's natural tendency towards distraction, ADD and momentum dissipation. A typical company is a wandering, wobbling hive mind, liable to spend all its time chasing distractions if you let it[.]

Groups of people don't naturally have collective agency. That only emerges when they're organized in a particular way. And for starters we need a shared, continuously rearticulated sense of where we are, where we want to go, and what we are doing to get there. This requires keeping nuance, complexity, subtlety, diversity, and lively internal debate under a certain level.

> When CEOs are doing this job well, they look like out-of-control assholes.
>
> They derp. They preach. They steamroll over people. They are painfully blunt and black-and-white in their responses to things people say. They make no effort to soften the blows they routinely deliver. They reduce people to tears. They appear to listen, but then they just do their own thing. When they exercise power, they make sure you know it. /---/
>
> If you didn't have a CEO serving as an orientation lock, you'd have governance by some sort of bickering executive committee. /---/
>
> Result: the irresolute Brownian motion of (say) a Parliamentary democracy. No compound interest. No network effect. No platform effect. No force-of-nature unleashed. No dent in the universe.

Those of us you can call nonconformist if you want to be respectful and a bit autistic if you don't, are instinctively resistant to this softly coercive homogenization necessary for collective action. I cannot and will not change this part of my psychology, but I have come to understand how rejecting background shared reality can come across. Where Christianity is the norm, "I'm an atheist" doesn't just mean "I have different factual beliefs than you on this issue", it means "I reject the entire system you rely on to coordinate with others and build trust". Or, in short, "you can't trust me".

Political slogans and corporate policy documents may be more prosaic than our stance on the divine, but they play the same role, and the implications of opposing them are the same. It pains me to say it, but that priggish, petty gossip of a personality that looks for signs of dissent and applies social pressure to root it out does serve a purpose. Nonconformists *are* troublemakers, in the literal sense of *making trouble,* by shrinking what can be taken for granted. For example, if gay people exist some assumptions around family formation and gender relations have to be brought from settled to open, so standards will become more complicated (examples with different politics, where other groups of people cause trouble by insisting on their rights, are left as an exercise).

Shared realities are power bases

Propaganda has the same purpose as the work CEOs do in Rao's model. People might occasionally believe its pronouncements, but that's not the point: propaganda is sermonizing, not lecturing. Even when most don't believe what they're told, it still establishes a dominant background reality everyone has in common and relates to. In authoritarian states it's there to be the only thing you know that everyone else knows. A colleague who worked in China told me that authorities there don't focus on censoring dissent, per se, but on preventing the construction of alternative shared realities that dissenters can organize around to become capable of effective collective action.

Shared realities are the basis of collective action—I might go as far as saying that a shared reality is what makes a group of people a community at all—and thus of power[69]. This is reflected in what one dominant reality called alternatives back in the day: *heresies*.

This informs some contemporary disagreements over free speech as well. "If you don't like what someone says, just don't listen" is an ineffective response to calls for censorship because it doesn't address

[69] Shared realities as a source of social power also explains resistance to large scale immigration even among those who don't dislike or disapprove of foreigners per se. They're fine with individuals of any ethnicity as long as they assimilate into the culture, but not as much with foreign cultures being present as wholes, becoming potential power blocs. If this were the issue, you'd expect immigration to be more controversial (holding pure numbers constant) if it's 1) from more culturally distant societies, 2) mainly from one or a few foreign cultures rather than many different ones, and 3) newcomers are clustered together rather than evenly spread out, making it easier to maintain separate shared realities.

the issue[70]. It's not about the right to speak per se, but the right to coordinate. Censorship isn't about protecting people from ideas they don't want to hear, but about preventing villains from coordinating.

How distasteful it may be for my liberal temperament, reducing diversity of ideas and pushing tensions and contradictions out of view is expedient, even necessary, sometimes. It still comes with an inherent moral cost. If I didn't believe that, I wouldn't be a liberal, but there are clear advantages. Part of the appeal of fascism after the First World War came from noticing how capable industrial societies could be when working towards a common goal. Endless debate is dysfunctional when action is required, and sometimes it's more important that we come to a decision than that the decision is correct and fair. Referee calls work this way, court verdicts work this way, and political votes (where having just 51% percent of the vote means you get your way) do too. It remains offensive to the liberal sensibility, and we for good reasons don't accept the conformity corporations enforce in democracies.

[70] More accurately, it *can* be effective precisely because it sidesteps the issue and addresses a different one. It's just not convincing to the other side.

PART IV

Partial Narratives

Chapter 12

Artificial Clarity

Facts are meaningless. You can use facts to prove anything that's even remotely true.

— Homer Simpson

For years I worked for a small strategy consultancy. I wrote reports about the state of an industry or about societal trends relevant to a client's business. To be successful they had to have a clear, consistent message, because people do not read such reports to stimulate intellectual reflection. They have jobs to do. The clear and consistent message must be justified by evidence and reasoning, regardless of how well the evidence available implies such a clear and consistent message. Clients pay for clarity, and to achieve it I had to take the facts and figures, select them, interpret them, and stitch them together to the best of my abilities to have them point towards a conclusion.

There's nothing nefarious about this, necessarily. I, and I trust others in my situation, do want to paint as correct a picture as possible. If there's a bias it's towards coherence itself. Early in my career I had a reporter from a business magazine email me to ask about a piece I'd written. I referred her to my boss because her questions made me uncomfortable. I didn't feel I could justify or elaborate on what I'd said with any confidence because I had no expertise or interest in the specifics, and no more to say than what had already been said. My piece wasn't the surface expression of a deeper, greater understanding that I possessed. I wanted to be honest and say something like "it says what it says because it can be plausibly argued given the numbers that are there and the assumptions I expect readers to share. It's a superficial exercise in narrative logic, not a judgment coming from domain expertise. I'm not an authority or guru; I'm a professional dot-connector." I could've put together a contradictory, ambiguous, and self-problematizing set of facts and figures instead, had I wanted to, but nobody wants to pay for that. Nobody wants to read a consultant problematizing, hedging, and qualifying. That's what you hire a consultant to *avoid*[71]. You can get your fill of "this is complicated and uncertain, more research is needed" for free on sci-hub.

Rohit Krishnan, writer of *The Strange Loop Canon* and former management consultant at the prestigious McKinsey, writes in his article *Why do big businesses seemingly suck at innovation?*:

> The biggest reason that consultants are hired though is because when something complicated needs to be done at any large company, which is almost everything by the way, then someone needs to help explain what needs to be done to everyone else. And to provide such clarification and business reasoning you do need a solution that makes logical sense, but will also be bullet proof at a later date when someone inevitably asks "why did you do that?"
>
> Clarification turns out to be a non-trivial skill.
>
> What the above means is that consultants try to make decisions that are legible (understandable to

[71] A common way to turn moderately meaningful information into captivating stories is creating types by essentializing differences. If a survey shows that 23% of group A likes cheese while 31% of group B does, then group A are now "Cheese Haters" and B "Cheese Lovers". While that's harmless, versions of the same trick like "demographic group A does Bad Thing somewhat more than demographic group B, so Bad Thing is an essential feature of group A" are not.

> everyone, within their own context), and defensible (one that's highly internally coherent, and if there's any fault it's not in the logic but rather some extrinsic dataset).
>
> And that's really where consulting shines. It creates a clear storyline that is both data backed and internally coherent that management can use to do things. Not necessarily evil or stupid or premeditated things. Just regular normal business things that otherwise would've been shrouded in confusion.
>
> Complexity taming is thus a big part of the value proposition.

Some treat consulting like a scam; "a consultant is someone who asks to see your watch and tells you the time" they say. While not a complete lie, it's far from the whole truth. As Krishnan points out, businesses need coherent internal realities, and for this they need to crystallize a strong story about the world and their place in it. A management consultant is not hired to bring you detailed knowledge about your own business, but to be an expert at producing and legitimizing an account of reality. They do this by anchoring it in as much real data and compelling reasoning as possible and putting their prestigious brand on it.

As part of it, consultants reject the difficult and theoretical language of academia but retain the academic norm of hiding their selves, i.e. minimizing the personal authorship behind what's produced. In a scientific paper you're not supposed to write "we did this", but rather "this was done", and the motivation is the same as with consultants' reports: we avoid saying "I" or "we" because we want to maintain the illusion that no individual, no subject with a personal judgment, is speaking to you. Rather, it's reality itself coming through.

The function of such a report is to be a bridge from reality and facts to policy and action[72], with minimal subjectivity. They translate the mess and complexity of the real world into a clear, crisp (clients love "crisp") story that also implies a way forward. The stronger both relationships—from reality to narrative and from narrative to action—the better.

Now, it's not just the narratives in boring corporate reports that do this. They *all* do. We tell stories because we want to say something, and we want to say something because it matters for what gets done. Narratives, whether supplied by consultants, politicians, artists, activists, CEOs, teachers, journalists, entrepreneurs, or academics, describe the world and tells us what to think about it—what is good and what is bad, who are the heroes and who are the villains, who owes and who is owed, what is possible and what is pie in the sky, which parts of ourselves should we value and cultivate and which ones should we get over.

Partial derivatives

With that in mind, let's take a small detour and talk about calculus. Or, let's talk about how narratives and ideologies are almost, but not entirely, unlike calculus. I was on the fence about including this mathematical metaphor at all. I first used it in a blog post from 2016 that this chapter is loosely based on, and while the article was appreciated, the metaphor alienated some. Still, according to several who said the post was revelatory to them, the metaphor was important for the message to click, and I'm wary of meddling with a winning formula. So, please, humor me.

A mathematical *function* is a description of a relationship between numbers[73]. For example, the function $y = 3x$ represents a relationship where for all values of x, the corresponding y is three times larger. Functions of this kind have a *derivative*. The derivative is an-

[72] If you're mathematically inclined: a transformation matrix from fact-space to policy-space.

[73] I'm using nonstandard, loose terminology to make it easier.

other function we get by applying a set of procedures you grind and grind in calculus class. The derivative describes not how to get the corresponding y from a particular value *x*, but how to get the *rate of change* of *y* at a particular value of *x*. In the $y = 3x$ example this is really easy: the derivative is 3 (i.e. $y' = 3$). There's no *x* in it, meaning it's always the same, for all values of *x*. This is easy to see if we make a graph:

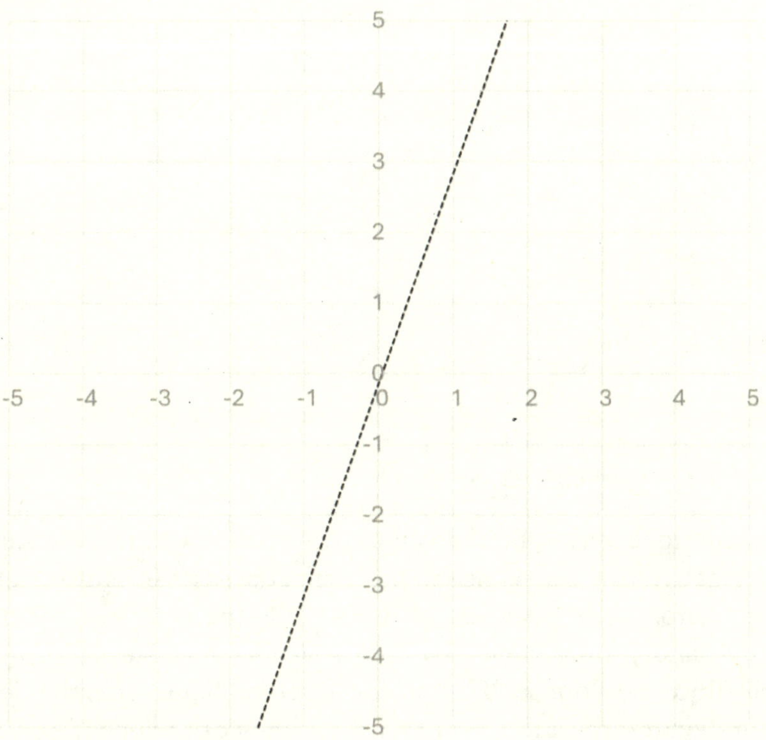

Figure 12, a graph showing y = 3x

If *y is 3x*, the relationship is a straight line, and the *slope* of that line (which is what a derivative describes) is always the same. A fixed number. For more complicated functions (relationships), that isn't the case. If we had a different formula and *y* would be equal to the square of *x* instead, the graph would look like this:

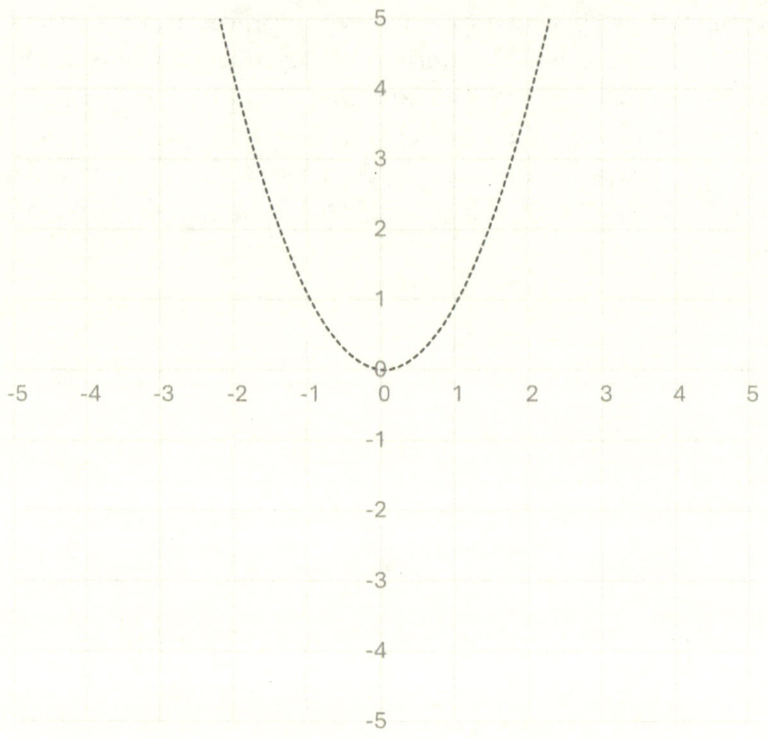

Figure 13, a graph showing y = x^2

Now the slope varies. Left of center, where x is negative, the slope is also negative (the line is heading down as we move rightwards). At exactly zero, the slope is also zero (flat). On the right half, when x is positive and grows larger, we get a steeper and steeper upwards slope. Since the slope is different for different values of x, the derivative of y with respect to x is not a fixed number but depends on x. I.e. it's also a *function* of x (the derivative of $y = x^2$ is $y' = 2x$).

Why is this important for our purposes? By itself it's not. I'm just trying to make sure that everyone who might not have known what derivatives are before this knows now. It's risky to use a mathematical metaphor since it makes people expect rigorous reasoning, but when I say that the derivative of a function is a bit like a narrative accounting for a certain set of facts and events, I mean this in a loose, metaphorical sense. The derivative can be considered a "depiction" of a function. The value "3" is a depiction of the formula "$y = 3x$" from a point of view, focusing on one particular feature: x's effect on how y changes. Now, what was a static, inert way of describing two entities has become a description of a dynamic, causal relationship.

Narratives are stories describing a set of entities and events, positing a causal, thematic, meaningful relationship between them. The narrative version of a trivial derivative like "3" is a simple story like "you dropped the plate on the floor and it broke" or "you pushed your little sister so she started crying". Many we come across in the real world are more complicated than this, however.

Derivatives *destroy information.* They're not complete depictions of their functions. In fact, "3" isn't just the derivative of "$3x$" but also of "$3x + 20$", "$3x - 159$", and an infinite number of other functions. This is because taking the derivative with respect to x (that is, centering this one relationship) removes any terms without x. Where this gets even more important—and this is the key point—is when a function involves more than one variable. If y is, for example, not three times x but three times x plus the value of some other variable z ($y = 3x + z$), then it no longer has a single derivative, and "slope" becomes less intuitive. Now it has two *partial derivatives,* one focusing on how y depends on x, and one focusing on how y depends on z. Its two derivatives are two different depictions, each centering one relationship while making the other invisible.

A complicated function may describe a relationship between, say, five variables, multiplied and divided etc. by each other in all sorts of ways. It will have five partial derivatives, five depictions from five points of view, each looking completely different while still describing the same underlying thing. Each partial derivative makes a different actor the lead, against which everything else becomes a supporting character at best, if not completely absent.

Partial narratives

I find the parallels between this and the relationship between narratives and the reality they depict quite striking. A strong narrative focuses on one aspect of reality and shapes itself entirely around the expression of this one truth. That which doesn't fit, that which points in the opposite direction, or meaninglessly out into empty space, is cut as irrelevant. What separates a narrative from reality is how everything is meaningful; everything has been selected, curated, and massaged to communicate something.

More artsy and intellectually ambitious narratives try to balance several partial derivatives, jumping between perspectives and avoiding a single point of view. This is difficult and not the norm, as most stories—certainly the most emotionally powerful and convincing ones (ask any journalist, propagandist or PR person)—are built from pieces pointing in the same direction. Sonya Mann, writing at *Sonya Supposedly* says, in *Notes on Narrative*:

> We expect coherence from narratives. Arguably, coherence is the point—we don't want to be bombarded with disparate factoids. Narrative ties all the threads together, braids them; narrative means synthesis into an intelligible whole. "Sense-making" means constructing and applying narratives, which are hypotheses of causality and importance. Especially importance.
>
> What makes a story a story? Riffing on "The evolution of stories: from mimesis to language, from fact to fiction" by Brian Boyd. A story is a salience line. A narrative isn't about causal A happened which directly triggered B, it's about A happened which is significant in light of B; assertion of the link between the two being salient rather than mere description of it being present. /---/
>
> In essence, narrative is a communicated hypothesis of causality, whether predicated on familiar reality or the strange dictates of a fantasy world. The very

> sequentiality itself, the assertion of connections between A and B—that is the narrative.

We're closing in on the essence of what it means to be human. As intelligent creatures we long to, well, *intellige*. The impulse has been most successfully pursued within the sciences, but it's everywhere, including in millennia of mysticism, philosophy, and religion: *we want to know the Truth*. We want to understand the hidden principles and rules that govern a world looking so chaotic. We want to peek beyond the messy details and see the order, simplicity, and perfection underneath—we call this "insight" or "enlightenment", and it's thrilling and satisfying.

It's all about separating *signal* from *noise*, to throw more technical language at you. The signal is the principle, the pattern, the content, the information, the "real stuff", while the noise is the randomness and incidental irrelevancies that interfere when we try to perceive the signal. Look at this graph:

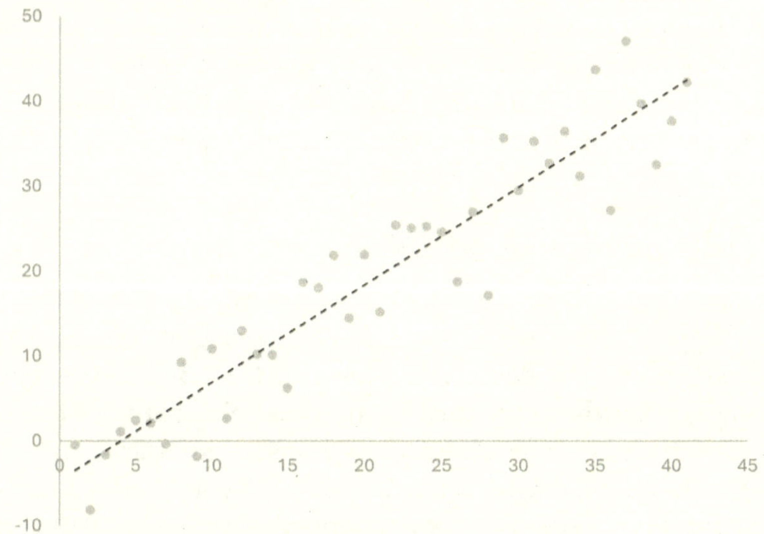

Figure 14, a simple relationship, with noise.

There's an obvious relationship here! The dots are almost on a single line! Whichever facts in the world this depicts, there is a rule, a deeper truth, to be found. That's the signal. Whatever is making the dots *not* line up perfectly is noise. It's not relevant to the underlying truth, so we exclude it from our mental model. When we replace the concrete and real with a generalized abstraction, we're apprehending a purer, truer truth, as we see it. This isn't a new idea, born of modern science or the mathematics of signal processing that brought us this jargon. It's straight up Platonism: messy physical reality is the noisy, corrupted, indirect manifestation of a realer-than-real reality to be found in abstractions. And while Plato was a pioneer for writing it down, he was clearly formalizing an inherent drive of human intelligence.

Now, combine this habit with how partial narratives work: 1) removing noise and irrelevancies to get a cleaner, clearer signal feels like apprehending a purer truth, 2) partial narratives select a particular point of view from which to make sense and then ignore everything that doesn't fit. Putting the two together implies that partial narratives are crack cocaine to intelligent minds.

We can pick an idea or relationship to center in a story and present it to trigger an experience of insight, regardless of how truthful. Intuitively we cannot tell the difference between what is presented as central vs. irrelevant in a story from what is genuinely signal and noise in the world.

Partial narratives as ideologies

This all came together for me when I read a summary of Ayn Rand's *Atlas Shrugged*[74]. As an erisology enthusiast I was attracted by the controversy around the book. Some love it, cite it as an inspiration and moral guide, while others call it horrible, plagued with terrible writing and reprehensible philosophy. Books with such power to cleave readers into lovers and haters this sharply are fascinating because they give us clues as to how people differ, like psychological litmus tests.

---

[74] I did not read the whole 1000-page novel. Life is too short.

Atlas Shrugged presents a view of how the world works and a set of values to go with it, wrapped up together in a story: innovators and industrialists carry the world on their shoulders. They are responsible for progress and prosperity, but the envy, pettiness, and ingratitude of others are keeping these heroes down. Compare this to the Marxist story, where laborers create all value while exploited and oppressed by the bourgeoisie. If Rand's and Marx's narratives were consultant's reports, they would close with opposite recommendations.

Those who find Rand's values off-putting do so because they don't buy the narrative. They think it's not a fair description of reality, and therefore that the moral implications are wrong. What stands out to me about her account is not its rightness or wrongness but its obvious *partiality*. It's not false, but features reality seen only from one specific angle, obscuring most of what we're accustomed to focusing on, especially in fiction. If the aspect she centers is central to your own life and experience as a reader, then depicting the whole world based on it and nothing else will work perfectly for you. It'll be just like removing all annoying noise, complexity and ambiguity to make things crisp and perfect. You feel enlightened and emboldened: *everything is so clear to me now*. It overwhelms you with a sense of insight that is powerful and beautiful. It is also how ideologues and fanatics are born.

If this aspect is *not* central to your own intuition and experience, it will not work for you. It will repel you. Its clarity looks perverted, gross, and twisted instead of insightful. Instead of removing the noise to get a clear signal, she's *removed the signal*, the key truth about how things work, and warped the noise left behind into something grotesque. A franken-narrative that can only be the result of blatantly ignoring the real, central truth that should be staring you in the face! You cannot be serious! It takes willful ignorance to believe something this upside-down. Clearly this is just self-serving bullshit, presented in bad faith.

It goes without saying that I don't think either the lovers or the haters are all wrong or lying. They've just derived with respect to different variables and got two worldviews that point in opposite directions. They live in the same world but disagree on what is signal and what is noise, what's central and what's marginal, what's the essence and what are its caveats we discard when rounding off and saving the result in our gray matter archives.

The supposed "true nature" of capitalism is one of the clearest examples of partial narratives I can think of. What *is* the true way to represent a complex reality in simple terms, with no self-evident standards on what to put front and center? Both "capitalism is when people can trade freely in voluntary agreements and create wealth through their own work and ingenuity" and "capitalism is when the rich can use wealth to assert power over the poor and extract surplus wealth from their labor" are partial truths, like a 3D object casting a different shadow depending on the angle of the light. Thinking in terms of partial narratives can square a circle, but it's nonetheless difficult to keep more than one in your head at once, since going from one to another requires a gestalt switch.

Now consider how this plays out when people argue. For simplicity, imagine that the world is just a set of dots like this picture:

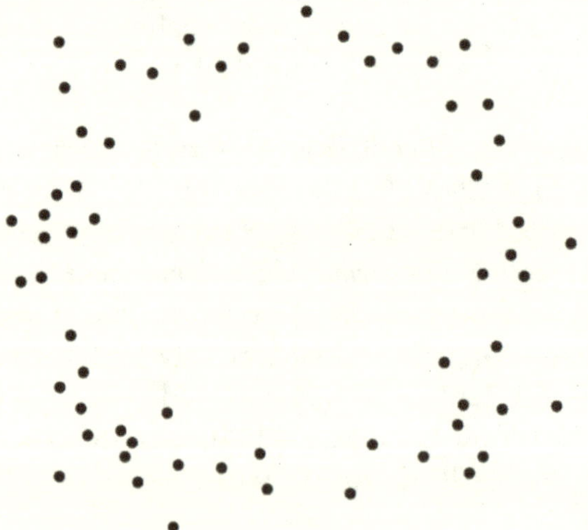

Figure 15, a small universe.

Alice feels that the world is, deep down, a square, like in the left picture below. She may think so because she has been told so, because her own personal experiences and self-interest are more compatible with that belief, or because her psychological predilections predispose her to thinking that way. Bob, for his own version of those reasons, believes the world is in essence a circle (right picture).

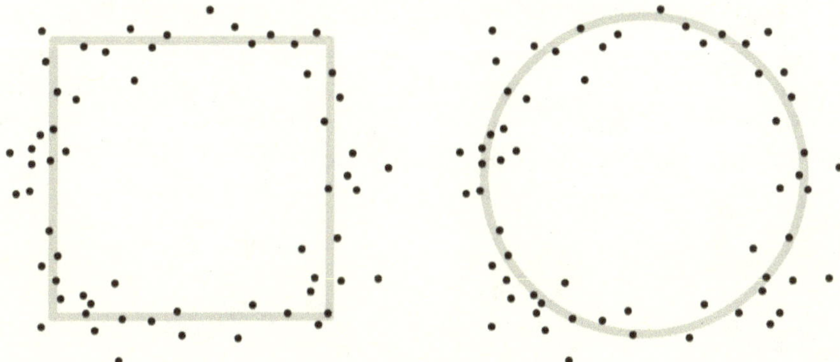

Figure 16, two ways to make sense of a small universe.

Alice and Bob now disagree on which dots are important. They disagree on which are expressions of a key, fundamental truth and which are just irrelevant, isolated exceptions. They will be interested in and eager to talk about the dots that make up their preferred shape, all of which speak volumes. *This* dot is different from this other one because it's not just a dot, you see, it's an instance of a pattern. But to the other party, it's just a dot.

When Alice talks about any dot in the square she's really talking about the square, the dot is just one example. Those outside it are beside the point, and to her, Bob is just derailing the conversation when he keeps harping on about some random dot that's supposedly part of some "circle" he's imagining. It's a distraction from *the real issue* (the square). If Alice is feeling uncharitable, she'll think Bob's just talking about irrelevant dots because he doesn't *want* to talk about the square, which he, like everyone else sane, *must* be seeing just as readily as she does. *Everyone* knows about the square and those who pretend they don't aren't being serious. Bob, in turn, thinks Alice is a hypocrite when she takes a great interest in dots in the square and dismissing dots in the circle as meaningless. She just talked about one single dot herself, why is *my* single dot less important?

Note that they don't have to disagree on which dots exist or where they are. Savage political fights can happen without any factual disagreement or ultimate value difference. We're perfectly capable of fighting over how to produce generalities from specifics (sensemaking) [75]. Look what happens if we don't add or remove any dots, but use size and darkness to emphasize or de-emphasize them based on how well they fit into each pattern:

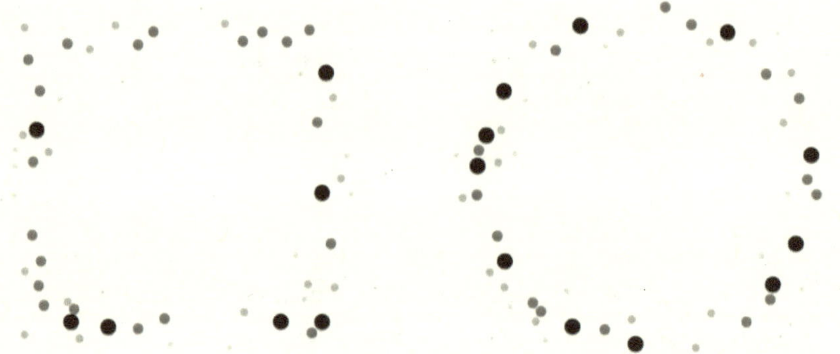

Figure 17, the exact same set of dots twice, but with different ones emphasized with larger size and darker color.

You can't even tell they're the same dots, just like you can't tell that Marx and Rand describe the same world.

Having internalized a partial narrative makes it easier for us to notice particulars that support it. In turn, the particulars confirm and reinforce the narrative. Everything ignored by that partial narrative, by contrast, we have no routine for integrating into our understanding of the world. When we come across such incongruous particulars

[75] Cf. matters of model, which are not simply half matters of fact and half matters of value.

we often don't notice them. If we do, we don't get the sense that they represent something bigger, nor do we experience that mental activation of related examples from our memories that makes it feel like an instance of a pattern. Partial narratives, like the types constructed by cat couplings, have *far sides* that they make invisible.

There are of course more examples of partial narratives pointing in different directions than Randian vs. Marxist descriptions of capitalism. "Nature and nurture" is a big one: "behavior is the result of socialization" and "behavior is the result of human nature and individual hereditary variation" are both partial truths.

The full truth, notably, is not "in the middle" of two partials but on another plane entirely: on a level with less generalization, abstraction, and narrativization—less aggressive sensemaking. In fact, people who disagree on generalities might agree surprisingly well on specifics. When I was at university there was this guy I used to hang out with at parties. He was a Gender Studies student and I, committed to natural science as a model for knowledge and intuitively aligned to biology as important for personality and behavior, was very much not. Philosophical differences aside, I tend to get along well with his type of person socially and we often discussed human nature and society. Despite both of us drinking too much (being students and all) to be at peak eloquence most of the time, our conversations did progress. The more we talked, the clearer it became that we disagreed very little on how the world worked. We had different interests and slightly different personalities that made us feel that different things were more central and fundamental, and because of that, our signal vs. noise attributions were often flipped. Like Alice and Bob, we agreed on where each dot was, but not on which overall shape to make from them.

You could say that we agreed or disagreed based on *resolution*; the more one simplified, generalized, and narrativized, the more we disagreed. When details were worked out and more specifics introduced, our disagreements softened.

Narrative (non) logic

Here lies a problem: narratives are partial and too vague, general and value-laden to be treated like facts (even though they are often phrased like facts). Therefore, normal logical rules don't apply to them, specifically the law of non-contradiction. Unlike the case with well-formed truth claims, if two narratives contradict each other it *doesn't* mean that one of them must be wrong. To contradict each other means, in this context, that they have opposing implications for moral valence, policy, and action, which our dumb monkey brains mistake for a logical contradiction. It doesn't in any way indicate a pathology like it does in logic, mathematics, or hard science. Look at these:

"History is determined by the actions of individuals" vs. "history is determined by large-scale economic and technological forces".

"Art subverts the audience's unexamined preconceptions" vs. "art is the creation of transcendent beauty" vs. "art is the expression of personal feelings".

"Sex is about satisfying basic, impersonal appetites" vs. "sex is an act of intimacy and an expression of love" vs. "sex is for procreation and anything else is a sin".

"Science works by accumulating knowledge about the world, asymptotically approaching perfect correctness" vs. "science works by replacing one paradigm with another in a series of revolutions".

"Prisons keep dangerous criminals off the streets" vs. "prisons oppress those who revolt against an unjust economic order".

"Societies who do certain things are more successful and survive better than societies that don't, therefore institutions and traditions are the result of beneficial cultural evolution" vs. "institutions and traditions arise as tools the powerful use to oppress the weak, and progress requires tearing them down".

"Misbehavior is naturally occurring, and people need to be disciplined to behave" vs. "misbehavior is caused by bad experiences and people need to be nurtured to behave".

"The industrial revolution lifted us all up from grueling poverty and made life better for everyone" vs. "the industrial revolution made life worse for the poor because capitalists forced them to work in dirty and dangerous factories" vs. "the industrial revolution made us destroy nature to satisfy our greedy hunger to consume".

"Music, books, and movies become popular when they appeal to people's inherent tastes" vs. "music, books and movies become popular because they are aggressively marketed".

"The Dark Ages was when European civilization declined and remained a shithole for centuries" vs. "the Dark Ages are a myth, and things were just as advanced as in antiquity".

"Wealth means access to resources, and wealth in one place has been diverted from somewhere else, robbing the poor of their right to an equal share" vs. "wealth is created by people's ingenuity and work, wealth in one place comes from nowhere else and no one has any right to anything but what they themselves create".

"Desperation and poverty cause moral corruption" vs. "power and wealth cause moral corruption" vs. "bad social norms cause moral corruption" vs. "individual weakness of character causes moral corruption".

"Raw economic incentives rule the world and will always produce races to the bottom" vs. "culture and values determine how people act in the economic realm".

"Children are born good and must be nurtured to thrive" vs. "children are born bad and must be socialized to behave".

"Bad things exist because of coordination problems, inefficiency, incompetence and irrationality" vs "bad things exist because people intentionally do evil" vs. "bad things are inherent to the world".

"Success comes from having talent" vs. "success comes from hard work and grit" vs. "success comes from connections, privilege and nepotism" vs. "success comes from the blind, dumb luck of being at the right place at the right time".

And so forth. Think of all of these in terms of how our experiences may reinforce or weaken them, and how internalizing one version and seeing the world through it biases our noticing, interpreting and remembering things. The philosopher Karl Jaspers wrote (*The Origin and Goal of History*, 1949):

> An ideology is a complex of ideas or notions which represents itself to the thinker as an absolute truth for the interpretation of the world and his situation within it; it leads the thinker to accomplish an act of self-deception for the purpose of justification, obfuscation and evasion in some sense or other to his advantage.

Known cognitive biases play roles here, most of all *confirmation bias*, which, according to Wikipedia, is

> [T]he tendency to search for, interpret, favor, and recall information in a way that confirms or supports one's prior beliefs or values. People display this bias when they select information that supports their views, ignoring contrary information, or when they interpret ambiguous evidence as supporting their existing attitudes.

There's also *source amnesia*:

> [T]he inability to remember where, when or how previously learned information has been acquired, while retaining the factual knowledge.

...which, slightly adjusted, means we remember the truth of a narrative and that we've got it confirmed many times, but struggle to recall the specific instances. This one can make us flustered and sound stupid when talking to people who disagree with us, when all we can muster is a handwave and a reference to "many such cases". Maybe we can produce one or a handful of examples, which looks feeble and far from justifies the confidence we display. It is, after all, just one dot.

It's hard, bordering on impossible, to communicate a narrative to someone who doesn't share it, while making it as convincing and evident as it feels from the inside. All the cross-references to supporting beliefs, facts, events, and experiences can't be articulated or communicated, and expressing yourself in those circumstances with the shorthand and emotional force appropriate from *within* the narrative comes across as hyperbolic and unhinged from outside it.

Gulliver problems as narratives

A lot of narratives are about problems. They say things like "there's this pattern, it's bad, and it should be dealt with". There's a type we can call "Gulliver problems", based on the story from *Gulliver's Travels* where the hero is lying on the ground in Lilliput, tied down by little threads. Each thread is weak enough for him to rip apart but put together they keep him trapped. Many, many social problems are like this, involving what is harmless, negligible, or justified in isolated cases, but adds up to significant harm. "Microaggression" was coined to point out some such problems. Funnily enough, others have given complaints about the use of that term as an example of the *same* kind of problem from the other direction—as in, individually minor instances of ~woke ideology adding up to an overbearing, oppressive atmosphere.

The erosion of privacy is also a Gulliver problem. It might not matter very much if the pizza place wants to know my email address, if a shop stops accepting cash, or if I can't even use my new TV without creating a Samsung account. But if we cast them all as instances of a pattern it looks different: they're not small, insignificant problems, they're part of one big, *significant* problem of encroaching surveillance.

Conceptualizing Gulliver problems involves building connections between disparate facts and events so that each individual instance comes to carry the full moral weight of the whole. If you *don't* assume all these connections, making a grand generality, then loading so much weight onto a single dot looks crazy (having to accept cookies isn't some great plot to oppress you lol relax). This mechanic lies behind a lot of disagreements over the existence and status of problems like regulatory burden, heteronormativity, grade inflation, environmental destruction, social isolation, credentialism, crony capitalism, consumerism (frankly almost anything ending in "ism").

It's worth pausing to consider the lesson. When another has an overly strong reaction towards some triviality, it's a sign that they're not seeing it the way you are. Their path through life and discourse has been different from yours, and thus they're seeing this trifle not merely as itself, but as part of a real and obvious square or circle that you and your ilk are stubbornly refusing to acknowledge. And furthermore, *that refusal*[76] is often amplifying the strong feelings.

Narrative humility as maturity

As we grow up, our very perception grows intertwined with acquired narratives. We experience fewer concrete events and facts, and more avatars of generalities: we didn't get punched, we experienced assault; we didn't not get a job, we were passed over for a diversity hire; we didn't meet an asshole, we witnessed the decay of manners first hand.

Ideologues are those convinced that these stories we internalize are the truth itself. Starting to perceive abstractions directly is, to them, not a corruption or a double-edged sword, but consciousness-raising. Taking them on isn't incorporating another device into your toolbox but a transformation into an enlightened being. It might be called being "conscious" but also "red-pilled" or—from back when the word was a self-descriptor more than a term of abuse—"woke" (awakened). The mechanism is the same.

Bright teenagers and young adults are the most vulnerable to ideology. It's the time in life when our ability for abstract thought is new and fresh, right out of the box, revving its engines, eager to pounce on the first sexy-looking insight that saunters along[77]. The

[76] Or sometimes, mockery: "haha imagine being upset about [thing]".

[77] I know that many disapprove of mixing metaphors. I do not.

young are prone to zealotry because they think that thrilling first love is The One. Cultivating maturity means mellowing our youthful tendency to think of such interpretations as *facts*. It constitutes arrested development to *not* gradually come to recognize and appreciate the multiplicity of narratives, and the divergent interpretations they imply, for each and every encounter with the specific. This is why it's dangerous and irresponsible when the supposed adults in the room defer to the young too much, treating them as superior repositories of wisdom.

To make progress we must keep gathering partials, keeping them on file, and train ourselves to switch between them so comfortably that we can almost see a fuzzy truth in the totality. That is, according to the *Stanford Encyclopedia of Philosophy*, how to handle incommensurability:

> To overcome the barriers posed by incommensurability to understanding antiquated sciences, and to understanding the special technical vocabulary used by contemporaneous, phylogenetically related subdisciplines, it is neither necessary not possible to translate between them. Rather, one must become bilingual, learning to use (and keep separate) the incongruently structured lexical taxonomies underwriting different laws and theories.

It's not just for scientific theories and philosophies, it's for everything. It's not easy, it's not cool, and you'll lose that exhilarating rush of moral clarity that *Atlas Shrugged* or *Das Kapital* offers the precocious teenager with a left- or right-leaning temperament awaiting ignition, but you're not quite a grownup without it.

Chapter 13

Truth at Different Resolutions

General claims have often experienced traumatic amputation of their contexts.

— 'Literal Banana', *Introducing the Extended Sniff Test: A Method for Recreational Hostile Fact Checking*

The partial narrative idea allows for a relativism that is necessary and true. They compress the full truth into a much smaller and simpler account, built around one particular feature of that truth. When doing so, they force harmonization of contradictory implications, making things look artificially straightforward. This is, in fact, their main function. There can be many stories told around the same set of facts, and they are not true or false the way facts are, but always somewhere in between. We don't want full relativism, however. We don't want to say that every story is just as true as any other. Not even people who sound like they want this really do.

This problem weighed on my conscience as a professional sensemaker. I always resisted hooking clients up with artificial clarity, and I at least wanted to be confident that I'd produced the "truest" description possible, given the length and complexity I was allowed. But how would you measure that? How would you determine which representation is truer than another? It's not obvious even for the easy task of compressing neat, unambiguous numbers. The *mp3* audio compression procedure shrinks the size of files radically by throwing out information about frequencies outside the range of human hearing. That seems obviously correct, but does assume that listeners are human. This makes it, strictly speaking, value-laden, and not completely objective.

There is obviously a spectrum. The circle and square in the last chapter are about equally true given the universe of dots, but I could, in theory, pick out any three of them, draw a triangle and declare "the world is a triangle" a partial truth along with the others. The hypothetical lazy relativist just grants this, but we all understand that this story would be more contorted, more partial, and less true.

There are ways to handle this in dot-only universes. When I turn large sets of multidimensional data into stories I often use *principal component analysis* (PCA). Simply put, PCA works by replacing many variables with fewer ones, where each new variable is a combination of the old, selected in such a way that you keep as much variation in the dataset as possible. For example, if data are body measurements like a person's height, weight, head circumference, arm length, leg length, foot width, etc., we can replace them all with a single "overall size" property and keep most of the information content with far fewer numbers. PCA is a mathematical procedure that does this in a rigorous, ~objective way—given a universe of dots[78].

Trying this sort of approach on the circle/square/triangle case, we'd calculate the average distance from each dot to the nearest part of the circle/square/triangle and see which was the smallest. We'd find that the circle and square would be similarly good and the triangle much worse. The real universe, however, is not made of dots. It doesn't even consist of things that convert neatly into dots, so we don't have procedures like PCA to create "correct" compressed accounts of it.

Claims are true or false depending on resolution

Compressions like PCA are not *true* in the sense of giving you exact facts about the underlying data, they are a *best effort* at approximating

[78] It's more complicated in that it matters what units you use and how they are scaled (and of course which attributes you include from the start), but the point stands.

it, given a certain level of detail. We often treat such approximations as truths in their own right, but unless they represent actual, underlying laws of nature they are not. They are "true only at a given *lower resolution*.

Think of it like compressing a high-resolution photograph with many millions of pixels into a much lower-resolution one, like pixel art. This creates an *incorrect* depiction in the sense that it's different from the original picture. It's a *correct* depiction at a lower resolution, however, if it's the most accurate way[79] to rescale the image to that resolution. Therefore, the truth of a simplification, generalization, or any statement in shorthand, is dependent on the resolution assumed.

Case in point: whether it's true that "the Earth is round" depends on how precise we want to be. The Earth isn't a perfect sphere. Its surface is uneven, and because it rotates it's slightly flattened, thicker along the equator. Does this make "the Earth is round" false? Does it mean that it's not a fact? Yes and no. It's true at the level we're implicitly expecting when hearing that "the Earth is round".

For a messier example: does the Earth revolve around the sun? Yes! Well actually… the sun and the Earth are both moving around a common center of gravity which just happens to be close to the center of the sun because the sun is so much larger and heavier. And *actually* the masses of the other planets also affect the movement somewhat, and so does the path of the whole solar system orbiting the center of the galaxy, and the movement of the galaxy relative to other galaxies. It's really a matter of frame of reference here… wait while I get my blackboard... And so on. If you increase precision to infinity, only a complete description of the movement of every particle in the universe is really *true*.

What happens when we get the implied resolution wrong is best illustrated by a joke:

> "This dinosaur skeleton is 150 million and two years old" said the guide at the museum.

[79] Given some reasonable objective-by-execution way of defining accuracy.

> "Wow!" said a visitor. "How can you know so precisely?".
>
> "Well," says the guide, "they told me it was 150 million years old when I started working here and that was two years ago."

Was it true that the dinosaur skeleton was 150 million years old? Yes, at certain resolution, and no at another. "150 million and two" is (most likely) false because it implies a resolution high enough to make the original 150 million number false. When you combine a low-resolution claim with a higher one, the result has the lower resolution of the two.

These toy examples are easy to follow because they involve numbers and shapes, i.e. mathematical objects that are easy to think about in terms of higher or lower resolution. There are well-defined ways to express numbers with varying specificity and we're pretty good at interpreting them right. We all get the joke. Other times it's not so obvious. Many methods in social science are attempts to gracefully turn masses of specifics into simplified generalities. It's a thankless task because, unlike physical scientists, social scientists have little hope of finding underlying natural laws that can compress its complexities fully and cleanly.

PCA is such a method. Descriptive statistics like averages and standard deviations are others. With them you can turn millions of numbers into one or two and come out with a low-resolution generality. Comparing averages, men are taller than women, but the compression is not perfect: we lose some information because some women are taller than some men, and this generality renders them invisible. But *if* we agree that we're using the particular procedure of taking the average to compress and simplify the complex relationship between the distributions of heights of two sets of people, then it's *true* that men are taller than women, while the reverse, that women are taller than men, is *false*.

Of course, what happens, typically in more fraught and less clear-cut cases than height, is that people *don't* agree on the appropriate procedure to lower resolution, or that there's a legitimate way to do so at all. Generalization is a virtue in science but a dirty word in human relations. According to one moral standard, the only allowable generalization when it comes to human characteristics is "we can't know, everyone is different" (which is also *true*). We can account for stereotyping being immoral even when stereotypes are statistically correct by considering it an obligation to avoid treating people at a resolution lower than the individual.

To make things worse, contradictory claims can be true at the same resolution, but according to different procedures. In a situation where income inequality is growing, we can get different answers to the question "are we getting richer?" depending on whether we're looking at the mean (all incomes summed up, divided by the number of people) or the median (the income of the person standing in the middle if we put everyone in a row by order of income).

These questions aren't curiosities of mere academic interest. We use claims at this resolution to assemble our understanding of the world, while having a habit of treating them as brute facts. It's the reason we can live in the same reality but wind up with radically different beliefs about it.

When we go further, on to simplifying and compressing the wholly non-mathematical, the situation turns outright anarchic. We just declare some properties more important than others. We say that grass is green and the sky is blue even though grass is often yellow and the sky is often gray (shoutout to my British readers!) or black, but we think green grass and blue sky are more typical, more essential, states of grass and sky, like a ripe, sweet strawberry is more essentially a strawberry and a tall man is "more essentially" a man. We might also say that "mosquitoes carry malaria" even though only a small minority do, just because it's important to us and mosquitoes don't know or care to be offended by it.

Suddenly, ghosts appear

As we've seen, some claims are of the "a thing exists" variety. If their truth depends on resolution, it implies that some things only exist at certain resolutions. Imagine an image entirely made up of blue and yellow pixels, arranged in a checkerboard pattern. If we zoom out so far that we can't make out individual pixels, it'll look green despite there being no green pixels. The "greenness" is there—just like it's there in green paint that's a mix of blue and yellow pigments—but it only shows up as we zoom out. Mathematical artifacts like average heights are also a kind of "ghost" that only exist at low resolutions.

In my bachelor's thesis I argued that some disagreements over free will result from lack of clarity on resolution. Traditional free will views the self as a unified whole, the sort of entity a property like free will can be ascribed to. Since we experience ourselves as unified centers of consciousness that can act according to their wishes and whims, clearly such selves have free will. The problems occur when we increase resolution so that we're looking *inside* the self, at individual components of the brain or the processes of decision-making. If we still assume the self is a single unified thing we look for it *inside itself*[80] and find nothing (in which brain cell is the self, and where in the choosing process do "I" step in?). We conclude that it must be some mystical, undetectable substance, and get scared shitless when we see decision-making seemingly working just fine as a physical process in the brain, without some external entity that is "us"[81].

My argument was that free will doesn't exist at the particular resolution where physics or cell biology are done. It's a ghost, like greenness or average height, and we have it on the resolution of psychology and experience, which is the level where it's appropriate to ask the question. I have a flat kitchen table, but if we look at it through an electron microscope we'll find that it's full of mountains and valleys and not at all flat. It is *still true* that my table has a flat surface in the ordinary sense, because an implied resolution comes

[80] This is like walking the streets of a city looking for "the city".

[81] It should go without saying that this is a simplified form of the argument.

with saying so. The same is true for free will. We have it at one implied resolution, and then we get confused and anxious when we don't have it at a different one. If we look back to collective action problems we can see that there's a similar confusion over levels there: we have free will and agency at the level of the individual[82], but if we continue to zoom out and aggregate to large groups, the ghost disappears again, and we get confused and frustrated by the spotty-at-best free will and agency of collective entities.

Social science can't give us what we want

The hard physical sciences aim for lossless compression. They're trying to find the real underlying rules the universe runs on, looking to nail down a few principles that explain the behavior of reality completely, without leaving anything unaccounted for. They're pretty good at it; physicists and chemists can describe and predict processes in their experiments virtually perfectly, and this knowledge has made it possible to control matter in such exquisite detail that we can create technological marvels like synthetic fibers, smartphones, and space stations.

This success can make physical scientists arrogant when looking at the comparatively meager achievements of social science. They're being unfair because social scientists have a more difficult task. They can't do perfectly controlled experiments, for one thing, but more importantly there's little reason to believe that there are the same kind of simple mathematical principles governing the object of their study. They have to do lossy compression, which means they get all the problems above.

We look to social science (and life science, which has some of the same problems) to give us Answers. We want narratives, and we want them to be as true as scientific facts. But social science can't give us that. Not directly. Not without stepping outside its boundaries. Specific observations and experiments are precisely that—specific—

[82] An individual is both cohesive and flexible enough to behave in a way apt to describe as agentic. Molecules or unorganized masses of people are not.

and to tell us things on the level we want to hear them, they have to be interpreted. When we want to know if building more housing raises the fertility rate, if remote workers are as productive as on-site ones, if SSRIs are effective against depression, if raising the minimum wage causes unemployment, if the death penalty reduces crime, if the keto diet is the best, if climate change is a threat to civilization, or which side in politics is right about everything, then we need to interpret scientific findings.

The sociology of science I was taught can be boiled down to the point that scientific research involves a lot more interpretation than people commonly believe. Years later I think of it as saying that the practice of science is much closer to the artful assembling of facts and figures I did as a consultant than I'm entirely comfortable with.

Since the interpretation of results that produces authoritative narratives is done not only by scientists but also by journalists, by activists, and by administrative bodies with one foot in science and the other in politics, *legitimation*, that central problem of postmodernity, becomes more complicated than slogans like "Trust the Science" imply. If rephrased into the more honest "Trust the Social Process That Turn Scientific Results into Authoritative Narratives", it's easier to understand why some don't always do so.

Operationalization is destruction

Things we want to know, like "does AI threaten jobs?" or "is globalization reversing?" or "why are people increasingly anxious and depressed?" or "how many people are LGTBQ+?" are not scientific questions in a strict sense. To be informed by science at all, they have to be translated into specifics. Scientists call restating and redefining a concept into something that can be measured "operationalization", and the hope is that it can be translated back into the original afterwards, i.e. that answering the scientific question also answers the question we actually asked[83]. We'd like to think it does. We'd like to think that truth can be preserved as we turn resolution up and down

[83] A.k.a the "validity" of a scientific construct.

as if by a knob. We'd like to think we can make broad and general questions precise and testable without destroying them[84].

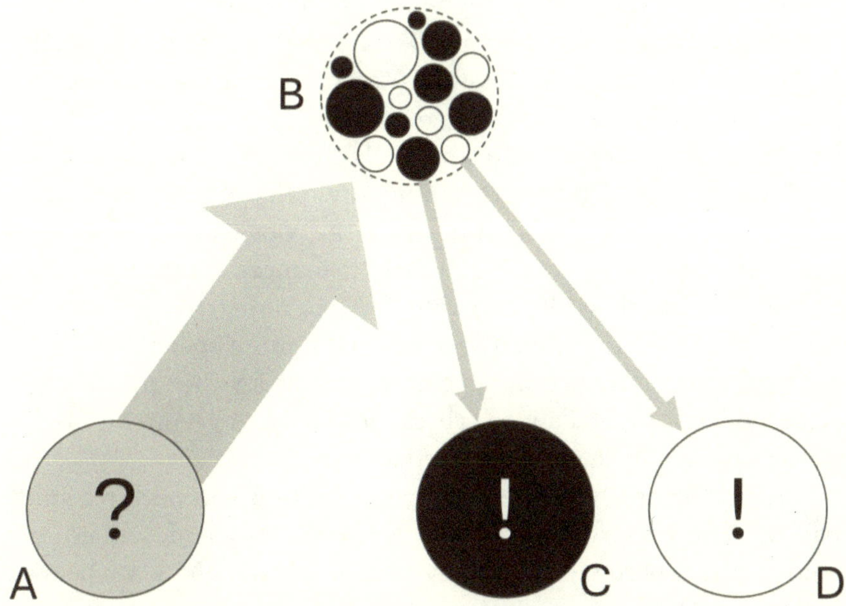

Figure 18, a general claim (A) has many possible operationalizations (B), and depending on which one we pick, it comes out true (C) or false (D).

In 2020 we wanted to know if lockdowns work against pandemics. This obviously depends on a lot of factors. Clearly, isolating people slows the spread of a contagious disease to some degree. How could it not? But how much? How much is enough? What exchange rate between effectiveness and costs is enough to classify something as "working"? [85] How do we add up different kinds of costs? And what

[84] We might also, if we have a narrow area of expertise and an agenda, pretend that knowing the answer to a precise question grants us authority to settle a much more vague and general question.

[85] Sometimes "work" can have more cynical interpretations. There've been plenty of thinkpieces declaring that diversity trainings "don't work" in the sense of reducing discrimination or improving attitudes, but "work", for those who commission them, might mean "keep the company from getting sued or dragged through the mud".

is effectiveness, what are we trying to minimize? Number of infections, or deaths, or total sick days, or hospital stays, or post-viral complications? Some kind of aggregated total suffering? It's obvious that such questions must be specified far further, so much further that they are not the same question anymore. Through a Faustian bargain we can have truth but lose relevance[86].

Let's look at one more example. Is "the death penalty deters crime" true or false? I'd bet everything I own that the right answer is "for some people, in some conditions". If the cops would shoot me on the spot for speeding, I would definitely take more care to stay below the limit. But will it work "generally"? Most research seem to claim "no", but the evidence offered answers much more specific questions about aggregate statistics in specific places at specific times where specific policies were changed, all capable only of giving an inkling towards a general rule implicitly hypothesized to exist.

I picked the death penalty example because it was part of a study I read on "the backfire effect". The backfire effect is described as a cognitive bias where we react to evidence the "wrong" way: hearing evidence or arguments against our beliefs cause us to become more convinced that we are right, rather than less. Like many others interested in psychology and epistemology I had heard of this, but once I made the effort to read the original paper I was unimpressed. The effect was fickle, only appearing on some issues, and depended on whether you discussed your opinions with others or not, and it mattered whether you did that before or after you saw the evidence, etc. It was not robust.

Other influential psychology results have similar issues, as you would expect when the observed facts are just how a few dozen psych undergraduates behave in highly unnatural lab experiments, which gets generalized into eternal truths about human nature. I've

---

[86] It's not *always* a tradeoff. Some results are robust in that most of their operationalizations point in the same direction. There's little doubt that "antibiotics work against bacterial infection" because the answer doesn't depend that much on the specifics.

seen attempts on television to replicate famous findings like "if people believe they're drinking alcohol they'll behave as if intoxicated" and "if you tell people they answered a survey the opposite way to how they actually did and then ask them to justify their answer, they'll go on to defend the answer they didn't give", and results were spectacularly underwhelming. A few who thought they were drinking felt a little intoxicated, many were doubtful, and some said they weren't. The survey effect was weak and only showed up on a few topics where people don't normally have strong opinions (like "it should be compulsory to vote"). Not robust, no general rule.

I don't mean to say such research is worthless or that it's hopeless to find truth on such matters. I just mean that it's harder than it seems and you risk looking for something that does not exist. With the (unstated) expectation that such principles are there to be found, the robustness, certainty, and significance of individual results are exaggerated as they take their place in public discourse and social reality.

In *The Wisdom of Crowds* (2004) James Surowiecki states four requirements for crowds to be "wise": there must be diversity of opinion or approach, individual judgments must not be affected by others, there may not be a central authority affecting judgments, and there must be some method of aggregating individual decisions fairly and accurately. Unsurprisingly, these qualifications got lost as the idea made it out of the book, and now "the wisdom of the crowd" gets thrown around even where those conditions don't hold. The pseudonym *Suspended Reason* puts it like this in the article *Discursive Games, Discursive Warfare*:

> It's not just that ideas become distorted, it's that they're distorted in a specific direction. They generalize claims from local to global, or from one local domain to another, and they increase their certainty or explanatory power from modest to strong. Boas's observations about Inuit linguistics didn't get less dramatic. Freud's theories did not get moderated

> and attenuated. TEDx speakers do not downplay the generalizability of a given psychology study. Rather, as ideas work through a culture they are slowly exaggerated; as ideas are constantly applied to new domains analogically, the territory they claim to explain expands. Repeated simplification and generalization (which are forms of decontextualization) ensures that ideas are weakened by their very advocates. The simplicity makes the meme easily communicable; the generalization makes it widely applicable; the combination means easy-to-use concepts that are equally easy to knock over.

Even when we've dealing only with numbers, where we have set procedures for how to lower resolution, we argue about whether we should, or which procedure is appropriate. With non-numbers, turning specifics into generalities is a matter of opaque human judgment. On top of that, social dynamics weaken the relationship between reality and narrative even further. We look to science for reliable and relevant knowledge, but it struggles to give us both at the same time. Studying the human and social world with scientific-like methods won't yield the general laws that the hard sciences have taught us to expect, yet we treat the results as if they were indicative of such underlying laws—as if there were rules on just the right level to answer our ill-posed questions[87].

We're stuck with narratives, and even though we know that some are more correctly descriptive than others, we don't have a neutral, objective way to determine which ones.

---

[87] When I see questions like "are people fundamentally selfish or unselfish" debated I want to tear my hair out.

Chapter 14

Mains and Correctives

That is what learning is. You suddenly understand something you've understood all your life, but in a new way.

— Doris Lessing

One of the best descriptions of how narratives can point in opposite directions is Scott Alexander's review of Samuel Shem's book *House of God,* in which Shem chronicles his experiences as a medical intern.

> *House of God* does a weird form of figure-ground inversion. An example of what I mean, taken from politics: some people think of government as another name for the things we do together, like providing food to the hungry, or ensuring that old people have the health care they need. These people know that some politicians are corrupt, and sometimes the money actually goes to whoever's best at demanding pork, and the regulations sometimes favor whichever giant corporation has the best lobbyists. But this is viewed as a weird disease of the body politic, something that can be abstracted away as noise in the system.
>
> And then there are other people who think of government as a giant pork-distribution system, where obviously representatives and bureaucrats, incentiv-

ized in every way to support the forces that provide them with campaign funding and personal prestige, will take those incentives. Obviously they'll use the government to crush their enemies. Sometimes this system also involves the hungry getting food and the elderly getting medical care, as an epiphenomenon of its pork-distribution role, but this isn't particularly important and can be abstracted away as noise.

I think I can go back and forth between these two models when I need to, but it's a weird switch of perspective, where the parts you view as noise in one model resolve into the essence of the other and vice versa.

And House of God does this to medicine.

Doctors use certain assumptions, like:

1. The patient wants to get better, but there are scientific limits that usually make this impossible

2. Medical treatment makes people healthier

3. Treatment is determined by medical need and expertise

But in House of God, the assumptions get inverted:

1. The patient wants to just die peacefully, but there are bureaucratic limits that usually make this impossible

2. Medical treatment makes people sicker

> 3. Treatment is determined by what will make doctors look good without having to do much work
>
> Everybody knows that those first three assumptions aren't always true. Yes, sometimes we prolong life in contravention of patients' wishes. Sometimes people mistakenly receive unnecessary treatment that causes complications. And sometimes care suffers because of doctors' scheduling issues. But it's easy to abstract away to an ideal medicine based on benevolence and reason, and then view everything else as rare and unfortunate deviations from the norm.
>
> *House of God* goes the whole way and does a full figure-ground inversion. The outliers become the norm; good care becomes the rare deviation. What's horrifying is how convincing it is. Real medicine looks at least as much like the bizarro-world of *House of God* as it does the world of the popular imagination where doctors are always wise, diagnoses always correct, and patients always grateful.

Alexander, a doctor, judges that both depictions are similarly true, even though they're entirely inverted. You can say he's a moderate or centrist on this issue (or he would be if this was a conventional political "issue"), not in the sense that he believes in some specific "in-between" narrative with all his heart, but in the sense that he accepts the partial truth of two opposing ones. Such in-between narratives can exist, but the deck is stacked against them. Those on the far ends, coming with clear, clean moral messages, are more engaging and simpler to process and remember. They have a fixed point to anchor and focus them.

This *narrative moralism* makes perfect sense given the function narratives fill. They have coherent morals because establishing shared judgments (i.e. sermonizing) is what they are for, and we've already seen how to produce artificial clarity by selecting what to focus on, what to ignore, and what connections to draw between which facts. The pull of artificial moral coherence is universal. It lies behind the "halo-/horns effect" cognitive bias, where we, for example, feel that better-looking people are nicer, smarter, and funnier, even when they aren't, and the "just-world fallacy" when we feel people must have done something to deserve what happens to them. We assume that good things (and bad things) go together, as if goodness and badness were natural properties like mass or electrical charge. I'm sure you've noticed how your political enemies are misinformed, stupid, *and* evil.

Like a consonant chord sounds settled and final, a narrative without internal contradiction is more robust than one full of "buts", which comes off unfinished, messy, and lacking proper payoff[88]. It ~wants to resolve, to collapse into a stable resting state.

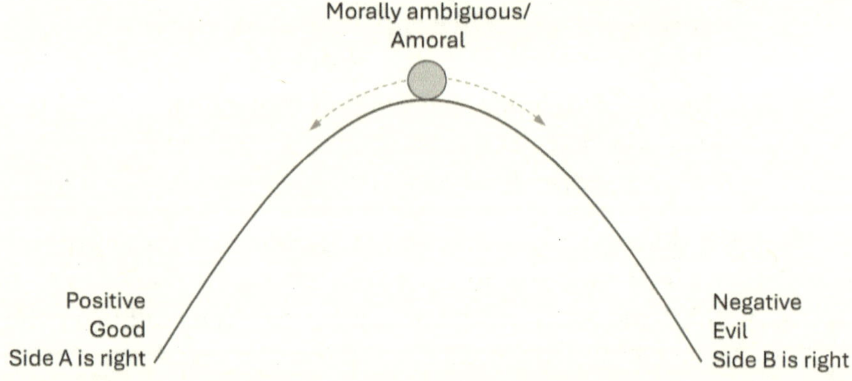

Figure 19, stories with internal contradictions feel unstable and unsettled, yearning for resolution like a dissonant chord.

[88] The minority of sophisticated narratives that make ambiguity a centerpiece demand more from their audience and will always struggle to compete in the market. To deny the mind its sugar and grease and cater to grown-up, acquired tastes is to tack against the wind. At work I used to follow a rule to minimize *buts*, i.e. the logic should flow naturally and obviously, without me having to redirect the reader from their natural path by saying "but". It was always a struggle to go against my pro-but values, but I can't deny that it worked.

Consider the genre of headline that asks us to choose between a flattering and an unflattering description, implying that one precludes the other. E.g:

> Are E-Scooters a Convenient Transport Option or a Public Nuisance?
>
> He sold everything and moved to a cabin—a bold return to simplicity, or just running away from responsibility?
>
> They turned their breakup into a podcast—clever emotional transparency, or monetized oversharing?
>
> They've transformed the old warehouse into an art space open to everyone. Is it a bold act of cultural revitalization, or just gentrification dressed up in gallery lighting?
>
> He asks tons of questions in meetings—engaged and curious, or performatively 'involved'?
>
> The new curriculum eliminates standardized tests and focuses on student-led projects. Is that a revolution in education, or the erosion of academic standards?

You'll notice that none of these pairs are mutually exclusive. No law of nature says only one of the descriptions may apply. It's all about what overall *moral* judgment we should make. But it's not just that, the judgment is not content to be applied on top of the facts at the end, it retroactively redefines the essential nature of what's being discussed. This type of headline goes through the motions of nuance by telling two stories, but still imply that one must take precedence over the other.

The slopes in the hill-like figure above makes a prediction I think is borne out by experience: although less powerful, it is possible to build a morally ambiguous narrative—as long as it's close to 50-50 (balancing on top of the hill). Maintaining stability on an incline, around "this is actually 80-90% good/bad instead of 100%", is much harder. I found a discussion on Swedish Reddit that illustrates this, where a poster asked why several of his immigrated Serbian friends were so overly sensitive about the Yugoslav war in the '90s. Another user responded (translation mine):

> "Wow you're so sensitive about how your relatives were killed in a genocide", says someone whose family comes from a safe country. OP, this was in 1995. Many Serbs who came to Sweden have relatives who died. Shit, of course they have strong feelings. You would too if you had parents/siblings etc. who died in ethnic conflict.

Who in turn got this response from a third user:

> I don't want to be that guy here, I really get what you mean. But most sources are in agreement that the Serbs were responsible for around 90% of genocides and war crimes. Of course it's awful when your relatives die, genocide or conflict alike, but have some perspective.

Whether this accurately describes the situation with OP's friends, or the war in general, I don't know, and it's not the point. Let's say it's accurate for the sake of argument, and note the difficult position it puts some people in. It may be correct that one side committed the overwhelming majority of atrocities and therefore are "the villains", collectively speaking. But for a victim of an exception, who may not have taken part in or supported the crimes of their own side, having their own victimization dismissed or downplayed adds insult to injury. If it's *just one dot,* it's not taken as seriously as one accompanied by many similar ones, even though it's just as real as any other dot representing the gruesome fate of a living, breathing human being. Each person has the capacity to suffer, while abstracted collectives do not, and what was done to you does not become any less real or significant just because "yes, sure, *you* were victimized by this other person, but overall, *your group* wasn't victimized by *their group*, so...". "So" what? As if it makes a lick of difference to you (and this is what the tone-deaf "have some perspective" is telling you to accept). In this situation, of course the difference between 90% and 100% becomes of vital importance. It's a fight against the steamroller of narrative moralism working to dismiss your human worth as meaningless noise because it goes against a bigger pattern. However, to others it comes off as an attempt to deny the larger truth, so it will always be an uphill battle.

Pardon the soapboxing but this does upset me. To return to detached theorizing: even this observation that 50-50 good/bad is easier to pull off than 80-20 good/bad can itself be explained by it being simpler and more categorical. If "this is a matter of right and wrong, good and evil" vs. "this is subjective, or just two sides fighting each other" are two different ways of looking at a disagreement, the second avoids taking a side but is not actually more morally complex, it just takes the morality out completely.

Order matters

Here's this chapter's big, key speculation: because moderate, morally ambiguous narratives are less robust than "clean" ones (especially if you want anything other than 50-50 a-moralization), moderate opinions tend to come in the form of *pairs* of contrasting partial narratives. This way, the internal tensions, the "buts", are relegated to a position between narratives instead of inside them.

If balanced views consist of one-sided narratives stacked on top of each other, partially cancelling out opposing strong implications, then it matters in which order they come. To use a silly example: we can all agree on what a zebra looks like, but some may think of them as white horses with black stripes, and some as black horses with white stripes. When we don't make an active effort to be fair and consider everything, this can simplify to "zebras are white!" and "zebras are black!". In the real world, the base color of zebras is (thank God) still not political, but two people whose views on, say, economics are

> "The free market will work best as a rule, but there are a few cases where it won't, and some people will be hurt so we should have a social safety net to soften the hard edges of capitalism."

and

> "Capitalism is morally corrupt and rewards selfishness and greed. A society run for the people by the people would be best, but planned economies don't seem to work very well in practice, so we need the free market to fuel prosperity."

have opposite fundamental intuitions but will in practice support a similar set of mixed-economy policies. We can think of them as having one "main narrative" and then another as a "corrective" to account for what the main misses—that is, tying those insignificant exceptions up into another, secondary narrative.

At the risk of showing too much nerdy naiveté, this is a case where I wish a mathematical concept was better known among the public. This "main plus corrective" idea is similar to how simple mathematical models work: a *first order* approximation means a model with a single parameter (one explanatory factor[89]). A *second order* approximation is a model with two parameters, where the first captures the truth as well as it can, given its limitations, and the second

---

[89] If I'm allowed to be a bit sloppy and ignore details about polynomials.

captures the remainder as well as it can, given its own limitations (and so on for third and fourth order approximations)[90].

The key similarity is the *reason* we do it: approximations make calculations easier, and simple narratives make thinking easier. A first order approximation (i.e. just a main narrative) is the simplest of all, so that's what we default to whenever our thinking resources are limited, like when we're in a hurry, when we only have 280 characters, when we don't particularly care, and when we feel threatened, insulted, or otherwise emotional—or when we can get away with being lazy because no one is challenging us. When we have more time, energy, and comfort, or are incentivized to be fair, we might add more components and admit correctives.

This main-plus-corrective model can make sense of a lot of things. For one, it gives us a new way to characterize zealots or ideologues: they lack correctives. And *groupthink* is a social dynamic where voicing correctives is taboo[91]. It also explains something that happens to me a lot, which is switching (apparent) sides when talking to different people. When someone disagrees with you on a fundamental level, you prioritize defending your own main narrative and ignore your own corrective that agrees with them. When they *agree* with you on the fundamentals, you may start to argue for your corrective, against your own main narrative because it doesn't need defending[92].

---

[90] Compare with the PCA discussion earlier.

[91] This leads to the sometimes-observed effect where a group can produce a collective opinion more extreme than that of any individual member.

[92] If you're in a social environment where everyone shares your basic narrative, and nobody ever mentions a corrective you may be tempted to defend something you don't really support. I've defended conservative Christians on the "war on Christmas" issue (and sometimes religion in general) and social constructionists before, even though I don't agree with them. I don't "agree with them" in the sense that I don't hold their views as my own mains on these issues, but I do accept that they are legitimate correctives. The standard meaning of "agree" fails to describe this situation.

Another way to look at it is that disagreement is a negotiation and depending on what the other party's "opening bid" is, we adjust our own to end up with an acceptable balance. For specific issues where there's a decision to be made and both are invested in coming to an agreement, this can lead to mutual acceptance of correctives. But if there is no need to agree, and the person on the other side offers an extreme view, the rational course of action, even for a moderate, is to counterbalance with an opposite extremism one does not actually believe in[93].

Mine first

Most of us are willing to entertain and grant some legitimacy to ideas running counter to our basic beliefs, but only if respect to those basic beliefs is paid *first*. Sure, go ahead and complain about some specifics of the free market, government, technology, democracy, or whatever, but only after you've admitted their fundamental goodness. Reasonable people will accept that their main narratives have correctives, but they will not accept that they should be rejected wholesale. It's a lot easier to install a corrective in someone than it is to dislodge their main narrative, and for something to be taken as a corrective it must be presented as such, not as a pretender at main status.

These are the rules, as we feel them:

1) My own main-plus-corrective is the truth.
2) Opposite main-plus-corrective is valid but suspect.
3) Just my own main is limited but valid, one may simplify this way.
4) Just my corrective is invalid and perverse, one may NOT simplify this way.

House of God is shocking not because of the issues it brings up, but because it portrays them as the essential truth and not just a corrective on the margin. The same goes for *Atlas Shrugged*, discussed before. Most who aren't hard-left ideologues recognize some truth to the idea that entrepreneurship is crucial for prosperity, that the

[93] The risk is that you come to believe in it by saying it enough times.

wealth of the industrialized world is disproportionally due to innovators and builders, and that being rich does not necessarily make you an exploitative parasite. The other side of the story has been told many, many times in fiction, with capitalist types cast as villains as a matter of course, rarely with a corrective in sight[94]. It's common in literature and entertainment to offer that tacitly-accepted-as-partial narrative, but controversial to offer its opposite. That's not because one has a legitimate point and the other doesn't, but because most people willing to acknowledge Rand's perspective only do so as a corrective. We're not used to it being told as a main narrative. Making these points without paying your respects to inequality and the plight of the poor first! How dare you... it's... *indecent*. It's also why the most committed pro-market crowd loves it so much: having your basic beliefs rendered in fiction is a rare treat for them, and without being lectured about inequality and the plight of the poor first! For *once*! Such luxury!

I notice the defensive mine-first impulse in myself too. There is a lot of valid criticisms of how science is done, of bad study design, weak methodology, unfounded assumptions, statistical illiteracy, publication bias, etc.—hell, I've just ranted about it myself in the last chapter—but I'm not willing to acknowledge any of it unless I'm convinced that you're fundamentally pro-science and aren't trying to replace it with religion, political ideology, crystal healing, tribal mythology, lived experience, feelings, or what's fashionable. And sure, criticize modern civilization for destructive wars and environmental degradation while you're at it, but not until after you've given proper thanks for everything good it's brought us and acknowledge how shit everything was before it. I need to know you're not a deranged luddite hippie who thinks we should all live on communes growing turnips and playing the pan flute, because even if they have some valid points on specifics, they are wrong in general.

---

[94] It may say something about my temperament that the comic novel I wrote at 17 had the moral that some people with power are ruthless assholes, but even so, their behavior could be necessary or beneficial on the whole.

I'm aware of the *paradox of choice* (having more options can make us feel less satisfied), and I have my reservations about consumerism and contemporary materialistic culture, with its wasteful consumption of zero-sum status goods. I think huge inequalities are corrosive to the social fabric, I dislike advertising and find the demand to be profitable and productive in my professional life psychologically oppressive. Those, however, are correctives to a rock-hard commitment to a liberal political order and free market economy. When a coworker who sympathizes with an actual communist party brings any of that up I hesitate to support him, even though I might have made the same points myself had I been speaking to a libertarian.

This also explains why criticism against a group is interpreted differently when coming from an outsider compared to a fellow group member. An outsider can't be trusted to share our core values, so criticism we would've considered a corrective if coming from one of us, is instead taken as a full-on assault on all that it holy. I don't want to join the choir chanting that techies must study the humanities to become well-rounded, even though I completely agree and have done exactly that myself. That's because I'm not convinced most people saying that would acknowledge my prerequisite in return: that humanists must study and understand science and technology to be well-rounded themselves.

"Extreme first" and "reasonable first" narrative pairs

Some narratives are about *other* narratives (or ideologies). We can for example tell many stories about Christianity:

1) It's a moral code that tells us to treat others with dignity, empathy and love.
2) It's a justification of bigotry towards those who are different.
3) It's a fairy tale for simpletons who just accept what they are told as children.
4) It's a proud intellectual tradition.
5) It controlled and oppressed societies for centuries.

6) It kept the light of civilization, learning, and compassion in the otherwise dark and brutal Middle Ages.

They're all partial truths (and note how they point towards an overall positive or negative judgment). We can do the same with other belief systems and their adherents, whether they're anarchists, trads, transhumanists, or metal fans. They'll potentially be all kinds of stories, but for any ideology or movement there's one type of main-plus-corrective pair you can always make: "they're reasonable" and "they're extreme". Putting them in order yields:

> "Those people are extremists with insane beliefs, even though a few make alright and understandable points if taken in isolation."

or

> "Those people have their heart in the right place, even though a few go overboard and say extreme things."

Holders of each pairing may agree on many specifics about a group but have opposite views about how they should be viewed in general. Should they be given power, or should every attempt by them to install parts of their beliefs as policy be resisted, even if reasonable on their own?

We can put four different types of believer in a 2-by-2 matrix. On one axis we distinguish between those who admit correctives (reasonable) and those who don't (extremists), and on the other between those who have the same vs. the opposite stacking order to ourselves.

Correctiveless zealots on your own side are an embarrassment you prefer not to think or talk about. They're crude unsophisticates who should honestly just shut up to not actively harm what they're trying to support. When outright denial of their existence isn't viable, the feature to highlight is their utter insignificance. Their equivalents on the other side, however, are a threat you can't avoid thinking or talking about. They're evil alien mutants, they're everywhere, and they must be fought like the armies of Mordor.

	Has **only** main	Has main **and** corrective
Has **same** main	*Embarrassing brute/naïf*	*Eloquent genius*
Has **opposite** main	*Evil monster*	*Terribly frustrating*

Figure 20, how other people come across to us, depending on whether they share our main narratives and whether they admit correctives.

Moderates with correctives also look different depending on order. Those with our own stack are smart and insightful. If they express themselves with grace and clarity beyond our own ability they're geniuses whose thoughts we hurry to share with our friends. *This is such a great article!* Those who stack in the opposite order are tremendously frustrating people. They're sane, well-informed, and can reason competently but have a nasty habit of focusing on the wrong things and drawing the wrong conclusions. They accept valid points and then just move on and behave as if they never heard them! What the hell do you do with someone who accepts what you say but refuses to take it seriously?

Correctives writ large: the dangers of overcorrection

Mains and correctives can be extended from the psychological level to the cultural, and some ideas are best understood as correctives to a culturally dominant main. However, there's great danger in this, because such ideas depend on that taken-for-granted background to stay sensible.

Once at a corporate strategy workshop I, an early millennial, discussed the future of work with a boomer. She kept going on about how anything is possible these days, the sky's the limit and you can achieve anything if you put your mind to it. All those clichés. Well, they were clichés to me, but maybe not to her. She'd been imprinted with another reality in her youth, one with opportunity far more limited by things like class, sex, or the right social networks. Against that background, today stands out in how accessible opportunities are. To get to an accurate description starting from the taken-for-granted reality she had once learnt, she applied a wildly overoptimistic corrective to describe what stood out to her, making it all add up. But I hadn't grown up in her cultural environment. For my generation, the "anything is possible, follow your passion" was the *main* narrative growing up, and we corrected for it with a certain cynicism when it sunk in that not everybody gets to be a rockstar-astronaut-fashion-designer. Since "you have to actually make a living" was taken for granted by our parents' generation they didn't feel it had to be said, so it wasn't hammered into us and thus not internalized. As a result, many feel disappointed or even betrayed when confronted with this corrective in adulthood.

What happened is that the story that started as a corrective eventually took over the role as ground truth. That is, the corrective became the main as the main it was supposed to correct for faded away.

Instead of getting a moderate new narrative we jump right to the opposite and culture swings like a pendulum. Think 80s-style Reagan-Thatcher neoliberalism as an overcorrective to 70s-style regulatory stultification—or narratives around mental illness swinging from shame to romanticism: some positivity as a counterweight to stigma brings balance, but when by-default stigma quietly wanes as its adherents age out of influence, the balance is no more.

My wife had a realization when working as a substitute teacher in a middle school for a few weeks. While a more sensitive, permissive, and egalitarian sensibility was an appropriate response to authoritarian schooling a few generations ago, that ethos is now running the show completely unopposed. That means catering to even the most absurd of personal quirks and behavioral dysfunction, making the students unaccustomed to having any demands whatsoever placed on them.

Writer and former AI researcher David Chapman argues that this happened with the postmodern critique of objectivity and knowledge in some academic disciplines. In his article *A Bridge to Meta-rationality* he says:

> In the 1970s and 1980s, the best postmodern/poststructural thinkers presented meta-rational views, based on their thorough understanding of systematic rationality. This first generation of postmodern teachers had a complete "classical education" in the humanities; they mastered the Western intellectual tradition before coming to understand its limitations.
>
> Deconstructive postmodernism, their critique of stage 4 modernism/systematicity/rationality, is the basis of the contemporary university humanities curriculum. This is a disaster. The critique is largely *correct*; but, as [Robert] Kegan observed, to teach it to young adults is harmful. Few university students

> have consolidated rationality. Essentially none are ready to move beyond it. Pointing out its defects makes their developmental task more difficult.
>
> You cannot understand what is wrong with rationalism until you are capable of being rational. You cannot go beyond rationality until after you can use it reliably. You cannot become meta to systems you do not appreciate and do not understand how to deploy.

The whole enterprise was a corrective to a hyper-rationalistic academic and industrial culture, nowhere near as dominant today as it was in the 1960s. Thus, in the present, it's not hitting as it should and not producing the moderate combination it once did. Sociologist and philosopher Bruno Latour, giant of the Science and Technology Studies discipline, was making the point himself in the late 2010s. In a 2018 article in the *New York Times Magazine* called *Bruno Latour, the Post-Truth Philosopher, Mounts a Defense of Science* he reflects:

> I think we were so happy to develop all this critique because we were so sure of the authority of science.

To be a bit harsh towards old Bruno (RIP), his regrets sound to me like he just realized something that should've been obvious from the start. Undermining trust in science and objectivity does not automatically serve the interests of progressive leftism the way '60s radicals thought it would. For a while now, as the sensemaking, knowledge-legitimizing institutions of academia, journalism, and education have grown more and more left-leaning, the shoe has been on the other foot. I could've told him this was a problem! Somewhere in a box in the attic I still have lecture notes from 2006, with my angry scribbles in the margins, arguing to myself that they should orient their scholarship around *balancing* the traditional and the critical conceptions of knowledge and *not* react to a preexisting slanted orthodoxy by putting up an equally slanted counterweight that can't even stand up straight on its own.

In their 2020 book *Cynical Theories,* Helen Pluckrose and James Lindsay also argue that today's "wokeism" is the result of once sophisticated high-postmodern correctives being transmuted into ground truths over a couple of academic generations. They've gone from a tempering critique of modernist rationality, via the cultivation of corrective narratives in their own right, to an orthodoxy[95] of outright hostility to enlightenment values as merely the peculiar habits of privileged white men.

Reaction to existing taken-for-granted norms play a huge role in the formation of beliefs and ideologies. The corollary is that they rely on these background norms staying in place to make good sense. It behooves us to keep in mind when reading Rand's novels that she grew up in Russia as the daughter of a small business owner who had his property confiscated by the Bolsheviks when she was an impressionable teenager. As far as she was concerned, concerns over inequality already *had* come first, in all too generous helpings.

Are you punching up or down?

Depending on what we as listeners consider the social norm, the same idea can come across as a moderating critique of the powers that be, or as aggressive enforcement of the party line. Here comes a whole set of complicating circumstances. "What the dominant narrative is around here" is *itself* a narrative, and it depends on the exact domain we refer to by "around here". We've already covered that it can depend on the time period: e.g. is smoking depicted positively in movies? Maybe if we take all of movie history into account, but not if we just look at the 21st century. What about homosexuality? Often the opposite. Is a certain artistic approach a bold break with convention, or a tired cliché? That depends on how fast we update our idea of the conventional. Subverting traditional notions of beauty has been

---

[95] Given the anarchic sensibilities of early postmodern theorists this is quite an irony.

the norm within high art for nearly a century, but if we look at all of history (or all of society, including the hoi polloi) we can still consider it subversive. At what point do we move on to problematizing the problematization, subverting the subversion, and transgressing against an ethos of transgression? The future is already here, it's just unevenly distributed.

We can pick and choose domain in other ways. Something might be the norm in this country but not the world, or in this city but not the country as a whole, or in this industry but not that one, in my friend group but not in school, in music but not in science, on the news but not down the pub, and so on. Norms around schooling differ between China and Sweden, for example, and when a colleague once said that a Chinese official who argued for less rote memorization in their school system *disagreed* with a Swedish politician known for advocating *more* grinding for children, he was probably wrong. More likely they had similar views on the ideal balance, but wanted to move in opposite directions compared to local norms, and thus the "disagreement" was an illusion. Is criticizing capitalism bravely punching up or an authoritarian rearticulation of orthodoxy? What about pointing out the wrongdoings of Israelis, or Palestinians? It depends on where you are and who's around you.

There may also be different norms implicitly and explicitly. Most people know that appearance matters a lot for sexual and romantic (and honestly, professional too) success, but if you only listen to what is said out loud you might come away believing the opposite, because everyone wants to sound nice. The same applies to corporations vis-à-vis the environment; looking at their public messaging we'd think they care a lot, but based on their behavior you can make a case for the opposite.

The personal, small-scale domain may have different norms than the public, large-scale domain. I can't help but notice, for example, how *utterly normal* it is to assume personalities and talents are inherited on a personal level. It's unremarkable to comment on how a child has her father's temper or his mother's musicality, but far outside the norm in public discourse to suggest that heredity plays some role in the structure of society (like reproduction of classes)[96]. So, what is *the* norm, against which we should interpret individual statements?

On top of all this, we like to cast our own opinion in the role of put-upon minority, with us bravely bringing balance to a society with our opponents in power. It's easy to do because we don't notice unstated standards when they correspond to our own views ("they're not assumptions, it's just the way things are"). When they don't, however, we do notice, so we feel there are more of those cases. The "hostile media effect" is an example. Wikipedia calls it

> [a] perceptual theory of mass communication that refers to the tendency for individuals with a strong preexisting attitude on an issue to perceive media coverage as biased against their side and in favor of their antagonists' point of view. Partisans from opposite sides of an issue will tend to find the same coverage to be biased against them.

I've been in conversations where I've held that the social pressure in favor of X needs to be taken into account, while the other person said the social pressure *against* X needs to be taken into account. And both can be right! There can and does exist social pressure in opposite directions depending on the context, and it's easy to overgeneralize (especially from cases where you are in the minority).

I'd go as far as saying that most argumentation is corrective, in that it says something the speaker thinks is underacknowledged. Thus it can only be properly understood given knowledge of how well appreciated the speaker thinks various things already are. Arguments are like jokes: they're meant to subvert or invert background

---

[96] Standard narrative moralism implies that everything ever said services a moral agenda, so just pointing out that these norms are different will make me sound, no matter how milquetoast liberal my politics are, like the villain from a hypothetical Charles Dickens novelization of *Gattaca*.

assumptions, and like jokes they only land right when those assumptions are shared between speaker and listener.

Cross-"cultural" communication is a minefield, and the appropriate attitude towards understanding where another is coming from can be nothing but severe humility. Everything requires interpretation, interpretation requires a background, people disagree on what the background is and therefore on the meaning of what is said. We're systematically prone to disagreeing with those on the other side not only on what the right opinion is, but also on who is on the side of moderation and of "punching up".

PART V

A Society of Minds

Chapter 15

People Are Different

One half of the world cannot understand the pleasures of the other.

— Jane Austen

There's a famous post on *Quora* by Mark Eichenlaub where he describes being anosmic (lacking a sense of smell) without realizing it. He thought smells were metaphorical, like "vibes":

> Each night I would tell my mom, "Dinner smells great!" I teased my sister about her stinky feet. I held my nose when I ate Brussels sprouts. In gardens, I bent down and took a whiff of the roses. I yelled "gross" when someone farted. I never thought twice about any of it for fourteen years.

We can talk about smell metaphorically, as in "this smells fishy" about something suspicious. Mark didn't understand that we don't *always* do so, because he, naturally, assumed that everyone was like him. It took him many years to realize he was wrong, even though "having a sense of smell" is a fairly obvious psychological trait. Subtler mental differences can go undetected forever.

Taking for granted that we're all alike inside, we do what Mark did and think people speak figuratively about experiences we don't have. If we happen to recognize our error, it can come as a revelation. In early 2020, a viral tweet set off such a mass realization:

> Fun fact: some people have an internal narrative and some don't
>
> As in, some people's thoughts are like sentences they "hear", and some people just have abstract non-verbal thoughts, and have to consciously verbalize them
>
> And most people aren't aware of the other type of person

The discussion spread to *Medium* and *Newsweek*, among others. Madison Epting, writing on Medium, said:

> As the individual who expressed his shock following the discovery, I too was surprised to learn that hearing voices in a true linguistic form within the parameters of one's own mind was both possible and involuntary for many.

James Felton, writing on *IFLScience*, came at it from the other direction:

> I assumed that everyone else had an internal monologue, and like mine, that monologue is voiced by Patrick Stewart. To think that some people don't have a monologue portrayed by Captain Picard was weird enough, without discovering that they hear nothing at all.

I have inner speech, but not always and it's not automatic. Like actual speech it's intentional and in "my own voice" with subvocalizing micro-movements, and it mostly occurs when I'm imagining explaining my thoughts to someone else. Others describe hearing *actual voices* that are not their own (sometimes several different ones), with distinct, vivid timbre and sound.

The surprisingly controversial mode of thinking

To me there's a clear and obvious distinction between thought and the vocabulary in which it is expressed. When putting my thoughts into words there's an element of translation: most often I didn't *literally* think those words, I thought something non-verbal and made an effort to phrase it for communication. But many seem to think directly in words and struggle to understand that for others, thought can be prior to language.

The psychologist Russell Hurlburt has studied what he calls "pristine inner experience" and argue in several books and articles that there are five categories of inner experience, and people vary greatly in how much of each they have. In *Not Everyone Conducts Inner Speech* in *Psychology Today* in 2011, he wrote:

> Subjects experienced themselves as inwardly talking to themselves in 26 percent of all samples, but there were large individual differences: some subjects never experienced inner speech; other subjects experienced inner speech in as many as 75 percent of their samples. The median percentage across subjects was 20 percent.

Inner speech is one mode of experience in Hurlburt's model, another is inner seeing (visual imagination), a third is emotion, and a fourth is sensory experience (the smell of roses, the sensation of wind on your face, or the sound of leaves rustling). Hurlburt's last mode is the most interesting, because apparently, well-informed, intelligent people disagree about whether it exists. He calls his fifth feature "unsymbolized thinking".

> An unsymbolized thought is specific: you're wondering what Feature 5 is. You're not wondering whether there are still other features, not wondering how Hurlburt knows this, not wondering what kinds of things go on in peoples' inner experience,

> not wondering about how inner experience is measured, not trying to recall what sensory awareness is, and so on. That is, you're wondering about what Feature 5 is, not about anything else that might be more or less closely related to that.

This is exactly how I think most of the time: specific thoughts not put into specific words. Then he hits me with

> Many people (perhaps most), including many (perhaps most) psychologists, believe that unsymbolized thinking is impossible.

What? This about what I find to be the most natural, obvious thing in the world—the one thing whose existence I cannot possibly doubt. Thought doesn't *feel* linguistic when finding the right words for them is effortful and has flawed results. If it was in words I could just... use those words? But this is not obvious to everyone.

> Our beeper studies show the full gamut of the frequency of experience of unsymbolized thinking. Some people rarely or never have such experiences, others experience unsymbolized thinking at nearly all their waking moments, and yet others sometimes do and sometimes don't experience it.

Findings like these are presented as curiosities, fun little tidbits that we hear about, go "huh", and then forget. I happen to believe that such mental differences have significant consequences for how we apprehend the world and what sort of beliefs we develop. For example, the clear separation I feel exists between thoughts and the language in which they are expressed might lie behind my irritation at words being "wrong". It bothers me, viscerally, when words don't match what I feel someone is trying to say, when the speaker has misunderstood a word's meaning, or when flaws in how words represent thoughts prevent those thoughts from being communicated. It's all wrong and ugly and it stinks (figuratively).

Much of this book is scar tissue around this. Perhaps—and I'm speculating—people for whom thoughts *are* words don't get this feeling. If so, then ambiguity and multiplicity of meanings, and the conclusion that a word means something different each time it's used and everything requires careful interpretation, might not be as bleeding obvious and important as it feels to me.

If you do think in words it makes sense to think of available vocabulary as much more strongly determining the thoughts we can have. I've stressed the importance of vocabulary myself, but I see its significance as mainly social, not psychological. It determines what we can effectively communicate, but not what we can think. These are clearly separate, and the thesis of *1984*—that language fundamentally constrains possible thought—is artistic hyperbole. But it could seem, or even *be*, literally true for some.

Missing a mind's eye

Hurlburt's second mode is "inner seeing", which brings us to another viral concept from a few years back. *Aphantasia* is the inability to produce mental images, and according to Google Trends, searches for it has grown about 3000% in the last decade. Neurolinguistics researcher Hélène Loevenbruck describes it (in *Live Science*, 2021):

> People who experience aphantasia don't experience visualizations in their mind; they can't mentally picture their bedroom or their mother's face.

Like inner speech and unsymbolized thinking, visual imagination isn't something you either have or not—it varies along a spectrum. In *Aphantasia: The science of visual imagery extremes* Rebecca Keogh et al. write:

> The ability to visualize has extreme variations, ranging from completely absent (aphantasia) to photo-

> like (hyperphantasia). The anatomy and functionality of visual cortex, including primary visual cortex, have been associated with individual differences in visual imagery ability, pointing to a potential correlate for both aphantasia and hyperphantasia.

Online quizzes and tests can tell you how good your visual imagination is[97]. My results point to "moderate to good" and I do feel I'm capable of producing quite detailed inner images, with colors and textures and such, and in some sense they are photo-like, but absolutely not as vivid and strong as literally seeing something. Nor do they appear automatically and effortlessly, which seems to be the case for some. Here's the signature "Naemi", blogging at *A Book Owl's Corner*:

> If someone says something like "love" to me, I immediately get hit with a ton of images and a sense of the feeling. I will see people I love, a heart, people holding hands, all super-imposed on one another. I am perfectly capable of seeing multiple images in my mind at once. And I will also see the actual word, "love", how it is spelled, in my head. This happens whenever people talk.

I suppose this is hyperphantasia, which I definitely don't have. To make mental imagery I have to purposefully turn my visual focus inward, towards "the back of my head", causing a sort of momentary blindness, and then work to hold the image in place. I tell you this, which seems perfectly unremarkable to me, because I'm now unsure if it is. Naemi also says:

---

[97] There is physical evidence of aphantasia. Kay, et al showed in *The pupillary light response as a physiological index of aphantasia, sensory and phenomenological imagery strength* (2022) that self-described aphantasiacs don't react with contraction of pupils when they *imagine* looking at a bright light, while others do.

> [I]t might explain why I love descriptions so much in literature. The more vividly you describe a world to me, the better I can actually picture what the author wanted me to see.

Another blogger, "Shell Child", in *The Joys of an Overactive Imagination*, says:

> I see so much when I read that it distracts me. It's not just images though. I hear, I smell, I taste. I get so wound up in exploring another world inside my head that sometimes it takes me months to finish a book. The more I love the book, sometimes, the harder it is to read.

This is likely the reason I don't much care for books trying to evoke sensory impressions, e.g. with descriptions. While I *can* produce imagery, the effort required combined with middling vividness means I don't get more out of it than I put in. The image, carefully built and held in place, doesn't come alive on its own and doesn't produce much of an experience over and above the description itself. I prefer literature about ideas[98], expressed in words (i.e. nonfiction or fiction heavy on narration, exposition, and dialogue), instead of taking the roundabout way through the medium of simulated sensation.

Taking difference seriously

Differences in Hurlburt's five modes of inner experience cause disagreements all by themselves, but more importantly: being aware of them helps us take differences in internal experience more seriously as significant components of disagreement. For example, I've come to understand that people may not be joking when they say they hate puns. I've seen it described as painful, at about the intensity of being

---

[98] Here I *do* often have Shell Child's experience of reading too slowly because it spontaneously and unavoidably provokes my mind into generating content. But that's unsymbolized thinking, not images.

poked in the ribs, and as an *act of aggression* for this reason. I find puns delightful, like having a small piece of chocolate. Perhaps I'd make fewer puns if could experience what a pun hater feels? More dramatically, would it change my philosophical beliefs if I could have the inner experience of a believer in new age spirituality, with "energies" and "auras" and whatnot? Experiencing spontaneous voices and images might make entirely different things feel plausible, compared to me thinking mostly in Hurlburt's unsymbolized abstractions. Some do report changing their beliefs after experimenting with psychedelics.

Inner experience can change in many ways. Aging makes you a different person. As a father I now understand why, to a child, adults seem strangely tired all the time. Alcohol makes me sociable in a way I guess tells me what it feels like to be an extravert. I also know how different everything looks during a depressive episode, with no change besides on the inside. A cup of coffee, by contrast, makes the world bright and inviting.

Some undergo more dramatic changes. One of the most interesting interviews I've ever heard is a short segment on an episode of *This American Life* from 2002. The theme is testosterone, and it has Griffin Hansbury as a guest. Hansbury is a trans-man, who as part of transitioning from butch lesbian to heterosexual man took testosterone injections. T-levels shooting through the roof produced a typically masculine sex drive *suddenly* instead of gradually during puberty in the normal fashion. Turns out that that can be quite a shock.

> Before testosterone, I would be riding the subway, which is the traditional hotbed of lust in the city. And I would see a woman on the subway and I would think, she's attractive. I'd like to meet her. What's that book she's reading? I could talk to her. This is what I would say. There would be a narrative. There would be this stream of language. It would be very verbal.

> After testosterone, there was no narrative. There was no language whatsoever. It was just, I would see a woman who was attractive—or not attractive. She might have an attractive quality—nice ankles or something—and the rest of her would be fairly unappealing to me. But that was enough to basically just flood my mind with aggressive pornographic images, just one after another. It was like being in a pornographic movie house in my mind. And I couldn't turn it off. I could not turn it off. /---/
>
> I felt like a monster a lot of the time. And it made me understand men. It made me understand adolescent boys a lot. Suddenly, hair is sprouting and I'm turning into this beast. And I would really berate myself for it. I remember walking up Fifth Avenue, and there was a woman walking in front of me. And she was wearing this little skirt and this little top. And I was looking at her ass. And I kept saying to myself, don't look at it. Don't look at it. And I kept looking at it.

Transitioning was obviously a disruptive experience, and I sympathize, but I won't deny that I found this a little funny too—as "just desserts" for being judgmental earlier about something he didn't understand. Part of me wants to have a go at him: "well, well... welcome to manhood, buddy! Did it have to take this for you to be accepting? How on Earth did you *think* this worked? Is it so hard to just listen to what people say and observe what they do to infer that maybe, just maybe, being them is different from being you? It shouldn't require something this drastic!". But this would be unfair, because yes, apparently it is very hard. Even I am not as understanding of people I dislike as I perhaps ought to be.

Hansbury was given a gift, of sorts, however harrowing, of going through a shift in subjective experience that produce a visceral understanding of what the rest of us need to learn through effort: people behave differently not simply because their rational minds and free wills make different decisions[99], but because their raw, subjective experience of life differs. That's not saying that no free will or responsibility exists, it's saying that we choose between options that are presented to us differently, with different saliency and intensity, and with different costs and payoffs.

Buckets and plates

This impacts how we feel about virtue and vice. That is, people differing in their inner experience makes them differ in what they find easy and hard, tolerable and torturous, heroic and the bare minimum. I find domestic chores crushing, to the point that it negatively affects my mental health. I know, I know, few people enjoy them, but there are some differences. My wife once told me she has a "stress bucket" that gradually fills up when new tasks come in, and when she crosses them off her list it gets emptied. As long as a reasonable completion rate can be kept, the bucket doesn't overflow and everything's ok, but if it does, due to sick kids or things going pear-shaped at work, she loses her shit—snaps at the rest of us, can't sleep, develops a whole-body rash, or eats too many unhealthy snacks.

As soon as she phrased it like that I realized that it's not how I work. That description wouldn't occur to me. I don't have a stress bucket, I have a stress *plate*. As long as there's anything on it I have to get rid of it before I can be at peace. I'm not fine and then suddenly lose my shit, no, I'm almost never "fine"[100], and I gradually lose more and more of my shit depending on how much is currently on the

---

[99] It could be that we assume this because we don't really think the mind is the brain. If we have immaterial souls equipped with a free will separate from the mechanics of base matter, then it makes sense for every such soul to be identical, with the same experience resulting from the same stimuli. Different "outputs", then, would be the result of different free decisions and the perfectly proper object of moral judgment. Thinking of us as material creatures, with material brains that differ on the hardware level, comes with different implications.

[100] Unless my perspective is drastically narrowed through intoxication.

plate. Despite the neverending deluge of chores family life brings with it, she's said she's fundamentally ok with our daily routine, and I can't say the same. She wants to improve things too, but I struggle to be enthusiastic because her solutions don't address what I consider the actual problem. With a bucket it's all about throughput, and she suggests ways to raise it. Great, but I want to *stop the inflow*. Treading water more efficiently helps keep your head above the surface, sure, but it's not solid ground.

Maybe being a "bucket person" and being ok with the existence of tasks as long as they don't overwhelm you requires getting some psychological reward from completing them. My favorite article on understanding the minds of others is *What Universal Experiences Are You Missing*, by the ever-relevant Scott Alexander. The post itself is good, but the thousand-ish comments where people discuss the peculiarities of their minds are the real gold mine. Consider this anonymous contribution:

> The little buzz of "reward" after accomplishing an extrinsically but not intrinsically rewarding task. After taking the stimulant "Vyvanse" for the first time, I saw what it was like to feel good after completing menial tasks like washing dishes. I thought people were just referring to the sense of relief from the stress of impending tasks.

Maybe "bucket people" feel some of this, I gather (my father-in-law once said he loves crossing items off lists), but I don't at all. There's no meaning or achievement in doing something just to stay in the same place.

I've also come to understand that some people enjoy exercise. That would certainly help with keeping fit. I never have; aerobic exercise in particular is nothing but pain. In other vices, I eat too much because it takes too long for me to feel full. I know that if I stop eating while I'm still hungry I *will* be satisfied in 20 minutes, but that takes active self-control. I'm not as bad as this commenter, however:

> I don't understand how people WANT TO stop eating. I can eat past the point of nausea and past the point of pain and if the food is in front of me I still want to eat it. I stop using willpower, not because I WANT to.

I guess this is why some people weigh 500 pounds, and I'm not necessarily any better than them. I'm just lucky it's not that hard for me. It would be even easier if I was more like my wife, who actually likes vegetables, as in, she looks forward to eating cabbage, cauliflower, and broccoli. I have never in my life *desired* vegetables. I'll eat them if they're in front of me, and with enough butter and salt I'll like them fine, but that's as far as it goes[101].

Does this come down to a difference in internal experience? Maybe one that can be traced all the way back to genes. Jennifer Smith at the University of Kentucky has done research on the TAS2R38 gene. It comes in two variants: AVI and PAV, and we have two copies, one from each parent.

> According to the study, the combination of these variants determines your taste. People who have an AVI/PAV gene perceive bitter tastes of these chemicals, while individuals with PAV/PAV make-up find the same foods exceptionally bitter – they're often called "super-tasters".

I could be in the middle with one of each, and she and her fellow veggie lovers could have double AVI, making green vegetables mild and sweet. There are other signs she's insensitive to bitterness, such as love of highly hopped IPAs and chocolate darker than the dead of night.

---

[101] She, on the other hand, struggles to believe anyone genuinely enjoys whiskey and has been known to accuse people of faking it for manliness points.

Is everyone gay?

Now for the *pièce de résistance*: assuming other people are like us can drastically impact even our deepest moral convictions. The article mentioned above has a comment noting that the gay rights activist Dan Savage gets letters from gay men in very conservative communities who don't appear to understand that most men are not attracted to other men like they are. Instead, they must just be hiding it. In a 1999 article in *Rolling Stone*, titled *The Holy War on Gays*, we find some revealing quotes from Dr. Paul Cameron, founder of the anti-gay *Family Research Institute*:

> Like many of his allies, Cameron believes that, if left unchecked, homosexuality will destroy America like God did Sodom. "Untrammeled homosexuality can take over and destroy a social system," says Cameron. "If you isolate sexuality as something solely for one's own personal amusement, and all you want is the most satisfying orgasm you can get—and that is what homosexuality seems to be—then homosexuality seems too powerful to resist. The evidence is that men do a better job on men and women on women, if all you are looking for is orgasm." So powerful is the allure of gays, Cameron believes, that if society approves that gay people, more and more heterosexuals will be inexorably drawn into homosexuality. "I'm convinced that lesbians are particularly good seducers," says Cameron. "People in homosexuality are incredibly evangelical," he adds, sounding evangelical himself. "It's pure sexuality. It's almost like pure heroin. It's such a rush. They are committed in almost a religious way. And they'll take enormous risks, do anything." He says that for married men and women, gay sex would be irresistible. "Marital sex tends toward the boring end," he points

> out. "Generally, it doesn't deliver the kind of sheer sexual pleasure that homosexual sex does". So, Cameron believes, within a few generations, homosexuality would become the dominant form of sexual behavior.

It's a revelation, one of the most fascinating things I've ever read. It's so odd, peculiar reasoning, that nonetheless makes perfect sense as the result of a gay man intellectualizing his desires under the assumption that everyone else is like him. Rather than understand that he's not typical, he thinks that "men do a better job on men" is why he prefers sex with them, and that everyone else would too if only they were allowed to. But no one who didn't would ever think that way, because it's just not how sexual desire works.

Under the assumption that *everyone is gay*, living a "gay lifestyle" or not does become a choice between giving in to pursuing sexual gratification or do your duty and raise children in an unsatisfying heterosexual relationship. For us straights this contradiction doesn't exist, but for him it does, and it slots perfectly into a Christian belief system because it looks like just another case of having to resist sin. Our whole life is an exercise in self-control, so why not this? *Of course* it's important for society to discourage "being gay" in the sense of choosing to indulge your desires, if social pressure is the only thing holding us back and making civilization possible, like with every other sin[102]. There's something deeply tragic about it, about a man who cannot in good conscience have what he wants, and turns the world upside down because of it.

Normal variation or "neurodiversity"

Given that diversity of inner experience is severely underestimated both in prevalence and importance, should I not be supportive of the so-called "neurodiversity movement"? It originated as an alternative

---

[102] This is of course not to say that all anti-gay sentiment is caused by being gay yourself, just that this is one way such sentiment can be intellectualized.

way to think about autism, as not a disability or medical condition but as a different way to exist normally and healthily. It has later expanded to include other neuropsychiatric conditions like ADHD, dyslexia, and Tourette's syndrome.

There's something sound about the idea, but it comes from the wrong angle. The antonym "neurotypical", meaning a ~normal person, gives me pause because it cements the idea that we're talking about a single normal state and distinct deviations from it. Ginny Russell, in a 2020 review article called *Critiques of the Neurodiversity Movement* argued that there is no bimodal distribution of autistic traits. It's not that you are "on the spectrum" or not—the spectrum stretches, continuously, all the way to "zero" (or neurotypical), and everyone is thus somewhere on it. In a 2017 article of my own called *The Nerd as the Norm* (my most popular piece ever, incidentally) I speculated that this spectrum could extend, like a regular bell curve, past the normal and towards another extreme on the opposite side. Regardless of how true that is, it seems obvious to me that the most natural way to make sense of the diversity of minds is as *continuous* variation, not as normality with a bunch of alternatives. Whether it's Hurlburt's modes of experience, the strength and orientation of desires, the ease or difficulty of doing different things, or clusters of traits like autism or ADHD, why not think of them as continuous normal variation, where extreme values can cause trouble, without us having to introduce falsely essentializing discontinuities?[103]

We notice the outliers, which is why we have terms like *aphantasia* and *prosopagnosia* (the inability to recognize faces) suggesting distinct conditions, when in reality these are the extremes of gradual differences. Just like hyperphantasiacs with uncommonly vivid visual imagination exist, so do "super recognizers" who remember every face they've ever seen. Most of us are in the middle of both.

There's good precedent. Personality psychologists model traits as continuums with most people in the middle. Their standard "Big

---

[103] Ok, so the "why" is that we like types more than continuous properties. That's not going to change, but please allow me some rhetorical questions.

Five" model consists of five axes called Openness, Conscientiousness, Extraversion, Agreeableness, and Neuroticism (making the acronym OCEAN), ideally other features of our psychology should be viewed that way too.

I say this because of who I am

I have more autistic-like traits than the average person, but not to an extreme or pathological degree. It's a personality, not a medical condition. I experience this in a way that to me feels obviously normal, but I'll describe it just in case it's not: my mind does parallel processing, with ~autistic style thinking and ~normie style thinking at the same time. It's handy, but the obvious discrepancy between the two can be unpleasant (sometimes enough to make you write books). My inner autist feels things should work a certain way, and my inner normie gets why they don't. The result is frustration.

Another personality-related part of the motivation for this book has to do with the Agreeableness trait. Wikipedia describes it:

> Agreeableness is a personality trait manifesting itself in individual behavioral characteristics that are perceived as kind, sympathetic, cooperative, warm, and considerate. In contemporary personality psychology, agreeableness is one of the five major dimensions of personality structure, reflecting individual differences in cooperation and social harmony.
>
> People who score high on this dimension are empathetic and altruistic, while a low agreeableness score relates to selfish behavior (often manifesting as stinginess) and a lack of empathy. Those who score very low on agreeableness show signs of dark triad behavior such as manipulation and competing with others rather than cooperating.

I've always disliked it because how awkwardly it fits me. On tests I score in the midrange, but that middling result hides huge internal differences in the sub-traits that go into it. I'm high on *forthrightness/honesty* and *cooperation* but low on *selflessness* and *tendermindedness*, meaning I'm agreeable in that I hate aggression[104], manipulation, and lies, but disagreeable in that I reject obligations to self-sacrifice and resist being moved by empathy. This is apparently not the standard, since them being facets of the same trait implies they go together.

Perhaps for what I write to resonate with you as a reader—for problems to seem like problems and solutions to seem like solutions—your personality must be similar to mine. I can't get around that my values are shaped by my personality. But I don't *want* that to be necessary for us to communicate. I want us to be able to break through such barriers and understand each other as we are. That's part of the point of this chapter and of the book as a whole. Whether I'm doing a good job is for you to decide.

---

[104] Maybe it's all self-interest, deep down. Would I be more accepting of aggression if I were big and strong and actually could use it to my advantage? In *The Evolutionary Foundations of Status Hierarchy* from 2015, Mark van Vugt and Joshua Tybur imply that I would:

> Men's physical strength predicts their quickness to anger and their likelihood of applying aggressive tactics to achieve their goals... Physical size at age 3 predicts aggressiveness and disagreeableness at age 11.

Other research by Sell, Tooby & Cosmides (*Formidability and the logic of human anger*, 2009) confirm that physically stronger men (and better-looking women and men) are more prone to experiencing anger, likely because the emotion evolved as a negotiation tool and they can get more out of it.

Chapter 16

The Political is Personal

People would never fall in love if they hadn't heard love talked about.

— Francois de La Rochefoucauld

I'm surprised by how often I see references to René Girard in my online neck of the woods. Girard is a historian, philosopher and social theorist mostly known for his theory of "mimetic desire":

> Man is the creature who does not know what to desire, and he turns to others in order to make up his mind. We desire what others desire because we imitate their desires.

This does not sound at all convincing to me, and looking further into it has done little to change that first impression. It's not that it can't be true for some things, superficially, but when we want what others want it's because those things are proxies for, or instruments towards, what we really desire, e.g. social status, admiration, power, sex, money. And those desires are pretty fixed. At least that's my headcanon and to the extent that such imitative wants exist, characterizing desire as imitative is at best a corrective. An account of human wants built upon that as a centerpiece is just bizarre.

I feel this way because of how my own wants and desires feel to me: stable and innate, strong and straightforward. If Girard's theories resonate with others, and if sentiments like the one expressed in this tweet

> [I] expect the vast majority of people decide what to do about sex entirely based on social convention. if society expects heterosexuality they'll be straight; if it expects bisexuality they'll be bi.

... are honestly held (and I believe they are), then it's simply not possible that everyone experiences desire like I do. My point is not that the tweet is wrong, necessarily. I could be mistaken, and my feelings could be far more determined by social influences than I think. I'm just saying that, based on my own experience, I would never, ever come to this conclusion.

What made this all click came from the article referenced multiple times in the last chapter. It's a transcript of a real-life conversation about food:

> Ozy: I am currently eating chickpeas and rice and I am delighted by the fact that I can eat this whenever I want. The nice thing about DISCOVERING YOUR FOOD PREFERENCES is that suddenly all the food in my cupboards is food I like and am looking forward to eating. And usually I get food I like by, like, luck? So this is excitement.
>
> Scott: I don't understand, why didn't you buy things like that before?
>
> Ozy: It took me a while to have enough of a sense of the food I like for "make a list of the food I like" to be a viable grocery-list-making strategy.
>
> Scott: I've got to admit I'm confused and intrigued by your "don't know my own preferences" thing.
>
> Ozy: Hrm. Well, it's sort of like... you know how sometimes you pretend to like something because it's high-status, and if you do it well enough you ac-

> tually believe you like the thing? Unless I pay a lot of attention all my preferences end up being not "what I actually enjoy" but like "what is high status" or "what will keep people from getting angry at me."

No I don't know, actually. I don't think I do that. I have many childhood memories around enjoying food, and I've always got a lot of pleasure from food I like and a lot of displeasure from food I don't. The idea that you can not know, not be quite aware, or just not pay attention to what kind of food you like is *wild*. I'm obviously aware of fashions and status and social expectations, but I've never confused them for actual enjoyment. But perhaps doing so is more normal than I think. Another story that's stuck with me was told by Jacob Falkovich (in a blog post called *Polyamory is Rational*):

> I told my coworker that when I'm in a rush and need a measured dose of caffeine I just chew on a handful of roasted espresso beans. The taste is not actually bad—if you like chocolate covered beans, you may not totally need the chocolate. I suggested to my coworker that she try it at least once, just to know what it tastes and feels like.
>
> She adamantly refused, citing "that's not how it's consumed" and "it's weird, people don't do that" as her main objections. I countered that these are facts about people, rather than facts about coffee beans. While you can infer some things about beans from observing people, the beans are right there in the office kitchen to be experienced directly. My coworker seemed unable to grasp the distinction, treating the social unacceptability of eating coffee beans as akin to physical impossibility.

Is it in fact normal, even typical, to experience social reality as solid enough to be indistinguishable from physical fact? If you do, and at the same time your own wants are weak and unarticulated, then the social could dominate the psychological so strongly that it *becomes* the psychological. Might you then experience your own personality as inseparable from your social environment?

This possibility has made me reevaluate some of my views. A while back a comedian on TV had a bit about Disney movies she watched as a child. She said she thought of the princesses as role models, and felt bad for not living up to that feminine ideal. Past me would have just thought it was her own fault for reading things into it that she didn't really have to. I never did that. I don't remember ever thinking of any childhood media as telling me what I was supposed to be like—or likely caring about it much if it had. Current me, however, understands that it's easy to ignore and dismiss implied social expectations if you are only weakly aware of them in the first place (especially if they're also drowned out by your own loud and clear wants). She may well have perceived those implied expectations as far more compelling and essential to self-formation than I can comprehend.

No auto-mute

Just like I experience wants as straightforward and innate while some do not, I also experience them as *stable and persistent*—which apparently some do not. When he was on the *Parenting Hell* podcast, the comedian Elis James talked about his adjustment to parenting a small child 24/7 during the first covid lockdown, including waking up before 5 every morning. He said:

> I would say I've got an almost superhuman ability to adapt to my situation, in this case complete lockdown because of coronavirus, and then find it completely impossible to imagine an alternative. So I actually wasn't that unhappy, I was like "oh well, I'm unable to leave the house—that's my life now". /---/

> If I'd been a character in the TV show *Lost* I would be the bloke who was quite happy to bed down for the night under the shattered wing of a stricken airplane "oh well this is my life now, I live under a wing".

It sounds like his needs, wants, and reactions to his circumstances are easily muted or even dissolved. He's right that this is a superpower, because being his opposite isn't great. I don't have much, if any, experience with getting used to or coming to terms with how things are, and I struggle to not constantly fantasize about how they should be different and better. When I cared for a baby that woke up every day at 4:45 in the morning I didn't react with passive acceptance. I had unceasing, desperate yearnings to get to sleep in to... like 6. Once back in our student days my now wife told me that her friend, then recently transitioned to working life, goes to bed every night at 10. Me, the life-long night owl, responded with "what the hell, what kind of a life is that?". Well, now I'm on my second decade of feeling "what kind of a life is this?". Ten years plus after becoming a father I still haven't got used to always being on duty. Hell, even before having children I never got used to the reduction in freedom and control over my time it meant to own a house, or to have a job, or even, at times, to have a girlfriend. I'm 42 years old, in a relationship itself old enough to order a strong drink, and I still look back to the freedom I had during teenage summers and feel that everything after it is an aberration, and that such a lifestyle will naturally return as soon as this temporary crisis that is adulthood blows over.

Elis James recognizes that he is unusual, but others like him might not. For them, others' inability to adapt and accept whatever happens to them may be cast as pigheadedness, immaturity, irrationality, or any other moral flaw.

Pick your motivations

Since I'm listing my personal shortcomings I might also mention my lack of rationality. I mean that in a specific way: I've tried to make the practical, rational choice when it comes to jobs, education, personal projects, etc., and just decide to do the thing with the best expected payoff. It's never worked. I have to do things I intrinsically enjoy or I'm miserable and can't hack it. To be able to suppress your lack of interest in things and simply do them to gain rewards like money/jobs/grades is also a superpower. Just like some experience their motivations as more socially mediated or even constructed than I do, or as more adaptable to circumstances, some also experience them as more subject to rational decision-making.

Amanda Mull wrote about her father in *You Can't Simply Decide to Be a Different Person,* in *The Atlantic* in 2022. He had the ability to decide he was going to do something like run every morning or stop smoking, and then just do it, forever, with no lapses or struggles.

> Stories like my dad's often serve as pop-psychological proof that you, too, could become a runner, if you really wanted to. But we all want things—human longing knows no bounds—and plenty of people do genuinely throw themselves into trying something new, without much success at converting those behaviors into lasting habits. If some people can just get up one day and decide to behave differently for the rest of their life, why do most people fail at it again and again?

Conventional wisdom says that people just make bad choices, and if you really want to, you can do anything. But newer research points in a different direction. Michael Inzlicht, a social psychologist at the University of Toronto, tells Mull we conflate two things with the word "self-control": there's a stable *trait* of self-control and there's the momentary *behavior* of self-control.

> "People who have high trait self-control, they don't actually engage in more restraint of their behavior and thoughts and emotions in the moment," he said.

> Instead, they just aren't tempted or distracted or diverted from their purpose as often or as effectively as the rest of us.

As opposed to Girard's mimetic desire, this immediately made sense to me: I have decent behavioral self-control, but pretty low trait self-control. Conversely, with high trait self-control you don't need to engage in the behavior of self-control as much[105]. If you generalize from that experience, other people's difficulties must look mighty odd. If you're also low on agreeableness they might just look like feckless degenerate children, deserving little sympathy.

The self-control aristocracy

Unless we take care to avoid it, we *will* generalize from our own experience to a Theory of Everyone. By extension that means a Theory of Society—of what is possible, what is desirable, what should and could be achieved and how, easily or with difficulty. In other words: *politics*. And it's easy to draw lines from intuitions about human nature derived from personal peculiarities towards common political stances. For example, Joseph Heath believes that members of what he calls "the self-control aristocracy" are more likely to be libertarians because they don't comprehend struggling against yourself. In the somewhat clickbaity-titled *What do libertarians and pedophiles have in common?*[106] he writes:

> [E]very academic proponent of libertarianism – understood loosely, as any doctrine that assigns individual liberty priority over other political values – is a member of the self-control aristocracy. As a result, they are advancing a political ideal that benefits themselves to a much greater extent than it benefits

[105] I grant that it's hard to say this without sounding like you're making excuses. It's still possible, even plausible, that it's true.

[106] The answer is that before the internet nobody knew how many there were.

> other people. In most cases, however, they do so naively, because they do not recognize themselves as members of an elite, socially-dominant group, that stands to benefit disproportionately. They think of liberty as something that creates an equal benefit for all. (Or, to the extent that it fails to benefit some people, it is entirely the fault of those people, for failing to exercise sufficient self-control.) /---/
>
> [O]nce you have a sufficient amount of money, it starts to become invisible. You have so much of it that you lose the ability to see the world through the eyes of someone who lacks it. The same is true with respect to self-control. Members of the self-control aristocracy have so much of it that they take it for granted. As a result, they have great difficulty seeing the world through the eyes of someone who lacks it. And so they spend their days advocating political ideas that would, in many cases, only benefit members of their narrow social class, and yet this never even occurs to them.

I'd quibble with his needlessly cynical "socially dominant" angle, since generalizing from yourself is a vice available to everyone, but I nonetheless think he's right about the connection between trait self-control and libertarian politics. The economist Bryan Caplan has, in an extended debate with Scott Alexander, claimed that mental illnesses are best understood as unusual preferences rather than constraints on freedom of action. Whatever people end up doing is what they wanted to do, almost by definition, so perhaps we should do away with the idea of mental "illness"? The physicist Scott Aaronson weighed in, speculating that Caplan's stance results from the specifics of his own psychology:

> I recently had the privilege of hanging out with Bryan Caplan, and I think it gave me insight into this mystery. Bryan, it turns out, has a superhuman ability simply to decide on his goals in life and then pursue them—to the extent that, for him, "urges" and "goals" appear to be one and the same. This ability is an inspiration to the rest of us, and is no doubt closely related to his having become a famous libertarian economics professor in the first place. However, it might make it difficult for him even to understand the fact that most of us (alas) are wired differently.

Heath's and Aaronson's conjectures suggest an inversion of the old phrase "the personal is political": *the political is personal.* Our political views owe less to rational reasoning, socialization or straight-up cynical self-interest than commonly believed, and far more to particular features of our mental architectures we assume are universal.

Caplan is an economist, and so are many outspoken libertarians. It wouldn't surprise me if those who experience their own minds as unified, without debilitating inner conflict, were drawn to economics as a field. *Preference* as an economic concept assumes, at least to a first approximation, cohesive selves with well-defined, non-contradictory wants. It abstracts away internal and intertemporal conflicts as if they were rounding errors rather than major components of behavior.

Interestingly, this top-down perspective of motivation plays nicely with Christianity as well, in that intentional action is assigned great power and thought of as separate from ordinary causality. It's flattering to think of resisting sin with your free will as the central moral concern if you have unusually good control of yourself, and both the Christian and the Economist agree on "bad choices" as the main source of problems in the world. We may pursue evil goals, lack moral fiber, or embrace decadence and irrationality, and the solution to all is the same: take responsibility and do the right thing.

This view is obviously "political" in that it implies that certain things would or wouldn't work to solve social problems.

I'm predictable

It's clear what question must follow. Is *my own* politics a result of personal psychology generalized into a theory of human nature? Almost certainly yes. My hands-off, anti-radical centrist liberalism is definitely driven in part by the clear separation between my personal self and my social environment.

This trait manifests clearly in how instinctively repulsive and threatening I find "protest culture"[107]. This comment (from the signature "Kaminiwa" in the same article referenced several times before) is the precise opposite of how I feel:

> [When] I'm part of a crowd or protest and I'm not actively opposed to what they're on about, I'll just naturally settle in to a sort of group-think where I... basically stop having my own emotions and motivations, and start being part of a larger "hive" organism, feeling the crowd's emotions and motivations as my own. /---/
>
> It's a really, really pleasant sensation regardless of whether I actually support the cause – I've accidentally ended up in a few marches and protests that I was entirely neutral about the cause, and I still got that same sense of being a somewhat-literal PART of the crowd.

[107] My belief in the innateness of this trait is reinforced by my 12-year-old daughter expressing revulsion against street protesters, unprompted and in the face of my mild moderating correctives. This along with a remarkable array of my own personality quirks from childhood, including an idiosyncratic way of holding a pen I trained myself out of 30 years ago and she's never seen.

Beyond that, my political stance does follow from me considering us walking bags of wants and needs, straightforward and unyielding to social influence, habituation, and deliberate choice. We don't get used to not having what we want and trying to ignore that fact requires constant struggle. The only way forward is "try to actually satisfy our desires". Life is largely about chasing what we want, and the tragedy of the human condition is that for the most part we won't get it. Social problems don't exist because of sin or decadence, but because wants are endless, and deprivation is the default state. Politics and life are about balancing wants against each other, either in the same person when we struggle for self-control, or in different people when we argue over how society should be set up.

The variety yet fixity and persistence of wants implies a conviction that preferences should be respected, and that individuals should be granted freedom to live their lives the way they desire. Personal rights are paramount and it's ineffective and evil to demand or expect that people change or deny themselves what they think they need to be happy. However, this doesn't imply full-on libertarianism, since struggle with ourselves plays a significant role in life.

I experience myself as more self-aware and cognitively capable but not fundamentally different from what I imagine it's like to be any other mammal. Given that, the account of the human condition put forward by evolutionary psychology makes a lot of sense. As does behavioral genetics and brain physiology—anything that traces mental phenomena back to the physical. These accounts click with me in just the way Girard's mimetic desire doesn't.

The top-down view

Not everyone is like me. Somebody who experiences their self as socially embedded is more likely to think preferences and behaviors are malleable, that human nature is not much of a thing, and thus that social engineering carries great promise for solving society's problems. Wants are primarily tied up with, and possibly even conjured by, cultural frameworks, learned expectations, and layers of symbolic representation. Cultural images and messages and the processes that produce them have great power to determine selves, not just affect superficial details of how they manifest. Choices about consumption, relationships, and politics are a function of cultural influences rather than reflecting innate, fixed personal tastes. Most often this is implied, but this comment I found straight up says it:

> Personal preferences are heavily influenced by cultural values that determine the markers of high and low status. Your travelling example proves the point, actually. The vibes around travel culture is very modern. People wouldn't get nearly as much utility from going on international vacations twice per year if they didn't feel like it was something that makes you a worldly cool open-minded person.

I think this person just doesn't like traveling and commits the all-too-common error of thinking that everyone with different preferences must be duped or brainwashed into them (because people can't *really* be different[108]). Obviously this kind of disconnect has big policy implications. In this case the topic was the lifestyle costs of children, which the poster thinks are illusory, so if you wanted to increase fertility, these beliefs matter for what you think will work.

In this view, everything about society could be different and better if only its dominant ideas changed, because the nature of individual selves is downstream from culture, not the other way around. Furthermore, if we, like Elis James but without his self-awareness, habituate easily to new circumstances and assume others do too, then major, invasive changes to how we live our lives are not oppressive or abusive. We'll adapt, no biggie.

---

[108] The same is likely true for masculine women and feminine men who find gender roles arbitrary and oppressive because they don't fit with their personalities. This is assumed to be true for everyone, leading to the belief that they are imposed on people through indoctrination.

You'd be frustrated with the pervasiveness and stubbornness of social problems, which should be eminently solvable, here and now, if only bad ideas could be removed from positions of influence and replaced with good ideas. Tragedy is not inherent to the human condition, nor does it stem from failures of individual responsibility, but is the result of corrupt institutions and the ideologies that justify their preservation. Radicalism becomes the appropriate attitude, and you have great confidence in critique of dominant ideas and various forms of instruction and education as the way to deal with almost any problem.

Intellectually, social learning models of the mind, and the accounts of society put forth by history, sociology, media theory etc., will resonate. References to biology on the other hand, look ridiculous, far-fetched, and politically suspect[109]. Economics elicits eyerolls since its model of fixed and socially independent preferences is so obviously and laughably naive that it corrupts and invalidates everything it touches. Putting either biology or economics at the center of our story of the human condition looks perverse precisely in that partial narrative way where the signal in the data is removed and the noise is stitched together.

The biology-centric account looks right to me based on my own inner experience. The other stories have some truth to them, but in my head they're just correctives to the main, and accounts of mental and social phenomena that rely on any of them as the root cause are not convincing. I will accept and believe them in specific cases when there's strong evidence. For other people, this relationship will be reversed, and we will fight over the right to install our own intuitions as social standards.

Note how similar these accounts are to consultant's reports. They go from observed reality to implied recommendations for action, not by directly appealing to values but by declaring some things easy and others hard by implicitly making predictions about what would hap-

---

[109] This makes perfect sense if ideas create selves and we therefore should evaluate ideas based on what kind of selves they contribute to creating.

pen if we tried them. We say politics is about values and it is, but I suspect those values are more informed by factual beliefs than we commonly think. Most of us want the best for society and the people in it, and apparent differences in what road we prefer to take are just as much about differences in beliefs about where they lead as differences in where we want to go. We get so confused, frustrated, and angry when we assume others are like us but stubbornly and inexplicably fail to conform to how we expect them to then act. This situation could be improved.

Chapter 17

The Communitarian and Libertarian Intuitions

There's no such thing as society. There are individual men and women and there are families.

— Margaret Thatcher

Earlier I discussed the difference between having a stress bucket and a stress plate. When you have a bucket you're ok with having things that need to be attended to as long as they don't become overwhelming. With a plate, however, you're not fine with any at all, and every task must be completed before you can rest. For example, my wife and I have different philosophies of tidying up. She's alright with leaving stuff (like empty packaging or potato peels) lying around for a while to put away later, while I insist such things must be dealt with immediately because if not, they stay as "open tickets" that burden the mind.

It's not the amount of work that matters, but the number of separate tasks. I'm not simply lazy; I'm stressed out by task management rather than task execution. If I can focus on a single project it doesn't matter that effort is required, the important thing is that I don't have to keep multiple parallel channels open, and that I'm not vulnerable to new tickets being opened unpredictably and uncontrollably.

Platist politics

Why return to this? Because I'm going to speculate wildly and suggest that this, too, affects political intuitions. Given that politics are about relationships between citizens in a society, it's likely that how you relate to others has bearing on which politics you prefer.

Think about what other people actually are: fellow beings with interests, needs, wants, and desires, which, unless you're a sociopath, deserve consideration. This means—*and don't misread the phrasing*—that other people are outstanding tasks. You need to keep them as open tickets, all the time. You need to actively think about others, model them in your mind, consider the resulting wants and weigh them against your own. You need to do this continuously. And to be perfectly frank: despite taking great interest in how other people think, I'm not particularly empathetic. Please understand that correctly—it's not that I don't wish everyone well, and I really enjoy making people happy, it's that I find it cognitively exhausting to constantly run mental models of other people to predict their wants and needs[110]. I even find it taxing (and more difficult than my 10-year-old daughter does) to watch TV shows with too many characters and relationships[111]. Therefore, I prefer to practice consideration by adhering to rules and embodying virtues. My idea of moral behavior is dutiful more than it is empathetic.

When modeling others is far more cognitively and emotionally draining than performing specific duties, blanket expectations to live your life taking everyone else's unarticulated needs and wants into account comes across as an overbearing, fundamentally aggressive demand. Extending this disposition to politics gets you a dislike of the idea that we, by default, have a bunch of broad, implicit, and unarticulated obligations to everyone else. The mere existence of such potentialities triggers a stress response. Obligations should be clearly

---

110 At work this manifests as not being much of a team player. I'm not disagreeable and I don't dislike people, quite the contrary, I just don't want my work activities to be *about* coordinating with others or intuiting what they want. Give me explicit tasks, or clear targets with a mandate to make my own decisions in how to reach them, not involving currying favor with any other person.

111 Perhaps some have "dedicated hardware" for this and do it with ease, while others have to run the "general intelligence" function at full throttle, and get worn out. This could be a reason introverts feel drained by social interaction.

circumscribed, enumerated, and dischargeable by fulfilling concrete, sensible duties. You should be able to keep your plate clean at a reasonable price (paid in effort), outside of rare crises. The fuller, thicker, type of responsibility where you care for another's welfare as if it was your own, you reserve for intimate relationships like family and close friends. Outside of such relationships you only have obligations you willingly take on, à la carte or as part of a general social contract.

What you do tend to like, politically, is *rights*. Rights cut through all the complexity that comes with having to consider fellow citizens' interests. They are, by design, "no questions asked". As part of a close-knit community, you're supposed to weigh all concerns back and forth—"consult the opinion of the group"—before you know whether you can do something. With rights, however, that gets short-circuited. If you have a right to do something, you don't need to perform any social labor to know if it's ok, nor do you have to justify yourself to anyone. You're not dependent on anyone's sympathy or loyalty to get what you have a *right* to[112]. Rights simplify and formalize parts of human relations, close off certain types of social negotiations and limit the power of the collective over the individual. In doing so, we cut down on a lot of cognitive work required to model other people and the status of our relationships with them.

This doesn't mean that it's not a good, virtuous thing to be considerate to others and help them. But it means that going above and beyond detached civility and politeness is voluntary.

The history of civilization in a caibus

To what extent we have such vague, open-ended obligations towards anonymous others is a BIG fault line in modern politics and modern life. "You're not entitled to put your interests above those of others", and "you have no obligation to self-sacrifice for strangers" are both reasonable-sounding ethical starting points, but from each you can

[112] This is why movements protecting the interests of groups that can't rely on sympathy and oppression credentials tend to use the language of rights (e.g. "men's rights").

derive entirely opposite moral systems. How did we get to this strange situation? To explain it, we'll start by noting how unnatural it is for human beings to live in societies of millions. The anthropologist Robin Dunbar is famous for *Dunbar's Number,* representing how many personal relationships the typical person is able to keep track of, which is about 150. Following the agricultural revolution (which is recent in evolutionary terms), societies grew much, much larger, and we're still dealing with the mess resulting from this fact colliding with our evolved impulses.

Note that the following is a mega-caibus and not meant to be historically accurate. The complexity of real human history is orders of magnitude greater, and I tell this fake story merely to illustrate a point. If you're allergic to speculation using evolutionary psychological scaffolding, you're going to have a rough time in the next few pages. Take it or leave it, but the following is *my* crackpot lens through which to view the human condition in the modern world.

For most of our history we lived in small groups where everyone knew everyone else, and our social instincts (for lack of a better term) evolved in that environment. When we all know each other we can use informal, personal means of governance, resource allocation, and dispute resolution (a.k.a "politics"). Economic exchange happens in the context of personal relationships, with implicit and holistic notions of obligation, credit, and debt.

Some hunter-gatherer peoples still exist, and they're often described as egalitarian (the anthropologist Richard Lee called them "fiercely" so). Come into a windfall and you must share, because what's mine is ours, and ours mine. And you must not think you're better and can boss me around or consume more because you're a better hunter, warrior, or artisan. In return we can all count on support from the group when falling on hard times. We exist almost as cells in a body.

That's the *ingroup,* the band, the tribe—the "us"—which is a small enough group for it to work. Then there are outsiders, "others", which are many and we don't see them as often. We have other words for them than for ourselves, and different rules apply. It's acceptable to kill or enslave outsiders[113], or we may trade with them or otherwise peacefully engage, depending on what benefits us. This sort of trade is less like the sort of mutual gift-giving we do amongst ourselves, and more like the bartering found in economics textbooks.

The distinction between us and outsiders means that we have two separate modes of engaging with other people: on the one hand we consider them full, three-dimensional human beings with whom we have personal relationships, while on the other we consider them more like ~objects, which means that trade, robbery, conquest, genocide, or any combination thereof is on the table.

Then came agriculture and later industry, and with them we've been able to sustain much larger and more dense societies, far beyond the point where it becomes impractical to do everything mediated by personal relationships. We can't treat millions as ingroup all the time, because it's impossible to keep track of and regulate everyone's behavior, reputation, and status that way. But we're also too close and too intertwined to treat each other like complete outsiders. Large, dense groups of people finding it acceptable to rob and murder their neighbors is a recipe for disaster, as agricultural civilizations soon realized[114].

Civilization is about regulating behaviors *towards outsiders* away from violence and towards trade. We've created formal structures like the rule of law, contracts, currency, and bureaucracy to make interactions with strangers work smoothly and constructively, with more cooperation and less war of all against all. Larger, more powerful and advanced civilizations are able to include more people in this

---

[113] This might sound extreme and savage to pacified, post-industrial westerners (or Western Educated Industrialized Rich Democratic/WEIRD, coined by Henrich, Heine, and Norenzayan in 2010 in *The Weirdest People in the World*), but has been common throughout history. We are the extreme ones.

[114] This is still growing more and more true. Just a few decades ago it was much more acceptable to view foreigners as outsiders we don't have to care about and could kill in wars without much issue. A global economy and more personal experience with ethnic and national mixing is changing this.

semi-awkward but useful "not quite ingroup but not outgroup either" category (indeed, that's what it means to be a large civilization).

Relying on arms-length transactions, mediated by currency rather than relationships, we can depend on people without knowing them. I have no idea who grew my dinner potatoes, who drove the truck that brought them to the store, or who programmed the credit card software that enabled me to buy them. I don't have to be related to these people, nor do I need to befriend them, invite them home and ask for a favor I'm then obligated to return at some point. None of it happens in the context of a relationship I have to put effort into maintaining. I just pay and it's done. This is amazing, because it enables vast, mind-bogglingly complex economics, making modern society *stupidly* rich by historical standards.

The system doesn't run on empathy, it runs on *rules*. I, as a plate person, find this a relief. I see it as a positive that we have decoupled our way to sustain ourselves from personal social relations.

The libertarian intuition

Thinking it's good and right and proper to relate to each other primarily through civilized outsider norms like rules and formal exchange, rather than ingroup norms like empathy and personal relationships I call *the libertarian intuition*. It says that in your relations with strangers you have to abstain from violence, respect rights, and honor agreements, but not more. You don't have to actively look out for the interests of people outside your social circle, just treat them according to the rules. Economic exchange does not necessitate or imply a social relationship of any kind.

In other words, it takes inspiration from contemporary sexual ethics and has an "affirmative consent" attitude to moral obligations. Acceptable means to get others to take on responsibilities are to persuade them or pay them, end of list. Social technologies like money and the market are great because they turn vague, all-encompassing obligations into something explicit, limited, and tractable.

An artifact of civilization like economic inequality is an emergent natural phenomenon, downstream of basically sound principles of voluntary exchange; it might cause problems (which can and should often be addressed just like other problematic natural phenomena) but are not inherently injustices. The main purpose of politics is to enforce the rules: to protect rights and make sure agreements are fulfilled.

The communitarian intuition and its dissatisfaction with modernity

Against this stands the expectation to treat all of society (or even the whole world) according to ingroup norms. The *communitarian intuition* contends that we're all human beings and our failure to treat each other with the care you'd expect in a close-knit community represents shirking of moral duty. Sure, we live in societies of millions, but if someone needs help you should, deep down, react as if someone in your 150-strong tribe were in need.

Accordingly, in this view, what may be morally required of you at any point is open-ended. Anything you do affects others and is thus everybody's business, and moral duties can never be discharged or fulfilled. Social problems are solved by everyone taking it on themselves to be less selfish and focus less on what rights they have to do what they want. We all have a duty to address any suffering in the world and it's problematic to enjoy yourself while others can't. Money and the market economy ("capitalism") are suspect precisely for the same reason the libertarian intuition values them: they decontextualize economic exchange, separating it from social obligations and relationships. This allows, even rewards, selfishness, exploitation, and sociopathy.

Economic inequality is a sign of societal corruption, an unnatural and pathological aberration in human affairs. The purpose of politics is to reshape society to be more in line with ingroup norms where all human interactions are characterized by care for the other party. The caring is central, and I think the key to how the communitarian intuition drives utopian and anti-capitalist thought. Consider Freddie DeBoer's sentiment in his book *The Cult of Smart*:

> As a socialist, my interest lies in expanding the degree to which the community takes responsibility for each of its members, in deepening our societal commitment to ensuring the wellbeing of everyone.

There are elements of much socialist writing, in addition to popular fantasies about living in communes, that do suggest that, for many, it really is the *caring*, specifically, that's the issue. It's less the results of profit-driven markets that make them bad than the sinful intentions we have when engaging in commercial exchange. In the eyes of the most utopian of communitarians, when Adam Smith said

> [I]t is not from the benevolence of the butcher, the brewer, or the baker, that we expect our dinner, but from their regard to their own interest.

it wasn't a piece of wisdom to build our economic system around, but an accusation of moral turpitude. I get this in part from Joseph Heath's paper *On the Scalability of Cooperative Structures*, which critiques G.A. Cohen's *Why Not Socialism?*. Heath looks at Cohen's model for an economy based on "mutual giving" as opposed to self-interested transactions, and concludes that with all the requirements Cohen introduces to make his system viable, the only thing that separates it from a market is people's *motivation* for contributing to the economy:

> Cohen's requirement that individuals must maintain a "noninstrumental" attitude toward exchange is impossible to satisfy. Smith's invisible hand permits mutual disinterest in transactions ("I give because I get"), whereas for Cohen, exchange should be based on a system of mutual giving ("I give because you need, or want"). But either way, individuals are go-

> ing to wake up every morning facing a set of prices. These prices specify how much an individual must be paid, when she "gives" something to someone else, in order to ensure that the requirements of reciprocity are satisfied, when it comes time to "get" something from someone else. Whether she is giving it to that person in order to get paid, or whether the payment is interpreted as a gift that expresses the appreciation of the nameless beneficiaries, is a distinction without a difference.

While in consequence it makes no difference, it appears to matter greatly on an emotional level. Cohen says he wants to organize society like a camping trip, where the "economy" is based on mutual, voluntary giving, regulated by informal social cues, and laments that modern society has replaced gratitude with cold hard cash as the way to maintain balance between giving and getting. Yes, people must give in order to get, or it all falls apart, but they must *not* be motivated to give *because* they will get, but rather because they care about the needs of others.

When you hear utopian anarchists fantasize about commune life, you hear this feeling. Instead of relying on a vast, uncaring market, we should get what we need by finding someone in the community who *wants* to offer it, in exchange for whatever we want to offer others ourselves[115]. This almost sounds like trade, but there's a key difference: you don't quantify or tokenize the value. This means that nobody can hoard it to create inequality, nor actually measure individual contributions in a way that justifies any.

Under communitarian norms, the "wealth" in terms of social credit you get in return for sharing what you hunt/gather/craft maxes out quickly. In no way can you get tens, hundreds, or thousands of times more wealth than anybody else. It also requires that people *like*

[115] Hence the mockery this fantasy elicits: "I want someone to build a working sewer system in exchange for my poems about having an anxiety disorder".

you. If you're unlikeable, you don't get full credit for how productive you may be[116]. When wealth is stored in a bank account instead of in the esteem of others, the natural mechanism that keeps successful individuals beholden to the group's opinion of them is illegitimately circumvented. A person should receive goods in proportion to how deserving we as a community think they are, and while it should not be possible to be much richer than others at all, it's especially offensive that people can become rich while being unkind and unpleasant. That's not supposed to be possible.

According to the communitarian intuition, a transaction-based society where we view strangers as ~objects that we interact with through a rules-based interface instead of fellow-human beings we interact with through caring relationships, is just deeply wrong. Popular pejoratives like "exploitation" and "objectification" express this view by condemning transactional stances towards others. That is, they object to wanting something from other people without wanting *them*, personally.

While typical of the utopian left as a large-scale vision, the impulse is not inherently partisan. It plays a major role in the Christian tradition, and Immanuel Kant, who urged us to "treat people like ends and never like means", was not a revolutionary (what is revolutionary is to try to make it a political system[117]). And while often obscured by modern political alliances, many conservatives have similar misgivings about the rootlessness and breaking up of familial and local community bonds that result from the modern market economy.

---

[116] It would be interesting to predict people's political views by their personal ratio of likeability to productivity.

[117] "Love thy neighbor as yourself" is a big ask; "love *everyone* as yourself" is flatly impossible. Both fascists and communists liken society to a family in an attempt to extend familial feelings beyond their natural scope (and in the communist case, deconstruct the actual family as a cornerstone of social organization).

Fronts in the struggle between intuitions

The fantasy of the commune is of course completely impractical. There is no way to live like that and sustain the wealth of industrial society, but it's understandable and expected that people have these feelings, given our evolutionary history in small communities. A functional society with healthy politics requires a give-and-take between the two intuitions—and they are intuitions, as in vague, general sentiments, not full, intellectually developed ideologies.

The communitarian intuition has the important advantage that articulating and defending the libertarian intuition makes you sound mean. While most of us make very few and small sacrifices for strangers[118], we're ~supposed to feel vaguely guilty about it and low-key accept that we should, ideally, self-sacrifice for those of greater need, whenever it's demanded of us[119]. Explicitly rejecting this vague, undischargeable duty makes you look bad because we morally evaluate people based on whether they'd make a good friend, and the whole point of friends is that they don't treat you transactionally. If I invite you home for dinner you're being rude if you insist on paying me, because you're rejecting my attempt to form a relationship. Someone who does that is not nice, and someone who flatly accepts, without discomfort, that society beyond personal relationships works transactionally virtually all of the time is probably less nice than someone who's at least a little uncomfortable saying it. "We're not friends and I don't view you with the same fully fleshed-out personhood as I view my friends" just sounds unkind, even from a stranger where it's plainly true.

The intuitions are not just about economics, they're all-encompassing ideals of how to behave and relate, or even different visions of what society *is*. Are we an overgrown close community who constantly falls short of treating each other like extended family

---

[118] The *Effective Altruism* ideal of giving 10% of your income to charity is quite extreme by normal standards.

[119] The uneasy compromise ~rests on pretending that what's stopping us 99% of the time is just not knowing that someone could use our help.

and must be scolded until we do better? Or are we a simply a set of people who've signed the same civilizing social contract? As with any pair of partial narratives, neither and both are correct. They come to blows on a number of fronts, and we argue over which has the right to be the default and which is the corrective that occasionally gets its way but has to justify it every time. Balance of power between the two can shift dramatically depending on context, creating unpredictable social norms.

The communitarian intuition recognizes no right to be left alone to mind your own business. Slogans like "there's no ethical consumption under capitalism", "no one get seconds until everyone's had firsts" or "silence is violence" are all about how you can't discharge your obligations to the collective by simply not violating others' rights. If taken to its logical conclusion, the communitarian intuition implies we should live on the brink of starvation, donating the rest of our wages for working every waking moment. Nobody does that, but where exactly the line is drawn is not clear. The theoretical duty to self-sacrifice may be invoked any time a specific demand is made on you. This unpredictability scares those with libertarian intuitions, since what you're socially obliged to do becomes precarious and unprincipled, the result not so much of an objective system of rules but of inscrutable processes of social negotiation dominated by the sympathetic, popular, and powerful. Similarly, awareness campaigns that come with the implication that distant problems require your attention land badly because they are claims to cognitive resources (*awareness*, literally) that they find particularly unjustified. Such campaigns make perfect sense from the point of view of the communitarian intuition, of course, since it's assumed that once you're *aware* of a problem, it is natural and obvious that you assume part of the responsibility to fix it.

In chapter 12 we discussed "Gulliver problems". That is, things that only become problems when many small, individually negligible instances add up. No single person bears significant responsibility for it, yet everyone contributes. In this case, the libertarian intuition says that since you are only responsible for your own actions, others have no right to make significant demands on you for making an insignificant contribution to a problem. The communitarian intuition doesn't see it like that. Given that all problems are everyone's responsibility by default, there's no issue with judging your individual behavior much more harshly if it's part of a problematic pattern than if it was an isolated incident.

Any "systemic" issue distributed over many actors has this dynamic. "It's not enough to not be racist, you must be actively antiracist" is profoundly unconvincing from the point of view of the libertarian intuition. The same is true for gender issues; the response to "you specifically might not pay women less than men for the same work, but inequality results from biases all throughout the system so you are still obligated to actively counteract that when you can" from the other side is just "no I'm not". Thirdly so for parents putting their kids in private schools, which to the communitarian violates a duty to self-sacrifice to keep public schools good and well-funded. The well-known communitarian maxim that justifies these positions is "if you're not part of the solution, you're part of the problem". The inverse, central to the libertarian intuition, makes just as much logical sense: "if you're not part of the problem, you're part of the solution", yet I've never seen it verbalized before.

If only these discourses could progress to the point where this disconnect is articulated and brought onto the table as common knowledge it'd be a tremendous achievement. But it's so rare that conversations get there that I almost jumped out of my chair reading the below exchange on Twitter/X in late 2024. Commenting on a post from a right-leaning user rejecting any collective guilt held by the west for colonialism and American slavery, the left-leaning user @dragoncobolt said:

> The right wing obsession with guilt and feeling bad is really funny like... I'm a leftist, I fully think that slaveowners and the American government was basically entirely evil for a distressing amount of history, and I don't...feel guilty? I wasn't alive at the time?

> It's just, like, I am aware that cause precedes events, so I figure that we should try and, like, do what we can to fix the shit that our ancestors broke? Since, like, the problems still exist?

To which user @zippkode chips in with:

> That's the disconnect, though. They think that an obligation to do something stems from culpability. If they aren't responsible for the problem, they aren't responsible for fixing it.[120]

This is a good example of a "scissor"—a controversial claim that appears *un*controversially right or wrong to each side[121]. Here, *zippkode* finds the libertarian intuition so obviously wrong that just articulating it counts as refutation. To the other side, however, it's as if someone had said "you see, these people are crazy enough to think things fall down instead of up and that bears shit in the woods". Given the libertarian model of responsibility—its paradigm, if you will—someone bringing up historical crimes to justify an obligation on you logically implies blaming you for those crimes (a Kuhn distortion), because *only that could justify such an obligation.*

Another time the intuitions fire in opposite directions is when people have special needs. Whether it's physical disabilities, "neurodivergence", special diets, or whatever, such issues create costs, and the question is who is expected to bear them. Do you have to kindly ask others to take on part of them and accommodate you, and be grateful for it, as if you were, by default, on the hook for the bill yourself? Or are we all part of an informal, mandatory insurance system for any problem befalling you that isn't your fault, meaning oth-

---

[120] The rest of the exchange solidifies the disconnect. @SillyworldI3 says "Correct. You nor anyone else deserve my resources because ancestors who looked similar to mine did bad things" to which @Zippkode answers "You should not be especially important. Even to yourself."

[121] See the short story *Sort by Controversial* by Scott Alexander.

ers must accommodate you without complaint or thanks for doing the bare minimum?

Do we also expect institutions to take on responsibility for problems just because they're important problems? What duties do corporations have besides obeying the law and honoring agreements? Do they have to solve social problems, clean up the environment and raise awareness of [issue]? Must they care about their employees' personal well-being? Are the police just supposed to uphold the law, or address any social conditions that cause crime? Are schools supposed to teach children to read and write, or are they obliged to be a complete supporting environment, fulfilling their every need? And so on. How accepted is it to say "not our responsibility"?

There are discussions to be had about the proper balance, as always (my own view is, for the record, that the libertarian intuition should be the default but the communitarian gets through quite a lot of exceptions), but we must keep in mind how people come to them from opposing starting points, and that this is often automatic and subconscious. I remember a work meeting with a nonprofit client dedicated to combating a particular social ill. When we were discussing who had the responsibility for it, we concluded that none of the possible answers really fit. My immediate thought that I did not say out loud was "yes, this isn't anybody responsibility in particular, so *nobody* is responsible", and I was ready to go from there[122]. However, at that exact moment one of them said "yes, this isn't anybody responsibility in particular, so *everybody* is responsible".

The intuitions also break differently in their standard view of rich people. When everything is everybody's responsibility, duty scales with capability to help, so the better off you are the more obligated you are to think of others instead of yourself. Rich people must therefore care much more for others and are much worse people if they don't. This breaks the contract-like symmetry of rights and responsibilities at the heart of the libertarian intuition. "Privilege" dis-

---

[122] According to the libertarian intuition we solve diffuse problems by getting someone (like government or volunteers) to willingly take on the task.

course is so infected precisely because it puts this fault line in focus: demanding that people, publicly and semi-ritually, acknowledge advantages due to race, sex, etc., serves the purpose of saddling them with open-ended, non-dischargeable obligations to put certain others ahead of themselves[123]. In each case, both sides accuse the other of entitlement, by wanting to skirt your obligations, and by making demands you're not entitled to make, respectively.

The struggle between communitarian and libertarian intuitions is an emergent result of human nature in large, interconnected civilizations. They inform but do not entirely define left and right (again, intuitions, not full ideologies). I only discuss this to suggest that psychological predilections can make us like or dislike different aspects of human relations, which in turn affects our preferred coalitions, non-negotiable values, and implicit assumptions about what's good, right, and important. A first step in negotiating them more effectively is bringing them to the surface as psychological features and interpretive mental schemas. Just making them part of our common lexicon would be tremendously helpful.

---

[123] Original sin fills a similar social function in Christianity (although applied equally to everyone). Making us all carry a debt from birth serves to stop us from rejecting obligations we haven't consented to.

Chapter 18

A Bundle of Axes

The question is not for or against dichotomies, but how they are used. Are they the final word on something, or only the beginning?

— Johan Galtung

To argue is to try to demonstrate how our agreed-upon beliefs imply your own opinion. That means assuming some beliefs are agreed upon, and if you're wrong the argument doesn't land. For example, when calling something racist we assume that the other person agrees that racist things are bad, saying "that's like being an anti-vaxxer" assumes agreement that vaccines are good, and "the Lord said 'be fruitful and multiply'" is worse than useless against a nonbeliever.

The less we can rely on assumed shared beliefs actually being shared beliefs, the less well arguing works. This is yet another way to capture what dysfunctional disagreement means: when the core mechanism of making logical arguments from common ground breaks down because common ground is misidentified. Communitarian vs. libertarian intuitions about responsibility is one of those things we assume is agreed upon when it isn't, and arguing fails.

Those two are not the only such pair in our sensemaking faculties, and in this chapter we'll get to sample some others.

Whig and Haan history

The economist Noah Smith wrote an article in 2015 called *Whig vs. Haan*, comparing two conceptions of history. *Whig* history arose in the late Enlightenment and told a story of continuous technological and social improvement, looking to the future with optimism and self-satisfaction. *Haan* history, whose name comes from a Korean word meaning something like "lament of unavenged injustice", is more pessimistic. It's not convinced by superficial improvement and not satisfied with simply forgetting the crimes of the past. While economic growth and reduction in violence and injustice cause Whigs to celebrate, Haans don't find it enough that past horrors are no longer ongoing. They represent an *accumulated debt* that must be acknowledged and repaid. "Forgive and forget" represents failure and humiliation; until vengeance and reckoning is achieved, the world is corrupt and dirty, and everyone living in it, let alone celebrating it, has blood on their hands. According to Smith, it's

> [T]he notion that no matter how much better things get, society is fundamentally evil and unfair.

He goes on to describe Haan mentality as characteristic of the "critical left":

> You see it, for example, in leftist resistance to Steve Pinker's thesis that violence has decreased hugely. Pinker brought huge reams of data showing that violent crime and war have been in a long-term decline for centuries now. Leftist critics respond by citing anecdotal examples of war, atrocity, and injustice that still exist. /---/
>
> I was talking about Pinker to a friend of mine, a very sensitive lefty writer type. Instead of citing ISIS or the Iraq War as counterexamples, she talked about the problem of transphobia, and how "trans panic"

> legal defenses were still being used to excuse the murder of transsexual people. I checked, and this has in fact happened once or twice. My friend presented this as evidence that—contra Pinker—the world isn't really getting better. Injustice anywhere, under Haan thinking, invalidates justice everywhere else.

Reading this you may note how Haan history relates to the communitarian intuition of shared, unlimited responsibility for each and every problem ("don't you dare celebrate anything or declare tickets closed and relax before every problem in the world has been solved"), but is not identical to it. Nor is it identical to critical leftism, since Haan sensibilities also sometimes animate right-wing nationalist fervor. It's its own sensibility that can be teased apart from others if you do it with care and precision.

Varieties of intuitive sociology

Simplified, there exists in sociology a division between *functional* and *critical* approaches. The question that defines the difference is: are there or are there not real, legitimate reasons for things to be the way they are? Do we assume social institutions and norms fulfill some necessary function, or are they arbitrary and corrupt? Assuming the latter means tending towards radicalism, thinking that tearing stuff down will be mostly good. The task of critical sociology is thus to expose the injustice of the status quo. Conversely, if we assume the former we'll tend conservative and do sociology to find out what purposes components of the status quo serve. That intuition is encapsulated in the famous parable from G.K. Chesterton (nicknamed "Chesterton's Fence"):

> There exists in such a case a certain institution or law; let us say, for the sake of simplicity, a fence or gate erected across a road. The more modern type of reformer goes gaily up to it and says, "I don't see the

> use of this; let us clear it away." To which the more intelligent type of reformer will do well to answer: "If you don't see the use of it, I certainly won't let you clear it away. Go away and think. Then, when you can come back and tell me that you do see the use of it, I may allow you to destroy it."

Functionalist sociology assumes the fence (any social institution) is there for a reason and we should at least understand that reason before changing it. The response from critical sociology is that we do know: legacy institutions exist to perpetuate existing power and privilege, and the burden of proof is on its defenders to show otherwise (although trying to do so is suspect). It's justified by a telling of history where morality has improved by consistently discovering that old, now abandoned social norms have been unjust, and there's no reason to think this has changed (from here comes the expression "the right side of history"). Note that there are both similarities (focus on old injustices) and contrasts (attitude to progress) between critical sociology and Haan history.

From here it's a short skip to thinking in terms of *positive-sum* or *zero-sum* processes. The language comes from game theory—which isn't about games in the ordinary sense but a branch of economics that studies strategic behavior—and refers to whether something produces more total gains than total losses. A typical positive-sum game is trade: you and I exchange money for an item, and since we both value what we got more than what we gave up, we're both better off. Typical zero-sum games are bets or straight-up competitions, e.g. if we play poker and you end up with all my money, your win is precisely equal to my loss.

Most real-world processes produce gains and losses that can be difficult to measure, and we can temperamentally tend towards seeing them in either positive- or zero-sum terms. Your default lean determines your reaction to a lot of the economy: positive-sum thinkers consider economic transactions beneficial by definition, regardless of power differences or how much of the benefit each party gets. Habitual zero-sum thinkers, by contrast, consider supposedly voluntary transactions exploitative under conditions of power differences that allow one party to gain much more than the other (that is, "win")[124].

It may sound like a straw man to suggest anyone genuinely holds a zero-sum view of the economy, but it does happen and doesn't seem to be all that rare. I don't want to put the specific poster on the spot, but in one discussion I read this:

> I'm not certain that all economics isn't a zero-sum game. Profit implies loss. Maybe there is no such thing as "honest" profit in any situation, someone or something loses. For example, in extraction-based capitalism, they don't even count the damage to the environment as a "cost", hence it's all "honest profit." Similarly much of globalization has meant more diesel ships at sea, worse working environments *somewhere*, etc etc, for that "honest" profit. /---/
>
> [W]here do I think all that wealth came from? Off the back of people and places that had no say in the matter and got nothing in return. It didn't come from nowhere.

And in another, this:

> The economy is a zero-sum game. If a rich group hoards more and more for themselves there's less for those on the bottom. Then, living standards and life expectancy drops.

I get the idea, I do, and there's certainly *something* true about competition for limited resources, and that producing value can also cause

---

124 This conviction is also supported by the communitarian intuition, which implies it's morally required to demand less from an interaction the better off you already are. From this point of view it's not just getting a bigger gain than the weaker party that's wrong, but merely being in a much better position in the end.

harm, but to have this as your main model of how the world works seems quite out of touch with reality, to be honest. To think that wealth, by some natural law[125], cannot be created but just taken from one place to another seems to me refuted by just using your eyes and ears, but I have to accept that, for some, it really doesn't look and feel that way, and that means finding reasons for why it can't happen, even in principle—e.g. that environmental damage automatically and precisely counterweights the value of industrially produced goods, or that wealth is synonymous with natural resources and therefore when we consume them the value is exactly counterbalanced by their disappearance (suggesting that the capacity to use the resources productively does not count as wealth).

I must assume that to this crowd, the positive-sum view looks as absurd when mostly ignoring the negative term (remember the free trade example from chapter 7) and pretending that just because the *sum* is positive, there's no downside at all.

Whether the economy, and thus society, is fundamentally zero-sum or positive-sum obviously implies quite different political stances. In a zero-sum world, any success will mean depriving others, while in a positive-sum world it is closer to the opposite. And if you win by making others lose, you might think making others lose will make you win, and vice versa (protectionism in trade can stem from this conviction). It also encourages cynicism about public discourse, because if it's all about who's getting a bigger slice of the pie, suggesting you want to make things better overall just makes you a liar.

The contingent and the determined

Science aims to be rigorous but is not immune to unarticulated intuitions. Segerstråle's account of the sociobiology debate (cf. chapter 3) includes a key unstated difference in what was considered "good science". "Planters and weeders in the garden of science" as she

[125] What mechanism could ensure this? I almost suspect there's an imagined rule like the first law of thermodynamics: "wealth cannot be created or destroyed, it can only change from one form to another".

called them, disagreed on how small-c conservative you should be as a scientist. Planters favor bold speculation, abstract models, and ambitious new theories, while weeders think science requires concrete, reliable facts proved beyond reasonable doubt, and value debunking theories that don't meet that standard. Combine this sticking point with political passion and you get a whirlwind of accusations of pseudoscience, bias, and anti-intellectualism.

No matter how much experience I have with these issues I keep making mistakes. A few years ago I was very confused when a friend declared his intention to own the chuds by "making veganism masculine". His plan was to eat only tofu for protein while lifting a lot of weights, so when he got muscular he could disprove that "soyboys" are weak and weedy. It felt like nonsense to me because you can't "make" something masculine. It either is or it isn't. Things that are typical of men, i.e. more common among men than among women, are masculine, and vice versa with feminine. As long as eschewing meat is more common among women than men, it cannot be masculine. It is a logical impossibility.

I understand in retrospect that he simply wanted to provide an example of a "strong manly vegan". It was the phrasing "make it masculine" that triggered the wrong intuition in me, and the fact that it did revealed a difference between us in how we think shared beliefs are supposed to be formed[126]. If they're the results of observing reality, changing them must mean appealing to reality: you show how current beliefs are false (actually, more men than women are vegan). If they *aren't* false (fewer men than women are vegan), you have to change the actual reality if you want beliefs representing that reality to change. You can just *lie,* of course (or "bullshit" in the sense the philosopher Harry Frankfurt meant it: speaking without concern for truth), but this isn't something well-behaved people even consider any more than they'd consider robbing a bank.

[126] Whether knowledge primarily comes from individuals observing reality or from social learning is part of the contrast between *phenomenological* and *constructivist* epistemology.

I have to turn my instinctive thought pattern upside-down to understand shared beliefs as *not* about faithful depiction, and cultural beliefs as *causing* behaviors rather than *describing* them. Now, if in upside-down world we don't expect shared beliefs to depict reality correctly, we also might not find efforts to engineer them independently of correctness to be dishonest (i.e. that there's nothing wrong about making people think of veganism as masculine even though it's not). It helps me attribute this to personality that the same guy defended giving the Nobel Peace Prize to President Obama back in 2009 (before he'd done much of anything as President), arguing that it's a legitimate function for a prize to encourage accomplishments rather than acknowledge them.

Why this story? Well, my crackpot belief is that our idea of concepts as free-from, vs. subordinate-to, firm objective reality relates to *another* difference in intellectual predilections I've noted over years of comparing schools of thought: some people prefer their sensemaking to emphasize *contingency*, while others are drawn to *determinism*.

The first group takes delight in learning about the complexities and arbitrariness of cause and effect. Consider a historian deeply engrossed by all the little tidbits, the seemingly random things that determine the fate of nations and cultures. If only this or that had happened instead, it all could have been so different. Isn't it *fascinating*? Isn't it rewarding to expand your mind, imagine the possibilities, and nerd out over all the colorful details and specifics? It's what makes history come alive! Now consider another historian who prefers to look at history as a science, their own task being to uncover the rules and principles that govern it—that is, all the ways things *couldn't* have gone differently. They're not about savoring the specifics and weaving wild, rich tales of slings and arrows of outrageous fortune. They want to *explain* history as a rule-bound process, with reference to factors outside itself like geography, human nature, or economic logic.

This is part of why Jared Diamond's *Guns, Germs and Steel* has provoked so much heated discussion (and continues to do so). It draws ire from historians partly for being a ~deterministic account that tries to explain the global domination of Europe with geographic factors. Once during a history seminar our professor pointed out its deficiencies by asking, almost in disbelief, how Diamond could have left out the key force. "But what about *culture*?" he said.

To the determinism enthusiast, "culture" doesn't explain anything. It cannot, because insofar as culture explains anything, the real explanation is whatever explains the culture in turn. *Why* did that place and time have that culture? It's a conduit, not a force. Most who use culture as an explanation, however, don't seem to want to go there, but prefer to use it as a cause in and of itself. This is strange to the determinist, because if culture isn't determined by anything outside itself, if it is inherently chaotic and contingent, then claiming it explains something becomes nothing but another way to say that there is no explanation at all. "This could not have been predicted, even in principle" is uncompelling to those on the lookout for underlying rules, so they are unlikely to be particularly interested in pursuing such narratives or studying such processes[127].

As one of those people, I want to emphasize that it's not, first and foremost, about truth—contingency can be correct, I just don't find it as interesting or satisfying[128]. It's about which partial narratives you're psychologically attracted to: the determinist wants to get the answer, solve the mystery, they want to know *why*. "It's arbitrary" is meaningless, with no resolution or satisfaction.

My interest in music theory points to it as a stable personality trait, because you can easily tell contrasting stories of contingency or determinism about music, and I know which one I prefer. You may emphasize how arbitrary and culturally specific music is, or you may focus on how it comes down to fixed physical and mathematical principles making certain ways of organizing music ~work better than others. Many musical scholars and knowledgeable amateurs,

[127] This describes how Richard Dawkins and Stephen Jay Gould differ in their views on evolution (see chapter 5).

[128] It makes sense that another history professor told me I have the attitude of a philosopher, not a historian.

however, prefer the other story. E.g., instead of looking for some basis for why minor chords are considered "sad sounding" that's indirect enough to account for the moderate cultural variation, it's often implied to be arbitrary, without any hint at a corrective.

What goes for music goes for food. We're often told how culturally arbitrary food preferences are, the implication being that there's no reason we prefer hamburgers to fried cockroaches in the West etc. There's an obvious truth to it, in there is a significant cultural and habitual component to food preferences, but I always find myself wanting to moderate these claims and point out that it's no coincidence ice cream, pizza, and tacos are more widely enjoyed than Swedish fermented herring and Chinese urine-boiled eggs[129]. There are physiological and evolutionary reasons we enjoy sweetness, fat, and protein, and to me the grounding of food preferences in that has to be acknowledged *before* we bring in the corrective of cultural variation. But many find culture more interesting than physiology and evolution, and this interest pattern matters for which stories experts tell us, over and above what the facts say.

Note how easy it is to grab one side of this kind of story and justify it. You can nearly always say both "if this was completely determined there wouldn't be this obvious variation" and "if this was completely arbitrary there wouldn't be this obvious patterning", and be right (the error lies in assuming that it has to be either or, and that refuting the purest possible version of the other side proves the opposite purism). This leaves a lot of room for personal predilections.

Granted, there's a reason other than personality that experts like to present contingency-type narratives. They're correctives to popular understanding, which tends to take cultural standards as given. While understandable, this carries the risk of overcorrection outlined in chapter 14. Authoritative accounts should be able to stand on their own, and popular understanding tends to be incomplete more often than straight-up wrong (cf. claim resolution in chapter 13). This give-

[129] A.k.a "surströmming" (which literally smells like sewage), and "tóngzǐ niào zhǔ jīdàn", respectively

only-the-corrective-making-it-sound-like-a-main dynamic is inherent to the relationship between experts and the lay public, and it makes experts and those who listen to them overestimate how wrong common-sense beliefs are[130]. This is what made social psychologists (a kind of psychologist attracted to contingency[131]) go overboard with results of the type "this minor manipulation can drastically effect how people act", which were severely hit by the replication crisis.

Are planters vs. weeders and contingency vs. determinism the same thing? No, but they are related. The controversy around *Guns, Germs and Steel* is about both divisions, and the combination of the two causes the specifics of the conflict. A contingency-type attitude contributes to a weeder position in the sense that it's fine to reject a hypothesis explaining why Europe came to dominate the globe if we don't *need* an explanation for that, because it was contingent (and I've heard exactly this argument). Determinists, however, tend to think we should assume there's *some* explanation for things, and one must be the most plausible.

As a planter and determinist at heart[132], I get frustrated with some weeders in the same way I am with the overzealous skepticism of some science advocates when they reject a theory, sometimes gleefully, because it hasn't been supported by strong evidence. I want to object that there should be some explanation for a phenomenon, and if not this one, what do you think it is instead? Nothing's proved, ok, fine, but what's the *most* likely, given what we know? There are degrees of plausibility, even absent direct evidence, and failing to reach confirmed status doesn't justify the scrap heap. To editorialize, it's a common and annoying weeder habit to use the phrase "no evidence for" to mean "not strong evidence from randomized controlled trials

---

[130] A classic example is the sociologist Pierre Bourdieu's tome on taste, *Distinction* from 1979, in which he ~argues that tastes are determined by social position and that personality is insignificant.

[131] Psychologists attracted to determinism tend to go into cognitive, evolutionary, or personality psychology.

[132] This book is very planterist: a rough, ambitious sketch going for plausibility rather than rigor, with detail and empiricism largely absent.

for" while intending it to mean "is false or not worth taking seriously at all".

Askers and guessers

Differing intuitions and temperaments don't just contribute to political and philosophical disagreements; they matter for everyday interactions. For example, a difference between "ask culture" and "guess culture" has been articulated recently. The following description comes from a 2007 comment on *Metafilter* by Angela Donderi, in response to a question about asking to stay with an acquaintance:

> In some families, you grow up with the expectation that it's OK to ask for anything at all, but you gotta realize you might get no for an answer. This is Ask Culture.
>
> In Guess Culture, you avoid putting a request into words unless you're pretty sure the answer will be yes. Guess Culture depends on a tight net of shared expectations. A key skill is putting out delicate feelers. If you do this with enough subtlety, you won't even have to make the request directly; you'll get an offer. Even then, the offer may be genuine or pro forma; it takes yet more skill and delicacy to discern whether you should accept.

The *Guardian* columnist Oliver Burkeman adds:

> Neither's "wrong", but when an Asker meets a Guesser, unpleasantness results. An Asker won't think it's rude to request two weeks in your spare room, but a Guess culture person will hear it as presumptuous and resent the agony involved in saying no. Your boss, asking for a project to be finished early, may be an overdemanding boor – or just an Ask-

> er, who's assuming you might decline. If you're a Guesser, you'll hear it as an expectation. This is a spectrum, not a dichotomy, and it explains cross-cultural awkwardnesses, too: Brits and Americans get discombobulated doing business in Japan, because it's a Guess culture, yet experience Russians as rude, because they're diehard Askers.

Blogger Julian Sanchez, in his article *Asking and Guessing,* suggests Guess culture is a way of navigating ambiguity in a way reminiscent of how the balance between communitarian and libertarian norms depends on how close we are:

> [Guess culture is] often a way of preserving a deliberate ambiguity, which we generally want to do in social relationships where there's an intermediate level of intimacy—whereas relationships at the poles, with either close friends or strangers, tend to be governed by more direct asks. So, for instance, a purely commercial transaction with a bartender will be ask-centered: "I'd like a Magic Hat, please." And if I'm at the home of a good friend I visit frequently, the same: "Hey, mind if I grab a beer from the fridge?". If I'm visiting an acquaintance for the first time, on the other hand, I'll probably wait for them to offer.
>
> We do this, I think, precisely because those intermediate relationships are ambiguous: We're indirect because we're negotiating just where on the gradient we fall.

Destructive sensemaking of the partially related

As you can see, many of these contrasting pairs relate to each other in that most difficult of ways: "somewhat". They have things in common but are not the same. In the figure below, A and B have a big overlap, B and C medium overlap, and A and C a very small one.

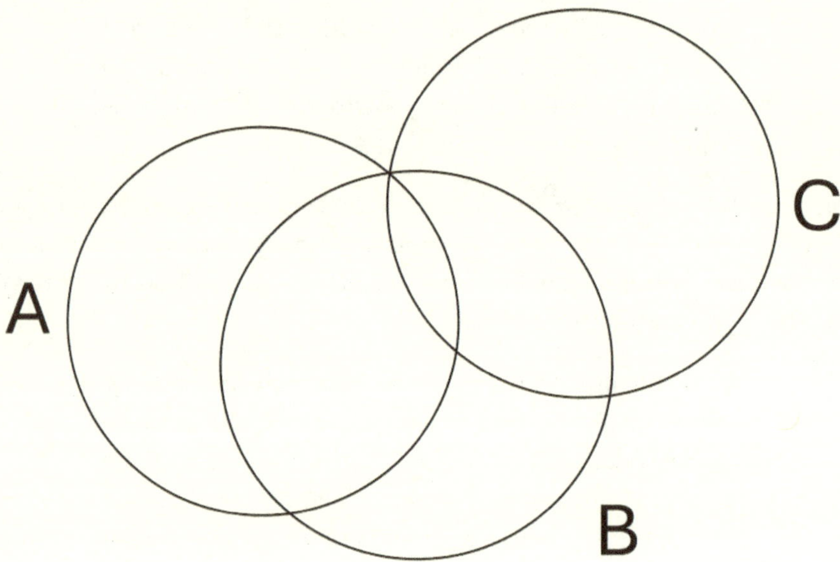

Figure 21, three different "things" that are partly the same, but to different degrees.

Since we like artificial clarity, we have ways to deal with this situation. Unfortunately, they are destructive. Since we need to think of things as either fundamentally the same or different, imperfectly related axes will be simplified either by being collapsed into one (like "left vs. right" in politics, or "STEM vs. the humanities" in scholarship), or by being made wholly disjunct. Visualizing it as arrows pointing in a similar but not the exact same direction (A, next page), destructive sensemaking will push them either together to become the same (B) or apart into a right angle where they vary completely independently (C).

This habit will make us critically wrong sometimes. We'll find that people having complex, dysfunctional disagreements vary along one or several axes in a complicated dance. What angle makes most sense depends on the specifics of the situation, so ideally we won't make any destructive simplifications until we have to, keeping the whole "uncollapsed" structure intact in our minds. Is this a Whig-Haan issue? Is it a contingent-determined issue, or a positive-zero sum issue? Or maybe an ask-guess issue?

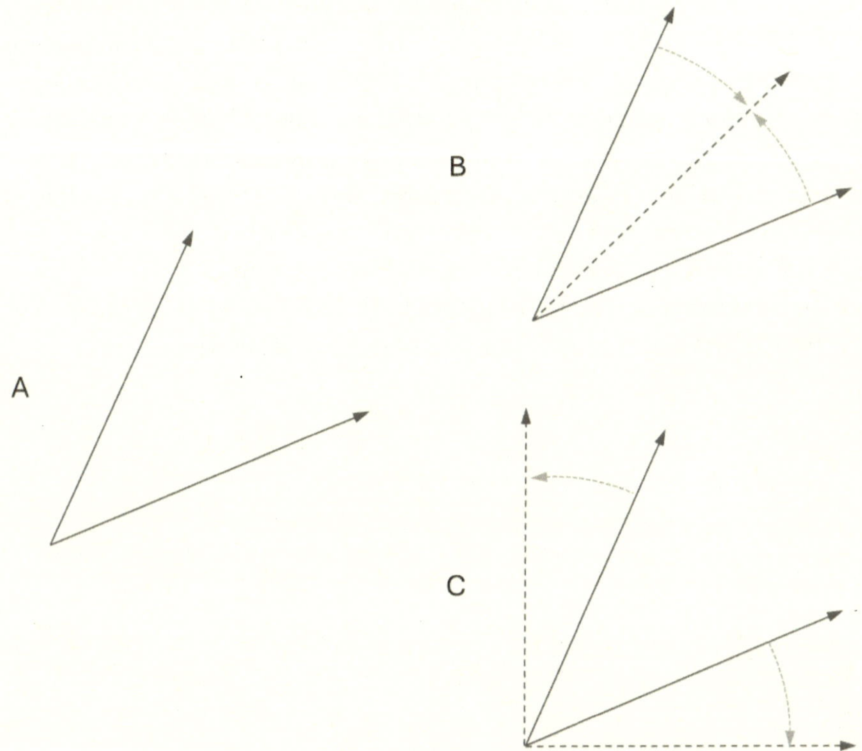

Figure 22, things that are partially related (A) tend to be sensemade as either the same thing (B), or entirely different things (C). Both introduce potentially critical errors.

Rather than keep black-and-white rules putting overlaps in "complete match" or "non-existent" buckets, we should fight our tendency to collapse them and learn to be comfortable with degrees of correlation. That said, the manifest difficulty of dealing with degrees of *anything* never ceases to amaze me. Hence the "main plus corrective" model: it is so counter to our nature to think in gradual terms that the way we do it when we have to is by putting different absolutes in hierarchical order. Rather than remember a number between 0 and 1 we prefer to think "0, but also 1", or vice versa.

Paradigms rebuilt

With this chapter we're back to where we were at the end of chapter 5. We're back to incommensurable frameworks across which communication suffers (if it works at all). This time, however, we encounter them reconstituted from the ground up. These frames, paradigms, proto-ideologies, whatever you like to call them, exist philosophically as systems of beliefs and justifications, they exist socially as shared realities we coordinate around for collective action, and they exist psychologically as enhancements and affirmations of the cognitive and emotional peculiarities of individuals. And as we shall see in part six, they are also the product of self-interest and self-deception.

PART VI

The Political Animal

Chapter 19

The Enemy Within

Remember, Jerry, it's not a lie if you believe it.

— George Costanza

My distaste for misrepresentation and my conviction that it's an alarmingly large component of rhetoric, need no further elaboration at this point. Now then, we come to the psychological mechanisms involved when we give the most uncharitable retelling possible of another's beliefs.

I used to ask myself at which point the distortion actually occurs. Describing someone else's beliefs is a two-step process: you have an impression of what they are, and then in turn describe that impression in your own words. When we misrepresent, at least one of those steps must be corrupted. Either we make a mistake and get a wrong impression that we communicate accurately, or we understand them correctly but choose to communicate something else, in which case we're lying.

The first possibility is off the table immediately. It just cannot be all honest mistakes, because we are nowhere near stupid enough for that. We make errors we would spot in an instant if done against us, and it always seems to be just the error that helps our case. When we want to, we all understand that a single counterexample doesn't disprove a pattern, that a single example doesn't prove one, that it's not fair to smear a whole group by pointing to a few bad apples, or that it's hypocritical to exaggerate the importance of one thing and minimize that of another. We still do these things. So, it must be the second. We're manipulative cynics who know we're twisting the truth but are willing to say whatever will help our side. Public discourse's passing resemblance to rational deliberation is a result of caked-on makeup, masking pure calculating sociopathy.

Call me naive but I don't quite believe it. No doubt gleeful assholes exist, but most of us are not them. We're good, honest people, or at least we want, and manage, to think of ourselves as such. Consciously and purposefully lying would ruin our self-image. Just like it's obvious that our selective stupidity is in fact selective, it's equally obvious that most of us don't mischaracterize others completely on purpose. We believe we're telling the truth.

Where does that leave us? It leaves us having to abandon the assumption of our rationality—the idea that our behavior is all conscious and intentional, that there is a coherent self in there making decisions with full awareness. Lionel Page's book on behavioral economics *Optimally Irrational* from 2022 says:

> Our naive psychology tends to look for black and white interpretations and suggests two types of behaviour: honesty and dishonesty. An honest person (let's say, Jane) would look at the objective evidence and make up her mind based on facts; a dishonest person (let's say, John) would hide his ulterior motives and act in a devious way while pretending that it was not the case. The prevalence of self-deception suggests that, instead, the reality most often comes in shades of grey.

Right, but I'm not satisfied with saying "shades of grey" and calling it a day. "It's a little bit of a mistake and a little bit of lying" doesn't bring us any closer to understanding what's truly going on inside our heads. It's like saying issues are "partly about facts and partly about values", which is true but says little about how the combination works in its own right (cf. "matters of model").

I think the real explanation goes something like this: since a lot of assumptions go into interpreting what others say, there are a lot of possible meanings for us to choose from whenever we hear something. It doesn't *feel* that way, however. We don't get a full range of possibilities listed in our mind, think about it for a bit, going through the options to then make a considered decision, taking all available information and our degree of uncertainty into account. Instead, one interpretation just pops up, feeling obviously correct. We don't even recognize a distinction between our interpretation and what was actually said. Somehow, our options are screened before they reach consciousness.

This pre-conscious screening process is heavily affected by motives and self-interest, making people capable of finding the most absurdly uncharitable readings nonetheless plausible. It's bleeding obvious how unfair it is when somebody misrepresents us or those we have sympathy for; it's clear to anybody not blinkered by ideology or cognitive biases, and nobody could be a big enough idiot to not see it. It makes us angry. Instantly. But when we or our friends misrepresent our enemies it's not like those same obvious objections are acknowledged and painstakingly refuted in our heads. Nor do we make an effort to suppress them and feel appropriately guilty about it. They are just not there. They don't automatically pop up and stand out the way they do when the shoe is on the other foot.

When some subconscious part of us decides what single interpretation will appear to us as the one true meaning, it doesn't feel like we're making a decision, it feels like we're just apprehending the truth. It's *judgment* that feels like *perception.* Consider the TEDx talk by Cassie Jaye, director of the documentary *The Red Pill* about the men's rights movement. In her talk she discusses what happened to her as she interviewed activists. A card-carrying feminist, she came to the project intending to "expose the dark underbelly of the men's rights movement", but as time went by her interpretation of what her subjects said started to shift.

> Looking back on the 37 diaries I recorded that year, there was a common theme. I would often hear an innocent and valid point that a men's rights activist

> would make, but in my head, I would add on to their statements, a sexist or anti-woman spin, assuming that's what they wanted to say but didn't.

She goes on to give examples which I won't quote in full because that's not what this is about, but the talk is worth watching if only as an account of having your mind slowly turned inside out. I see no reason to believe she's lying when she says that her interpretation changed, and this *surprised* her. There was no cynical ploy at work here. Her initial assessment of misogyny was perhaps uncharitable, but honest in the sense that she believed it. This was a "choice" in that it could have been made differently (as her change of heart shows), but not a deliberate action.

I sympathize with her because it's what happened to me about, broadly speaking, postmodernism problematizing stuff like objectivity, the authority of scientific knowledge, the stable and objective meaning of words, the straightforward truth of facts, etc. When I first saw claims like it, I remember reading all kinds of things into them that weren't necessarily there. I wasn't always wrong—there are bad motives in that crowd just like there are among men's rights activists or any other group—but I did make extrapolations I didn't realize I was making. It took hearing it phrased differently, from people who didn't feel like enemies, before I could see the valid points in what they were saying (and presumably Jaye's perception changed because she developed sympathies for her interviewees and internalized parts of their paradigm, which stopped the Kuhn distortions).

Now I've made the slipperiness of meaning, the partial relativity of fact and truth, and the social process of legitimation of knowledge into cornerstones in my belief system. That doesn't mean I've "switched sides" any more than Jaye did. At the end of her talk, she says she now has a more nuanced view, and so do I.

The Elephant in the Brain

It's not news to me that automatic hostile interpretation happens. When I first wrote about the "War on Christmas" in 2016 I had noticed a Reddit comment arguing that those complaining about it didn't genuinely believe it was real ("they are lying"). That felt obviously wrong to me, and the odd, unjustified confidence with which it was said made me think there was some specific mental machinery at work.

When your coalitional instincts sense that a statement open to interpretation (what does "war on" mean?) is part of a rival political narrative, you'll automatically interpret it to mean something false or unreasonable (and then think you disagree with people politically because they say false and unreasonable things). This belief forms part of your background assumptions, further informing your interpretation of other statements, and so on. And presto, polarization is bootstrapped.

It wasn't until a few years later that I came upon the final puzzle piece. In their 2018 book *The Elephant in the Brain,* Kevin Simler and Robin Hanson argue that much of what goes on in the mind is hidden from conscious awareness, not as a bug but as a feature, because knowledge of it would interfere with our self-image. The title is a play on "the elephant in the room", referring to what everyone knows but avoids talking about for reasons of propriety. That "something" in this case is hidden motives—not the kind where we lie to other people, but the kind where we lie to ourselves. Hence "in the brain": our mind politely avoids looking at parts of itself to not cause internal awkwardness. It is

> built to sabotage information in order to come out ahead in social games. When big parts of our minds are unaware of how we try to violate social norms, it's more difficult for others to detect and prosecute those violations.

Social standing is important, and we seek to impress others with our intelligence, wealth, generosity, and virtue. But since it's unvirtuous to toot our own horns, we have to do it surreptitiously. *The Elephant in the Brain* argues, persuasively, that many behaviors don't make sense if their motivations are what we say they are, but do if they're about gaining advantages and signaling flattering things about ourselves. This, of course, works better when we actually think we're being good—hence a faculty for self-deception.

Before this, I believed unconscious "thought" only dealt with low-level processing for perception, movement, and animalistic urges and appetites, while complex thought of the kind involved in social maneuvering *required* conscious deliberation. Simler and Hanson make a strong case against this. Unconscious processes are more sophisticated than we give them credit for: we can make up songs without needing a degree in music theory and catch a ball without solving quadratic equations. Wielding natural language is even more complicated, yet we do it with little trouble. It often requires logical operations complicated enough to confuse us if we try to do them explicitly (e.g. cat couplings), but it doesn't *feel* confusing, ambiguous and overcomplicated. Just looking at how people argue, even small children, reveals that we're capable of making complex rhetorical maneuvers exploiting subtle philosophical ideas without exceptional intelligence or training.

According to *Elephant*, the conscious self is smaller than we think and more the mind's PR officer than its dictator. It works on a need-to-know basis, having access to just enough and just the right information to do its job of managing our relationships and reputation.

> Knowledge suppression is useful only when two conditions are met: (1) when others have partial visibility into your mind; and (2) when they're judging you, and meting out rewards or punishments, based on what they "see" in your mind. These two conditions may hold for nonhuman primates in some situations. In the moments leading up to a fight, for example, both animals are struggling frantically to decipher the other's intentions. And thus there can be an incentive for each party to deceive the other, which may be facilitated by a bit of self-deception.

> Just as camouflage is useful when facing an adversary with eyes, self-deception can be useful when facing an adversary with mind-reading powers.

Read the last sentence again, it's the key to this whole thing. It's out of scope to repeat their full argument about charity, medicine, consumption, conversation, politics, and other things here. If you're skeptical, consider reading *The Elephant in the Brain* in full.

Having this all laid out in front of you makes you look a little closer at your own thoughts and behaviors. Particularly, sudden emotional reactions become suspect. I've always been curious about feelings of righteous certainty that just show up, uninvited and unannounced, telling you with little to no explanation what's good and bad, right and wrong, what must and mustn't be done. The authors suggest that these pop-ins are opaque by design. They are in fact coolly calculated to advance our interests and/or paint us as valuable social allies—to convince others of our competence, loyalty, power, and generosity—while costing as little as possible and without making it too obvious what we're doing.

These hidden systems are clever, and they know more than us. I don't keep track of favors between me and my friends, but there's clearly something within me that does because if it gets too unbalanced I instinctively react with either resentment or guilt depending on which way it leans. And this isn't some rare exception, according to the authors, it's central to how we function.

> Our main goal is to demonstrate that hidden motives are common and important—that they're more than a minor correction to the alternate theory that people mostly do things for the reasons that they give.[133]

---

[133] The book is trying to do a main-corrective inversion, trying to take what most will, when pressed, allow as a corrective ("we are fundamentally honest *but* flawed and sometimes corrupted") and put it as a main instead: this strategizing

If they are right, it explains how we can interpret unfairly without it being a mistake or cold sociopathy, but a secret third thing.

Not real and not fake

The phrase "virtue signaling" is used to accuse people of being motivated by appearing virtuous when they give their opinion, make sacrifices, or express anger, instead of genuinely wanting to do good or expressing consistently held values. Psychologists Jillian Jordan and David Rand wrote *Are You 'Virtue Signaling'?*[134] in the New York Times in 2019, arguing that yes, expressions of e.g. moral outrage do have this quality, but that doesn't mean they're not genuine.

> You may not realize it, but distinguishing between genuine and strategic expressions of indignation assumes a particular scientific theory: namely, that there are two separable psychological systems that shape expressions of moral outrage. One is a "genuine" system that evaluates a transgression in light of our moral values and determines what level of outrage we actually feel. The other is a "strategic" system that evaluates our social context and determines what level of outrage will look best to others. Authentic expressions of outrage involve only the first system, whereas virtue signaling involves the second system.
>
> This theory may be intuitively compelling, but new research suggests that it is wrong. Psychological studies reveal that a person's authentically experienced outrage is inherently interwoven with sub-

---

is the core mechanism of behavior, while honesty and consistency emerges occasionally when properly incentivized.

[134] Note how the scare quotes suggest this is a problematic concept.

> conscious concerns about her reputation. In other words, even genuine outrage can be strategic.

Jordan and Rand close their article by arguing that since strategically motivated expressions are still genuinely felt, it's wrong to dismiss them as "mere" virtue signaling. I'm sympathetic but doubt this implies what they want it to imply. It is indeed wrong to dismiss an argument based on nothing but the supposed motivation of the arguer, or to call someone a liar absent *mens rea,* but it *is* a valid reason to doubt that what you're hearing is a fair, unbiased assessment of reality, or the expression of consistent moral convictions. And it is a fair reason to reject an implied bid for moral superiority.

Whatever the implications are, we can't work them out until this not-either-or nature of beliefs and their expression is understood and accepted, even if that means questioning one of the central assumptions, even dogmas, of modernity: that a rational, coherent self is in charge of the mind. As long as we maintain a false dichotomy between "real" honest reactions and "fake" strategic ones, people will be talking past each other. When faced with the behavior of others, friends and foes will pick whatever angle that suits them, simplify in opposite directions, and cling to whatever partial narratives result, all before consciousness is even on the scene.

The Prince and the Figurehead

While Jordan and Rand argue that the mind does *not* have two separate systems that generate expressed beliefs, Simler and Hanson do seem to suggest a separation. What gives? My reading is that we indeed have two systems, but they are not parallel and don't do two versions of the same thing. They are parts of a single mechanism where one part feels genuine feelings and honestly believes in its own goodness, while the other does selfish, strategic calculation to select and trigger the exact honest and heartfelt impulses that best line up with our self-interest.[135] It's like a nice, popular entertainer who has their agent be the one ruthlessly grubbing for money.

Given that we get fed what is often misinformation by an internal shadowy advisor acting in our interests but not telling us the details so we can avoid getting our hands dirty, we have good reason to doubt that "obvious" interpretations of others are fair and accurate when we're dealing with an enemy (nor are they sufficiently critical when hearing an ally). Considering how Machiavellian it all sounds we should call this "advisor" *The Prince*. And while good for making the point in *The Elephant in the Brain*, "PR officer" is a little pessimistic for the conscious self. It can, if it knows what to look for, question and critically examine what the Prince is telling it. It can even assert power if so inclined. I prefer to call it *The Figurehead*.

Semitentional (neither intentional nor unintentional) misrepresentation thus results from the Prince and the Figurehead working together, with neither having full power nor full responsibility. The Prince is a sociopath without self-awareness or a conscience, and the Figurehead is a naif without all the facts. We're *neither as evil nor as stupid* as we would have to be for the state of discourse to look like it does with us as cohesive agents. However, through the miracle of division of labor, the Prince and the Figurehead can, as a team, produce stupid and evil behavior while being smart and good.

---

[135] Our inner strategist isn't all powerful. There are limits to what it can do and when it's not quite enough, we notice and feel cognitive dissonance over our actions not lining up with our values. When we do things we don't approve of so unambiguously that our subconscious strategic system struggles to reframe it as justified, we reach for explicit rationalizations like "I've done a lot of exercise this week, so I deserve a tasty treat" or "this is a white lie for the greater good". Perhaps this is a last-ditch effort at preserving our self-image when the subconscious system can't handle its own job and needs help from our conscious intelligence.

Chapter 20

The Two Faces of Reason

'Can a magician kill a man by magic?' Lord Wellington asked Strange. Strange frowned. He seemed to dislike the question. 'I suppose a magician might', he admitted, 'but a gentleman never could'.

— Susanna Clarke, *Jonathan Strange & Mr. Norrell*

If you've had your finger on the pulse of discourse for the last two decades, you know that human beings are *irrational*. We're heaving with cognitive biases, we make bad decisions, and we believe all kinds of things without sufficient evidence. Psychologists have shown us time and time again how we fail even the simplest of tests for rational thought. The message is clear: that divine spark of reason that separates us from animals fails a lot of the time. For unclear reasons.

This does not actually make much sense. Why would we have this capability that barely even works? Other functions—vision, hearing, movement, drives and appetites—don't just fail all the time for no apparent reason. Maybe our thinking isn't just rationality with random, unprincipled failures. Instead, think of "rationality" as having several meanings that can, much like the long list of examples in chapter 8, on occasion contradict each other.

We do speak of two kinds of rationality: *epistemic* and *instrumental*. To be epistemically rational means trying to have accurate beliefs, while to be instrumentally rational means pursuing your goals in the most effective way, given your beliefs. They're treated as two facets of the same thing because, obviously, having true beliefs can be nothing but beneficial in pursuing your goals, right? Of course, just like it could be nothing but beneficial to make sure your company hires the most capable employees.

About that... I'll call on Kevin Simler once again, this time not as the author of *The Elephant in the Brain* but of a 2016 blog post called *Crony Beliefs*. To understand why we believe all kinds of strange things, he invites us to liken beliefs with employees. Firms hire workers because they need things done, but employing people costs money and everyone you hire has to earn their keep.

> [W]e can think about beliefs as ideas that have been "hired" by the brain. And we hire them because they have a "job" to do, which is to provide accurate information about the world. We need to know where the lions hang out (so we can avoid them), which plants are edible or poisonous (so we can eat the right ones), and who's romantically available (so we know whom to flirt with). The closer our beliefs hew to reality, the better actions we'll be able to take, leading ultimately to survival and reproductive success.

Then he asks us to consider Acme, a company in the fictional town of Nepotsville. Everyone in Nepotsville knows you give the friends and family of local politicians cushy jobs if you want permits to get approved on time and the local papers to write nice things about you. In this environment it's in fact *not* beneficial for Acme to only hire the most qualified people. They have two separate and diverging purposes when hiring: there are meritocratic incentives to hire the best workers, but political incentives to engage in cronyism and hire a few well-connected warm bodies to keep the city council on their side.

> Suppose Acme has just decided to hire the mayor's nephew Robert as a business analyst. Robert isn't

> even remotely qualified for the role, but it's nevertheless in Acme's interests to hire him. He'll "earn his keep" not by doing good work, but by keeping the mayor off the company's back.
>
> Now suppose we were to check in on Robert six months later. If we didn't already know he was a crony, we might easily mistake him for a regular employee. We'd find him making spreadsheets, attending meetings, drawing a salary: all the things employees do. But if we look carefully enough—not at Robert per se, but at the way the company treats him—we're liable to notice something fishy. He's terrible at his job, and yet he isn't fired. Everyone cuts him slack and treats him with kid gloves. The boss tolerates his mistakes and even works overtime to compensate for them. God knows, maybe he's even promoted.
>
> Clearly Robert is a different kind of employee, a different breed. The way he moves through the company is strange, as if he's governed by different rules, measured by a different yardstick. He's in the meritocracy, but not of the meritocracy.

Of course, "Acme" is the mind. Like them, we have to balance different incentives; there is "meritocratic" incentives for beliefs to be as accurate as possible, and "cronyist" incentives where accuracy matters less than what our beliefs do for our relationships. Both "merit beliefs" and "crony beliefs" add to our bottom line and they are both *rational* to hold. Crony beliefs are instrumentally but not epistemically rational, and guess what, now we've shown that rationality is not one, coherent thing whose components necessarily point in the same direction.

It's importantly *not* the case that crony beliefs are false while merit beliefs are true. Crony beliefs can be true (Simler's example is "climate change is real") and merit beliefs can be false (you can be honestly mistaken). The crucial difference is whether critical examination is welcomed or met with hostility. Do we actually want to know if this belief is false? Are we making trouble rather than helping when we evaluate Robert the Crony's performance by objective standards?

Cronyism affects our reasoning across the board: what beliefs we adopt, which ones we look at closely, and what evidence we seek out. The social pressures that undergird it can be extremely strong, like in revolutionary France or contemporary North Korea. Simler:

> Even mild incentives, however, can still exert pressure on our beliefs. Russ Roberts tells the story of a colleague who, at a picnic, started arguing for an unpopular political opinion—that minimum wage laws can cause harm—whereupon there was a "frost in the air" as his fellow picnickers "edged away from him on the blanket". If this happens once or twice, it's easy enough to shrug off. But when it happens again and again, especially among people whose opinions we care about, sooner or later we'll second-guess our beliefs and be tempted to revise them.

Do we do this fully consciously? No, the Prince and the Figurehead are doing their usual dance, making it feel like what's socially convenient for us to believe is also most likely to be true. Simler goes as far as arguing that social incentives are at the root of all of our biggest thinking errors. Or maybe "errors" is the wrong word, because they aren't the failures of epistemic rationality they're typically cast as. They're *successes* of a particular social kind of instrumental rationality. In line with the book he co-authored, he adds that we know this, deep down, but we still underplay its significance. *I* might add that our *shared* common knowledge understanding underplays it even more. That shouldn't surprise us, because us collectively pretending not to see it is necessary for it to work. If we began to talk freely and openly about how some employees are cronies it would be a lot harder to give Robert the special treatment he needs.

I mean it when I call this rational—not just because it benefits us to fit in, but because it makes sense to associate with others who hold similar beliefs, and to enforce a shared belief system among those we associate with, because shared belief systems allow us to coordinate and collaborate. The problem lies in adopting a self-contradictory definition of rationality and ascribing the unavoidable fallout to random failures. It's a fundamentally broken understanding of thought. Epistemic and instrumental rationality would be aligned if we lived in an inanimate world without other social agents, like Robinson Crusoe on a desert island. Then, and only then, would it always be in our interest to have true beliefs. This is not a normal kind of life, however, and coordinating with others is an essential function of beliefs.

Haidt's moral intuitionism

Historically, moral argumentation has been considered applied reason, and reason the dispassionate application of logic in pursuit of truth. Deviations from it, a.k.a. "irrationality", has been dismissed as mere error, undeserving of examination as a phenomenon in its own right. This has recently changed. Among the best-known champions of this low-key revolution is Jonathan Haidt, familiar from back in chapter 11. In *The Righteous Mind,* he says that we don't in fact use reason to come to conclusions on moral issues. We have intuitions, emotional and immediate, and reason works to justify those intuitions after the fact. This emotional override isn't a failure or contamination, he says, it's an evolutionary design feature. Sound familiar?

> Moral intuitions arise automatically and almost instantaneously, long before moral reasoning has a chance to get started, and those first intuitions tend

> to drive our later reasoning. If you think that moral reasoning is something we do to figure out the truth, you'll be constantly frustrated by how foolish, biased, and illogical people become when they disagree with you. But if you think about moral reasoning as a skill we humans evolved to further our social agendas—to justify our own actions and to defend the teams we belong to—then things will make a lot more sense.

Haidt and *The Righteous Mind* are most known for a set of experiments where participants read little stories about people doing strictly harmless but disgusting or disrespectful things, like have sex with a dead chicken or cut up and sully a flag. He notes that the reasons people give for condemning these acts are made up to justify a preexisting judgment:

> [I]t was obvious that most of these supposed harms were post hoc fabrications. People usually condemned the actions very quickly—they didn't seem to need much time to decide what they thought. But it often took them a while to come up with a victim, and they usually offered those victims up halfheartedly and almost apologetically.

Even when they couldn't find any concrete harm, they didn't change their mind. Haidt points out that they were definitely reasoning, and making quite an effort at it, but it wasn't to reach a conclusion. It was to justify one.

> The social intuitionist model offers an explanation of why moral and political arguments are so frustrating: because moral reasons are the tail wagged by the intuitive dog. A dog's tail wags to communicate. You can't make a dog happy by forcibly wagging its

> tail. And you can't change people's minds by utterly refuting their arguments.

The Prince hides his work well, but if you know what to look for you can observe it through introspection. Haidt notices it happening to him:

> When my wife reprimanded me for leaving dirty dishes on the counter, I honestly believed that I was innocent. I sent my reasoning forth to defend me and it came back with an effective legal brief in just three seconds. It's only because I happened—at that very moment—to be writing about the nature of moral reasoning that I bothered to look closely at my lawyer's arguments and found them to be historical fictions, based only loosely on real events.

Simler's crony beliefs and Haidt's moral intuitions are obviously related. Both are *defended* rather than *evaluated,* with reason playing a justificatory role. Likely the same mechanisms are involved; the Prince understands that it's important for us to come to a particular conclusion and drums up the right emotional reaction while commissioning arguments to match.

When we don't have enough information to spin fictions credibly, this can be so obvious that it's funny. The psychologist Fiery Cushman, when answering 2011's Annual *Edge* question "What scientific concept would improve everybody's cognitive toolkit?", picks *confabulation,* that is, the tendency to make up fake explanations for our behavior:

> Some of the most famous examples of confabulation come from "split-brain" patients, whose left and right brain hemispheres have been surgically disconnected for medical treatment. Neuroscientists have devised clever experiments in which information is provided to the right hemisphere (for in-

> stance, pictures of naked people), causing a change in behavior (embarrassed giggling). Split-brain individuals are then asked to explain their behavior verbally, which relies on the left hemisphere. Realizing that their body is laughing, but unaware of the nude images, the left hemisphere will confabulate an excuse for the body's behavior ("I keep laughing because you ask such funny questions, Doc!").
>
> Wholesale confabulations in neurological patients can be jaw-dropping, but in part that is because they do not reflect ordinary experience. Most of the behaviors that you or I perform are not induced by crafty neuroscientists planting subliminal suggestions in our right hemisphere. When we are outside the laboratory—and when our brains have all the usual connections—most behaviors that we perform are the product of some combination of deliberate thinking and automatic action.

We're usually better at it than this, but there's no reason to think the ability magically appears in split-brain patients. It just makes it easier to spot.

Don't overcorrect

Some use this evidence to argue that all talk of reason is a sham. There's no "there" there, and all attempts at honest, unbiased thinking is doomed to fail because there are self-serving intuitions all the way down. This would be an overcorrection (much like the one-sided arguing against scientific objectivity I was taught at university). The social dimension is the part that philosophy, science, and general psychological theorizing have been ignoring as noise, corruption, and "software bugs" instead of what it is: another partial narrative about reason. Now that it's been brought out and formed as an explicit account for the first time, it's easy to go overboard.

A balanced view acknowledges that while many of our epistemic irrationalities are not mistakes but another mechanism working correctly, "traditional" rationality is also a mechanism that can work correctly. When we're not dealing with crony beliefs and it genuinely is in our interest to find out the truth, we're perfectly capable of reasoning to that end. If that wasn't the case, it's hard to see why we would even try to defend our intuitions with logical arguments. If there were no such thing as real reasoning, that can yield reliable knowledge, why would anyone be convinced by its imitation? For rhetoric to impersonate rational thinking there must exist rational thinking to impersonate. It's a key feature of crony beliefs that they look and feel like merit beliefs (they are at least partially about matters of fact or look like they are), and that requires the existence of such merit beliefs. *If there wasn't any real money, there could be no counterfeit money.*

Our capacity to reason is governed—designed, even—by two goals working at cross-purposes, yet deeply intertwined. This is what makes it such a mess, as disagreement so dysfunctional. As we become more aware of this, we also become more able to steer our cognition in more constructive directions. I don't know how much is temperament and how much is training by excessive introspection, but I've managed to cultivate conscious awareness of both systems over the years. Now, whenever I hear a claim, I *do* have multiple interpretations popping into my head. And I cannot help being aware of unstated assumptions behind what I say myself, and possible objections.[136]

Scout and Soldier mindset

Rationality lecturer and podcaster Julia Galef encourages cultivating something similar in *The Scout Mindset,* her 2021 book about two modes of reasoning. The *scout* in our minds, she explains, is a different creature from the *soldier*. The soldier wants to win and does it by

[136]To some extent. I'm *not* saying I've Achieved Enlightenment, but it has happened on occasion that I've counterargued myself into submission.

fighting enemies and coordinating with friends. The scout also wants to win but has a different job and gets there by a different route.

> The scout isn't indifferent. A scout might hope to learn that the path is safe, that the other side is weak, or that there's a bridge conveniently located where his forces need to cross the river. But above all, he wants to learn what's really there, not fool himself into drawing a bridge on his map where there isn't one in real life. Being in scout mindset means wanting your "map"—your perception of yourself and the world—to be as accurate as possible.

Galef's book trains the reader to tell the difference between scout and soldier mindsets in themselves, and asks us to unlearn certain habits of soldier mindset, such as considering it a failure to be proved wrong, or engaging in motivated reasoning.

> The best description of motivated reasoning I've ever seen comes from psychologist Tom Gilovich. When we want something to be true, he said, we ask ourselves, "Can I believe this?," searching for an excuse to accept it. When we don't want something to be true, we instead ask ourselves, "Must I believe this?", searching for an excuse to reject it. /---/
>
> Even if you've never heard the phrase motivated reasoning, I'm sure you're already familiar with the phenomenon. It's all around you under different names—denial, wishful thinking, confirmation bias, rationalization, tribalism, self-justification, overconfidence, delusion. Motivated reasoning is so fundamental to the way our minds work that it's almost

> strange to have a special name for it; perhaps it should just be called reasoning.

It's not that Haidt, Galef, and Simler have discovered something groundbreaking. The idea goes back all the way to the origins of philosophy. Argumentation was big in ancient Athenian democracy, and teachers of rhetoric made a living helping people win debates. The very short story of Western Civilization is that Plato disapproved of this use of reason, calling it "sophistry". He contrasted it with "philosophy"—using reason to find the truth, i.e. genuine "love of wisdom". The lineage starting from him forms the western philosophical and scientific tradition, and it pushed accounts of reason as *fundamentally social* to the sidelines for millennia, where it's been invisible to the conversation responsible for our collective self-understanding.

That's changing, which makes these books and their message a big deal. The journalist William Saletan referred to *The Righteous Mind* as a "landmark contribution to humanity's understanding of itself" in his New York Times review. Likely he was right, because to truly know and understand something, it isn't enough to have vague intuitions in the right direction. We need explicit accounts, and we need them to be common knowledge.

Solving the enigma

Enter *The Enigma of Reason*. Published in 2017 by cognitive scientists Hugo Mercier and Dan Sperber, it presents a theory of reason as a social phenomenon. Familiar to us now, they say reason is badly flawed according to the standards of "The Dogma", which is what they call the traditional view of reason as a faculty of a rational individual. If that's what it's supposed to be it does its job badly, since reasoning on our own leads us astray as often as it produces good decisions and true beliefs. The world is too complicated for us to understand everything ourselves. Wisdom is by its very nature socially distributed, and so is the process that yields, refines, and preserves it. According to Mercier and Sperber, reasoning isn't about forming a personal belief system, but playing a part in a collective process that produces one for the whole community.

Taking part involves 1) devising arguments to convince others, and 2) evaluating arguments put forth by others. Skilled reasoners in the former sense are first and foremost good at justifying their beliefs, and this isn't "doing individual reasoning badly", it's "playing your part in collective reasoning well". Laboratory experiments that show us being incompetent individual reasoners lack proper argumentative framing, they say, and once people are given such context they are skilled arguers. When trying to convince others, we want arguments supporting our view, and this is what we focus on finding even when we're alone—hence the famous "confirmation bias". It's not a mistake, it's us proactively building our case in anticipation of having to make it. From this point of view, evidence supporting our beliefs *is* more valuable and *should* be focused on and retained more.

Our reasoning ability is bad at individual rational thinking because it has what Mercier and Sperber calls a "myside bias". Arguments we come up with in our favor get the crony treatment, but when we hear the arguments others put forth we are more discerning, and, they say, more fair.

> [T]here is an asymmetry between the production of arguments, which involves an intrinsic bias in favor of the opinions or decisions of the arguer whether they are sound or not, and the evaluation of arguments, which aims at distinguishing good arguments from bad ones and hence genuine information from misinformation. This asymmetry is often obscured in a debate situation (or in a situation where a debate is anticipated). People who have an opinion to defend don't really evaluate the arguments of their interlocutors in a search for genuine information but rather consider them from the start as counterarguments to be rebutted. Still, as shown by the evidence reviewed in section 2, people are

> good at assessing arguments and are quite able to do so in an unbiased way, provided they have no particular axe to grind.

Our faculties for the generation vs. evaluation of arguments are separate because it's not our job to find the flaws in our own reasoning—that's for others to do. And while we're not likely to be fair to an opponent, third parties can be capable of judging both our motivated arguments and our opponent's motivated rebuttals.

> [C]ontrary to common bleak assessments of human reasoning abilities, people are quite capable of reasoning in an unbiased manner, at least when they are evaluating arguments rather than producing them, and when they are after the truth rather than trying to win a debate.

Sure, but that's a big "when" you've got there. That social reasoning can be rational in the aggregate even when the people involved in it aren't is an important result, but obviously not enough. We've seen how social reasoning gets co-opted and hijacked to fulfill all kinds of purposes aside from collective epistemic rationality. In Simler's words, we use expressions of belief to "blend in, stick out, suck up, show off, cheerlead, jockey for the high ground, posture and perform". This is all run by the Prince, who keeps the fair evaluative function Mercier and Sperber talk about—let's call it *The Analyst*—under his thumb. She only gets to speak when the Prince deems it to be to our advantage to make a rational judgment.

Misrepresenting others' beliefs, the subject of the last chapter, can now be accounted for in this way: the Prince won't let the Analyst do a fair evaluation, even though she can. He decides to trigger an immediate "this is OUR opinion" intuition, which activates the justificatory function instead. And that starts off by assuming whatever interpretation makes the job easier—"obviously my enemy meant this dumb, evil thing I can easily refute".

When collective reasoning works and when it doesn't

Mercier and Sperber's theory hints at what the modern world does to our reasoning systems, compared to the environment in which they evolved. Specifically, are there features of modernity (and post-modernity) that affect the balance of power between the justificatory and evaluative faculties?

Perhaps it's natural to only *argue* within our own tribe, "the in-group". We all have to live together, we're dependent on each other and know that it's in our interests to be mostly fair, show respect, and avoid escalating conflicts and alienate those we rely on and can't escape. But the out-group, our *enemies*? We don't bother arguing with them. What's there to argue over? We want to beat them and they want to beat us. We might talk *about* them, but then there's no reason to be fair. On the contrary, we should make sure we're as united as possible against them.

It's a great achievement of civilization that fighting has largely been replaced by arguing since modernity and democracy, but maybe it's caused some unintended weirdness: *we were never meant to argue with the enemy*. Maybe there's no natural way to handle this, and what we inevitably get is a messy, borderless mix of two completely different things: fair among-the-ingroup reasoning where we try to be convincing and honestly evaluate what others say, and unfair towards-the-outgroup reasoning where we just try to rile up our own side and, if having any contact with them at all, demoralize and humiliate the enemy.

Furthermore, the split into subcultures of diverging taken-for-granted beliefs ("filter bubbles") means we won't get the unbiased evaluation of our beliefs and arguments that collective reasoning depends on. We weren't built to be able to surround ourselves with only those who agree with us. Now that we can, the result is hive-minds that recreate all the biased tendencies of the individual. Not having to convince any nonbelievers allows our unprincipled argument-generation modules to coast. They spit out low-effort trash, which gets coddled like cronies by our friends, and in turn used by our enemies to show each other how awful we are. Yes, ideological bubbles even replicate, on a collective level, the Prince's ability to pick the worst possible interpretation of what our enemies are like. Instead of giving us the full set, they make sure it's the dumbest, meanest, most ridiculous specimens we know about.

Our argumentative faculties weren't designed to deal with disagreement *systems* either. They're an artifact of modernity bringing us together with people who don't just disagree on one or two things, but have entirely different belief systems, making interpretation a bigger challenge. This unprecedented complexity strains the Analyst, who then struggles to speak loudly and clearly. For the Prince, however, confusion and ambiguity are resources to exploit.

What can we do? For individuals: empower the Analyst. Give her the tools to understand these unnaturally complicated disagreements and speak with greater confidence. As Figureheads, we should remember to be skeptical of what the Prince tells us, to pause for a second, and address the Analyst directly. Often that does work, and do it enough times and she might grow confident enough to start speaking over the Prince. This is not the same thing as "teaching critical thinking". We *don't* lack the ability to be critical or to evaluate fairly, what we need to learn is to override our social self-interest and apply our abilities consistently.

For collectives, their ability to reason depends on their norms and their internal composition. While people are not designed to be individually rational in a social setting, we are designed to take part in a rational process. Collective rationality can handle individual bias as long as there is diversity of opinion that is accepted and respected, and disagreement is functional, i.e. that parties have good enough erisological competence to manage the diversity without failing to communicate.

If we're low on ideological and temperamental diversity, the only choice is to force a community to replicate the strict, individual-style reasoning Mercier and Sperber called "The Dogma". That is, to maintain collective rationality by ruthlessly calling out motivated cognition and cronyism in each other, and create a culture where contrarianism, pedantry, and playing devil's advocate are valued for their own sake. This is *much* harder than ideological diversity, but a community that is neither ideologically diverse nor saturated with such quasi-autistic behavioral norms will not have functioning collective reasoning[137].

[137] Note how we're back in chapter 3: functional disagreement requires at least one of two things: people must respect each other even when they disagree (like in personal relationships), or they must agree to seek truth and have strong norms against myside bias (like in science).

PART VII

Decoupling

Chapter 21

Decoupling Introduced

To read between the lines was easier than to follow the text.

— Henry James

Reason isn't all about dispassionate truth seeking, nor is it all about social maneuvering. It's a process constantly constructing, deconstructing, and reconstructing shared belief systems that bridge the gap between brute physical reality and the moral order, constituting what we call "social reality"—or, if you're a constructionist, "reality". We've learned that among its components—its types, labels, facts, narratives, tropes, valences, and imperatives—some can be tightly connected to reality but irrelevant to the moral order (like "oxygen" or "octopus"), while others (like "responsibility" or "credential"), are at best loosely rooted in physical fact but closely involved in regulating social behavior. Many, (like "victim" or "disorder"), are like little consultant's reports, stretching all along the spectrum, tying the ends together and justifying prescribed behavior by rooting it in reality.

We like that. We like it when the ends meet neatly and nicely. It creates certainty and clarity ("this is the natural and proper order of things"). However, making that neatness happen, making our moral goals justified by the facts, is an exercise in sensemaking, not mere discovery, and it can require more or less work. In other words, some moral agendas are more easily compatible with reality than others. It is for example much harder to justify putting people in quarantine if the disease they carry isn't contagious. But the relationship is rarely that simple, and there's no logical principle or natural law that guarantees that honest truth-seeking will yield the results that most easily justify the actions we prefer. Maybe cigarettes *do* cause cancer (but suppresses appetite and helps weight loss), maybe these otherwise useful chlorofluorocarbons *do* destroy the ozone layer, maybe capital punishment does/doesn't work as a deterrent, and maybe day-care/stay-at-home-moms *are* better/worse for kids' development (cross out as preferred). What if, hypothetically, vaccines *did* cause autism sometimes? What would we do then? We'd have some difficult decisions to make.

If the sides of the reality-morality equation happen to fit together, then happy days! That troublesome claim is also false! That ethically problematic method is also ineffective! *Phew!* If they don't, we experience cognitive dissonance, that unpleasant sensation of noticing that our worldview has contradictions in it.

When discussing labels back in chapter 10, we saw that they do on the one hand refer to reality ("does this label accurately reflect the nature of what we apply it to?") and on the other, to morality ("are the consequences of applying this label good?"), and that these are separate questions. To repeat once again because it's so important: *There is no natural law or principle whatsoever guaranteeing that these two types of judgement, made from opposite ends, will agree with each other.* It is accurate to refer to some people as "ugly" or "stupid", but we may justifiably think it's morally wrong to do so (and also that it's a moral problem that these attributes tend to come with worse life outcomes). In the same vein we might understand that some stereotypes are statistically accurate but also disapprove of applying this knowledge to individuals. These come with inner tensions and conflict, but they are not logically inconsistent or in any way less expected than the reverse.

Towards "decoupling"

It was in this context of relating the true with the good that I discussed *decoupling*, the concept I've helped spread more than any other, more than partial narratives, correctives, cat couplings, or "erisology". Triggered (it seems) mostly by me writing about it, it has become standard parlance in some subcultures and occasionally made its way into the mainstream. Its most high-profile gig so far is in Nate Silver's 2023 book *On the Edge,* where it's described as a key characteristic of gamblers and technologists.

Here's what happened: in the spring of 2018 I wrote an article that went, for some meaning of the word appropriate for a small blog, "viral". The 9000+ word autopsy of a spat between public intellectuals Sam Harris and Ezra Klein grew my audience tenfold overnight, and the term "decoupling" slipped loose. It had all started a few weeks earlier when I stumbled upon a link to a collection of emails between Harris and Klein. The two argued about a critical article that Klein's site *Vox* had published in response to Harris's podcast interview with controversial political scientist Charles Murray. While starting off amiably, the conversation turned hostile, and whatever good will was there in the beginning had run out by the end, spent on—apparently—failed attempts to get on the same page. Many thought Harris came off as the unreasonable party, and I could certainly see why. I came away with the impression that he had lost his cool and retracted an invitation to Klein to come on his podcast for no good reason. His anger was out of character; I'd listened to a few of his podcast episodes and he had come off well-reasoned, balanced and rational. Nonetheless he appeared to be the one responsible for the conversation deteriorating somewhere in the middle. And he had released these emails himself, obviously thinking people would take his side and it'd reflect badly on Klein. Why this reaction? To find out I had to follow the conversation backwards.

I grew low-key obsessed with their fight. There was so much complexity and history behind this conversation, all ready to be uncovered. The article I wound up writing is already a short summary, so I will not even attempt to do justice to it all here. The core, however, was that Harris had invited Charles Murray to his podcast for a generally friendly conversation. Murray is famous for co-authoring *The Bell Curve* back in the '90s, and for holding the view that there is some significant genetic component to the observed differences in measured intelligence between Americans of different ethnic groups (of which the one between white and black is what people care about). Murray, popularly known primarily for this belief, had recently been assaulted by activists when giving a (itself politically innocuous) speech at Middlebury University, and Harris wanted to show some support.

In response Klein had, among other things, as editor, let *Vox* publish an article by three other researchers, condemning Harris for not challenging Murray enough on his signature issue, arguing that his interpretation of intelligence research is illegitimate and pseudoscientific. They stop short of calling their conversation racist, but only by as little as is humanly possible. Harris considered himself smeared, and saw the article and Klein's tweets and later writings on the issue as a violation of civil discourse norms. It all culminated in a two-hour podcast conversation between them that did little to resolve the disagreement. For a full assessment, look up the article (*A Deep Dive into the Harris-Klein Controversy,* 2018*)*. Here I will jump straight to my conclusion: their disagreement was, in essence, over whether Murray's take on the scientific evidence was legitimate, and by extension whether the issue belongs under the jurisdiction of science or of politics—two magisteria with big differences in how claims are understood and evaluated.

Here's where the word "pseudoscience" comes in (which bothered Harris so much). Meaning "something trying to look like science when it isn't", it typically refers to whole fields that pretend to be sciences but don't abide by scientific standards—common examples include homeopathy, graphology, and cryptozoology. However, "interpreting results further than is justified" can also fit the definition "tries to look like science but isn't" if we by "science" mean "scientific facts established beyond reasonable doubt". Murray's interpretation of the evidence was then pseudoscientific because it went too far beyond the facts, according to Klein's side. Harris, supported by Richard Haier, a prominent intelligence researcher, argued that Murray's interpretive jump was in fact small, because there was no strictly scientific reason to consider it particularly implausible to begin with. Klein and the authors of the article that enraged Harris didn't explicitly deny this. Instead they said that the interpretation had such tremendous *political* significance that it became "a big deal", making the jump big, and thus unjustifiable as science[138]. The size ("big-dealness") and thus the legitimacy of the jump, therefore depended on whether it was considered a scientific or a political claim – and a case can be made for either.

I would've ended the article with that conclusion if I hadn't, around the same time, read a blog post.

From Stanovich through Constantin and Keer

The mathematician Lucy Keer published *The Cognitive Decoupling Elite* on her blog *Drossbucket* in April 2018. In it, she quotes another blogger, Sarah Constantin, discussing the work of psychologist Keith Stanovich:

> Stanovich talks about "cognitive decoupling", the ability to block out context and experiential knowledge and just follow formal rules, as a main component of both performance on intelligence tests and performance on the cognitive bias tests that correlate with intelligence. Cognitive decoupling is the opposite of holistic thinking. It's the ability to separate, to view things in the abstract, to play devil's advocate. /---/
>
> Speculatively, we might imagine that there is a "cognitive decoupling elite" of smart people who are good at probabilistic reasoning and score high on the cognitive reflection test and the IQ-correlated cognitive bias tests. These people would be more likely to be male, more likely to have at least under-

[138] It was a great source of confusion that they used this as an argument for their point of view instead of what it really was: the very issue under dispute.

> grad-level math education, and more likely to have utilitarian views. Speculating a bit more, I'd expect this group to be likelier to think in rule-based, devil's-advocate ways, influenced by economics and analytic philosophy. I'd expect them to be more likely to identify as rational.

Keer described the disembodied rule-following of cognitive decoupling as alien and unpleasant, despite having a physics PhD and working as a programmer. She quotes Sylvia Plath's *The Bell Jar* as illustrating a more extreme case of her own discomfort:

> Botany was fine, because I loved cutting up leaves and putting them under the microscope and drawing diagrams of bread mould and the odd, heart-shaped leaf in the sex cycle of the fern, it seemed so real to me.
>
> The day I went in to physics class it was death.
>
> A short dark man with a high, lisping voice, named Mr. Manzi, stood in front of the class in a tight blue suit holding a little wooden ball. He put the ball on a steep grooved slide and let it run down to the bottom. Then he started talking about let a equal acceleration and let t equal time and suddenly he was scribbling letters and numbers and equals signs all over the blackboard and my mind went dead.
>
> I may have made a straight A in physics, but I was panic-struck. Physics made me sick the whole time I learned it. What I couldn't stand was this shrinking everything into letters and numbers. Instead of leaf shapes and enlarged diagrams of the hole the leaves breathe through and fascinating words like carotene and xanthophyll on the blackboard, there were these

> hideous, cramped, scorpion-lettered formulas in Mr. Manzi's special red chalk.
>
> I knew chemistry would be worse, because I'd seen a big chart of the ninety-odd elements hung up in the chemistry lab, and all the perfectly good words like gold and silver and cobalt and aluminium were shortened to ugly abbreviations with different decimal numbers after them. If I had to strain my brain with any more of that stuff I would go mad.

Keer's own observations follow:

> The botany classes ground out in vivid, concrete experience: ferns, leaf shapes, bread mould. There's an associated technical vocabulary – carotene, xanthophyll – but even these words are embedded in a rich web of sound associations and tangible meanings.
>
> In the physics and chemistry classes, by contrast, the symbols are seemingly arbitrary, chosen on pure pragmatic grounds and interchangeable for any other random symbol. (I say 'seemingly' arbitrary because of course if you continue in physics you do build up a rich web of associations with x and t and the rest of them. Esther doesn't know this, though.) The important content of the lecture is instead the structural relationships between the different symbols, and the ways of transforming one to another by formal rules. Pure cognitive decoupling.
>
> There is a tangible physical object, the 'little wooden ball' (better than I got in my university mechanics lectures!), but that object has been chosen for its utter lack of vivid distinguishing features, its ability to

> stand in as a prototype of the whole abstract class of featureless spheres rolling down featureless inclined planes.
>
> The lecturer's suit is a bit crap, too. Nothing at all about this situation has been designed for a fulfilling, interconnected aesthetic experience.

Her final remark made a bunch of things snap together in my head:

> Strong coupling in this sense is like being a kind of sensitive antenna for your environment, learning to read as much meaning out of it as possible, but without necessarily being able to explain what you learn in a structured, explicit logical argument. I'd expect it to be correlated with high sensitivity to nonverbal cues, implicit tone, tacit understanding, all the kind of stuff that poets are stereotypically good at and nerds are stereotypically bad at.

I took this and ran with it. In a fit of passionate speculation, I suggested a connection between how you felt about the relationship between science and politics and how you felt about cognitive decoupling as described by Stanovich, Constantin, and Keer.

Stanovich meets Mercier & Sperber

Cognitive decoupling is like what Mercier and Sperber calls "reason in the classical sense": individual, disinterested, and divorced from emotion and intention. Stanovich agrees with them that this isn't a natural feature of the mind and it's wrong to regard it as synonymous with reason itself. I found this out when I, to get to the root of things, went back to look through his book *What Intelligence Tests Miss: The Psychology of Rational Thought* from 2010. He says that rationality in the sense of reasoning logically, explicitly, and formally, to form beliefs without emotion, motive or intuition tipping the scales, is a learned skill. Proficiency with it *requires* intelligence but is not *equal* to intelligence. He refers to developmental psychologist Alan Leslie:

> Leslie modeled the logic of pretense by proposing a so-called decoupling operation, which is illustrated in Figure 3.1.7. In the figure, a primary representation is one that is used to directly map the world and/or is also directly connected to a response. Leslie modeled pretense by positing a so-called secondary representation that was a copy of the primary representation but that was decoupled from the world so that it could be manipulated—that is, be a mechanism for simulation.

This is, in Leslie's conception, the mechanic behind our capacity for pretense and "as if" thinking. By creating a secondary, *decoupled,* mental representation of an object to manipulate in a sandbox, the primary representation can retain its place directly influencing intuition, emotion, and behavior. According to Stanovich, this operation enables abstract and hypothetical thinking, where we can entertain and evaluate an idea *without* necessarily believing it, endorsing it, and acting on its implications. This is, however, costly in terms of cognitive resources[139]. And that's a good thing:

> Evolution has guaranteed the high cost of decoupling for a very good reason. As we were becoming the first creatures to rely strongly on cognitive simulation, it was especially important that we not become "unhooked" from the world too much of the time.

[139] The general principle has been familiar for a long time. Although likely apocryphal, the quote "It is the mark of an educated mind to be able to entertain a thought without accepting it" is often attributed to Aristotle.

Getting "unhooked" from the real world by excessive cognitive decoupling risks damaging our motivational system and capacity to make appropriate, timely decisions, which Stanovich calls "The Mr. Spock problem". We therefore don't do it automatically, regardless of intelligence, but only when we tell our "algorithmic mind" (Stanovich's phrase) to get to work. We avoid this because of the effort required, a fact he highlights by calling us "cognitive misers". The main thesis of *What Intelligence Tests Miss* is that tests only measure the *capacity* of our algorithmic mind, not our proclivity to use it, which is his definition of "rationality". Mercier and Sperber are on a similar track:

> [I]ndividuals may develop some limited ability to distance themselves from their own opinion, to consider alternatives and thereby become more objective. Presumably this is what the 10% or so of people who pass the standard Wason selection task do. But this is an acquired skill and involves exercising some imperfect control over a natural disposition.

For those unfamiliar with it, the Wason selection task is one laboratory experiment among many where the intuitive solution is wrong and getting the question right requires executing explicit logical operations.

When decoupling works and not

That type of thinking, i.e. actually trying to reason something through, step by step, overriding what seems intuitively correct, is perfect for the particular class of situations when we have complete information about a limited, closed domain. That is, when we know all the rules that govern our object of analysis. The real world is rarely like this. Most often we *don't* have all the information and *don't* understand the underlying rules and mechanisms well enough to apply them in our heads to get a reliably correct result.

We can make mental simulation artificially powerful by isolating a system from the rest of reality, formalize inputs and outputs and set up clear, unambiguous rules for it. We can then internalize the system and play around with its representation in our heads, which enables us to predict and manipulate it. Some people enjoy this. *Nerds* enjoy this. Hell, I'll even say that enjoying this is the *defining feature* of nerds. It's how mathematics, computer programs, and board games work. And to a point, leveraging rule-bound predictability to simulate things in the world less than perfectly but still well, and find ways to accomplish results from this knowledge, is the basis of *all technology*[140].

When our object of study *can't* be represented this way, we *can't* rely on such formal mental simulation. Thus, we should be wary of decoupling in situations rich with ambiguity, unpredictability, and unknown unknowns. When we have little chance of figuring out what we're up against, it's safer to defer to tried and tested community knowledge like tradition, authority, common sense, and social norms. You are not smarter than everyone else, you know! Reading the room is the superior choice when something is too big and too hard for your mind to work through on its own.

Cognitive decoupling (or "classical reasoning" in M&S's parlance) is thus a small act of hubris: "I can *actually understand* this, using the power of my thought, instead of relying on socially acquired and transmitted rules-of-thumb, because I, unlike others before and beside me, *sniff*, have the capability." This is why those who decouple the most, like physicists, mathematicians, and engineers, have a reputation for intellectual arrogance.

Science is, for all its success, a ~hubristic attempt to leverage our capacity for decoupling and formal, abstract reasoning to get to the real bottom of how things work, far beyond memorizing useful surface-level regularities like "this fruit is good to eat, and this type of

140 The corollary is that technology advancement accelerates dramatically when liberated from the inexactness and unpredictability of the physical world, i.e. digitized.

rock is good for making arrowheads". It does this by institutionalizing this one type of occasionally appropriate reasoning and jealously protecting it from influence by the regular type. It's astounding that it works as well as it does.

The other half: Segerstråle's "coupled thinking"

That's cognitive decoupling. But there is more. In my head this came together with something Segerstråle had said in her account of the sociobiology controversy—not surprisingly, since it has a lot in common with the Harris/Klein conflict in that it involved the biological roots of human behavior, an issue always right there at the intersection of science and politics.

Segerstråle refers to what she calls "coupled logic" on two occasions. Once it means the belief that good scientific practice and progressive political views go hand in hand (and therefore, by extension, that correct science can virtually by definition never support socially regressive or conservative ends). The second time she uses it more generally to mean the belief that anyone disagreeing with one's scientific views does so for political reasons. Paraphrased, I take "coupled logic" to mean the idea that scientific and political views come as a package and cannot be meaningfully discussed separately. She refers to some players in the controversy, like Peter Medawar and Richard Dawkins, as "uncouplers" who do try to keep the science and the politics separate.

Stanovich's cognitive decoupling and Segerstråle's coupled thinking looked like two sides of the same coin. This impression, ironically, wasn't based on any particular evidence or logic; it was driven by pattern-matching and narrative elegance. They fit together too beautifully for a consultant's sensemaking muscles to ignore.

Harris and Klein and their two camps disagreed about 1) whether the scientific, logical, and evidentiary status was all that mattered for politically consequential scientific claims, and 2) whether you have a right to be evaluated on what you explicitly say, or whether you're also responsible for all the implications, interpretations and associations around it. With "high-decoupling" logic, Harris and Murray had discharged all their responsibilities by pointing out, again and again as their conversation went on, that it was wrong—irrational even—to discriminate against any individual based on average characteristics of demographic groups. When explicit, formal reasoning in "sandbox mode" is the norm, then all you need to say to isolate an idea from its aura of implicit associations is to say so: "by *this*, I don't mean *that*". When this magical ritual has been performed, no one is entitled to claim that you support the *that* or are responsible for it any way (this is what I'm doing above when I call this speculation; it's code for "if you take this too seriously it's not my fault").

This is the norm in some contexts. It's standard practice in science, which works by isolating variables, teasing out causality and operationalizing claims into carefully delineated hypotheses. They rely on explicit, logical reasoning and, as an ethos, eschew tradition, (untrained) intuition, and socially negotiated common sense. Thus, science, mathematics, and engineering disciplines (and analytic philosophy among the humanities) attract people with a knack and an appetite for decoupling, like Harris the trained neuroscientist and Murray the quantitative political scientist.

Other disciplines are dominated by the opposite of "the Scientist" in the gallery of brainy archetypes: the literary or artistic intellectual. Coupling, viscerality, embeddedness, and rich, implicit associations are the tools of their trade. Novelists, poets, artists and more prosaic storytellers like journalists, politicians and advertisers wield symbols to evoke just the right feelings and thoughts in their audience. The very words "artistic" and "literary" means using idea couplings well to subtly and indirectly push the audience's buttons to give the impression you want. It's the water they swim in. Being good at their job means being good at navigating and working with these unarticulated associations, as-is. Trying to work against them or outside them is idiotic and weird, like making foul-smelling food and blaming the customers when your restaurant fails.

To such a "coupler", decouplers trying to fence off any unwanted implications and pretend they don't exist looks bizarre and disingenuous. You don't get to remove associations that are *an inherent part of a concept's meaning* by decree! It's not a legal move. It doesn't even make sense, because the whole point of saying anything at all is to influence the minds of others. To think (or to dishonestly claim) that you have no responsibility for implications that naturally arise in your audience shows not just foolishness, but a disturbing recklessness and lack of empathy for those affected.

At the same time, to the decoupler, the coupler's insistence that it's not possible to consider an idea purely on its scientific or logical merits looks like naked bias and an inability to think straight. This is what Harris means when he says Klein is biased in their conversation. Of course, to Ezra Klein, the journalist and former political campaign worker, thinking in moral and political terms is not a bias, it's his entire job.

Not just an ability

I put the section on this expanded notion of decoupling at the very end of my Harris/Klein article. It was just a little extra, a bit of apophenic dessert after what I considered the meat of the issue. It placed the controversy in a grand narrative about human nature and difference—pretty, but too speculative to be a load-bearing part of my argument. Of course, it ended up being what most readers took from the article. Had I known that[141] I would have phrased things differently. Reality is complex and I regret describing it as two classes of people ("high-decouplers" and "low-decouplers") rather than two patterns of thought that can coexist in a person. Grouping people instead of ideas encourages identity formation and stereotyping, which makes the concept worse at doing what I intended it to do: help people make sense of complex disagreements.

It hardly makes it better that the concept, which I do think is valid and useful when considered with care, through my treatment, became associated with one of the most inflamed centers of discursive

[141] One could argue I *should* have known, but at the time I was not yet used to anything I said being taken seriously.

toxicity in the world: American race relations. That was unwise, and it contributed to the terms being used as insults. One tweeter I won't name suggested it was "quite obviously invented on the spot to justify ignoring political enemies" which is very much the opposite of the truth (he may or may not believe me, but it is). I invoked it specifically to avoid accusing anyone of dishonesty and instead suggest that Harris and Klein were involved in a collision of honestly held but incompatible norms.

But as the law says: *if a term can be used as a weapon, someone will use it that way*. The only way to avoid it would be to stick to concepts that can't be used as weapons, which I fear may be impossible given that even something as pacifistic as the principle of charity can be abused. Still, you can make abuse more difficult, and one thing I should have done was avoid framing "decoupling" as an *ability* the way Stanovich's version is. In fact, that aspect doesn't transfer well from his cognitive decoupling to this fusion with Segerstråle's coupled thinking. While there is some asymmetry in that abstract and hypothetical thinking uninfluenced by real-world implications don't come naturally to humans but have to be learned, the difference between decoupling and coupling in this sense isn't mainly about ability, but about moral conviction. In this, it inherits more from Segerstråle than from Stanovich, since her coupled thinking is never talked about as a matter of ability.

You can flip things around and characterize decoupling as an *inability* if you like. There exists a certain naive, socially clumsy, nerdy blindness to social implications that's characteristic of autism but present in varying degrees in a much larger group of people. Being "literal-minded" is not typically a compliment, and "tone-deaf" is never one. Not "reading the room" is not unlike lacking a fashion sense—a combination of not picking up social cues and not thinking or caring about how others perceive you. They're deficiencies in our "social antennae", in Keer's parlance. As described in the section on partial narratives, we teach ourselves to notice/posit (cross out as preferred) broader meaning in things, and a lean towards decoupling can come from not cultivating the skill of interpreting symbolism, intention, and vibes.

It can also be described as a personality trait or behavioral disposition. Different people find it differently easy and enjoyable to think in formal logical vs. social and emotional terms, and therefore do it more or less eagerly. As mentioned it's also a *local social norm* (e.g. in some academic fields or subcultures). Analytic philosophy in particular has strong norms to maintain affective neutrality when dealing with emotionally charged topics, and to respect the implied right to be taken at your word when you propose a narrow, specific meaning of a term for use in a given argument.

Finally, there was some justified criticism of the decoupling concept that pointed out that people don't couple or decouple across the board. Someone arguing that biological accounts of human behavior lead to fascism is *not* more likely to also argue that complaints about economic inequality lead to communism. On the contrary, they're almost certainly *less* likely to. When it comes to hot-button issues, coupling vs. decoupling is, perhaps most of all, an *opportunistic practice*—one that nonetheless feels perfectly honest and consistent, because of the Prince.[142]

After mulling this over for a few years, I do think there is a "there" there. Decoupling is real and significant, but it's not just an ability, it's not always the right thing to do, it's not simply determined by an immutable characteristic, and it has limited value for explaining where people land on controversial issues. Even so, it helps us to recognize when disagreements are made more complicated by an ancillary disagreement over whether decoupling is appropriate.

---

[142] Like with self-control, we can likely talk about "trait decoupling" and "behavior decoupling" separately but relatedly.

Chapter 22

The Silent Agreement

Fine manners need the support of fine manners in others.

— Ralph Waldo Emerson

There's nothing odd, unexpected, or paradoxical about the fact that evaluating an idea from the "physical facts" direction and the "social significance" direction can yield different answers. There's no reason to expect the two to agree; no physical or logical mechanism ensures it. Of course, it requires that we ask ourselves which side takes precedence when determining collectively endorsed social reality. Do we privilege the quasi-autistic pursuit of truth, or the quasi-sociopathic pursuit of outcomes?

There are dangerous ideas

Decoupling in one sense, ignoring neurological facets like mental simulation and only looking at social behavior, means thinking that the "facts end" comes first by default. Truth is what matters, and looking at the social consequences of particular beliefs is an illegal move that renders reasoning invalid. Social implications cannot reach back into what's logically prior and *make* something true or false retroactively. And bringing in moral implications as a factor in collective reasoning is equivalent to motivated cognition in individual reasoning, with the same corrupting influence.

Decoupling as an approach to collective reasoning has something else in common with decoupling in individual thought: *trust in the process*. Decoupling means you believe we have the capacity and wisdom to master the issue at hand. If we assume this, there is, notably, no such thing as a "dangerous idea". A dangerous idea would be one that is bad, yet we might adopt. This is a contradiction in terms since we can't both be justifiably confident an idea is bad *and* believe rational evaluation could have us adopt it. I used to think exactly this way, and this was my reason: to not trust public debate to come to the right conclusion is so cynical and condescending towards the intelligence of the average person that it could be ruled out on moral grounds.

Take a few seconds to appreciate the irony.

Sunlight *is* the best disinfectant. However, only if ample sunlight can be counted on at all times is it true that there cannot be any problem with opening up any issue for discussion. I've grudgingly come to respect the "coupling" position that we can't always trust public debate, no matter how much wishful thinking committed decouplers project onto it. Collectively we don't have the necessary information and self-discipline, and the risk of half-reason leading us astray is significant. Thus, the case can be made that we should instead rely on socially distributed rules-of-thumb like taboos and propriety. Once you accept that limitation, the coupling position becomes difficult to dismiss. There is a lot of bad stuff out there that isn't getting effectively countered.

We can try to make public discourse a little bit more precise, careful and rational, and more tolerant of ambiguity and complexity. But as long as we're not there, as long as it looks less like a philosophy seminar and more like random words being thrown into a pit of chaos, then there is such a thing as dangerous ideas.

An audience makes decoupling risky

Accepting what someone says only in a particular narrow meaning and agreeing to disregard all wider associations is necessary to communicate on delicate and complex issues, but it requires good will, which can be exploited. As frustrating as it might be to the devoted decoupler, refusing to decouple is a rational and appropriate stance in low-trust situations, when what you say can be taken out of context, or when there's an audience. With others watching, we're reluctant to accept anything "for the sake of argument" because we know that decoupling is unstable, like Stanovich says. Things readily collapse from the abstract and hypothetical back into the real if they escape a carefully fenced context.

Let's say I have this belief system I want to explain to you. It relies on certain assumptions and priorities that you don't share, but if one accepts them it all makes sense. Your natural impulse is to refuse to play along: "no that's not right, and it's irrelevant what would follow if it were". I can complain that it's not fair that you *won't even engage* with my reasoning. You don't have to *really* accept it but how can you even consider it unless you try to understand? If I'm being less than perfectly honest, or just a true believer whose Prince puts his thumb on the scale enough to make me feel that what I'm doing is perfectly innocuous, I'll do this with the hope that your decoupling *will* in fact collapse. You know this, and this is why you resist.

Even if decoupling won't collapse for you, it might for third parties. To an audience, perhaps seeing parts of a conversation out of context, agreeing "provisionally" will look like "actually" unless you keep protesting at every step. Just hearing someone say things we disagree with and not object is stressful, because we know in our bones that it looks like acceptance. And if others see you act as if you agree with me, or accept my authority, it helps legitimize not just what I am saying but what anyone else might think I'm saying. Thus, also refusing to disregard all interpretations besides precisely what is explicitly said, is rational and appropriate in a world where de- and recontextualization is the norm, and speakers lack the power to assert authority over the meaning of their speech. In other words, in our world of bite-sized, disembodied, cross-paradigmatic communication.

Science's dilemma

There is a context in which these concerns aren't supposed to dominate. Theres an institution meant to examine reality systematically and exhaustively, and where we do go in with the expectation that our faculties of reason are up to the task: *science*. Science approaches the world with a one-eyed focus on the truth and nothing else, and in return we trust it. Politics, by contrast, is all the way over at the other end of the spectrum. It's about coalition building, which means that the purpose served by its social reality ("the party line") is coordination for effective action, not correspondence to material truth (insofar as we "trust" anyone in politics, it is to look out for our interests, not to tell the truth).

Naturally then, when claims make science and politics meet, it results in turf wars just like those between academic disciplines. We might wish there was a clean split we could find through careful analysis, and sort science and politics into non-overlapping magisteria, but no such luck. It is not possible to completely remove motivated thinking from scientific practice because, as we have seen, modeling reality requires making choices, focusing on some features and playing down others. And as much as we'd like to think scientific knowledge (that-which-gets-taken-for-scientific-knowledge) is "just the facts", it is not. That much my professors managed to convince me of. This can on a few occasions be *significant* for the hard sciences like physics and chemistry, but it's *essential* to the human and social sciences.

The big question for science becomes "what responsibility do scientists have to consider the possible political uses of their research?" More starkly: *how much should they engage in motivated thinking*? Outright lying about results is beyond the pale in almost everyone's book, but just choosing questions, concept constructs, framings, methods, and interpretations gives *a lot* of leeway. And social implications do obviously influence purportedly scientific judgments; left-handedness and homosexuality were reclassified to not count as disorders not because we discovered new facts about them, but because moral attitudes changed. It is reasonable to do this on issues like what counts as disorders, but—and this is a big *but,* I cannot lie—doing so means deviating from the one-sided, nothing-but-truth norm that is essential to science. That means you lose some of your right to call it "science" or "scientific", and the more a discipline does this, the less legitimate authority it has.

Few would bite the bullet and argue that we should never, *ever* allow any such influence. There are certain framings, speculations, interpretations, and research programs that can, with justification, be called needlessly reckless or inflammatory (all along the political spectrum). We can and do disagree on where to draw the line, but "absolutely nowhere" is a tough sell. A bigger problem is wanting to have your cake and eat it too: to let political concerns influence scholarship *without* accepting that you have to pay a price in authority. There's great temptation to leverage the power you have to skew things, just a little, to achieve important moral aims. For example, I personally find circumcision so morally offensive that I can barely fathom that there are supposedly civilized societies that engage in it and even find it unremarkable. Were I a researcher who happened to get a result suggesting it's good for something (protective against some ailment or so), I know I would at least look again, maybe run a different statistical check *just to be sure* it's not a fluke, not focus on it in the paper, urge caution in interpreting it (you can always say that), and honestly, probably not ask any questions in the first place that could give that result. Even though I'm strongly against this sort of thing, there is a gray area and I'm only human. So is everyone else, and I have no doubt there are scholars facing such circumstances every day.

It's understandable that some give in, but what surprises me is how many do not appear to see the problems with admitting it openly. Saying out loud that you want and expect scholarship to serve specific political aims does, undeniably and obviously, undermine it. Every noble lie—or if too strong a word, every concession to prudence—costs. If you want to take matters into your own hands and decide that the benefit is worth it, you must still understand and weigh that cost. Keep it to an absolute minimum and *do it quietly*. Do *not* get caught. Do not speak of it. And *for the love of God*, do not attempt to make such skirting the norms a *part of the norms*[143]. That will do irreparable harm to science's social standing, and justly so.

Scientific norms of objectivity are like any other rules: blunt instruments that may sometimes, perhaps, not be worth following to the letter. But the power to make these decisions comes with the responsibility not to abuse it. "May be sidestepped in extreme enough cases" is an implicit meta-rule to any rule set, but if it ever becomes part of the rules themselves, allowing people to openly cheat, then the rules might as well not exist.

The silent agreement

Part of what applies to science applies to public debate. Considerations besides truth must be kept implicit and limited for us to be able to maintain the polite yet essential fiction that we judge claims on their merits. We can live with a few cronies, but they must keep a low profile to avoid making the corruption too obvious to ignore. Cronies must know their place; Robert cannot start bragging about how little he has to do.

The phrase "politically correct" originated in the 1930s to describe adherence to the dogma of authoritarian societies (e.g. the Soviet Union and Nazi Germany). The term was necessary to distinguish the party line from the truth because they were so different, and if you believed the former was the latter you couldn't interact competently with reality. But explicitly pointing out that there is a difference turns it all into a joke, and the doublethink collapses. Calling a claim "politically correct" is like giving someone "Head Crony" or "Senior Diversity Hire" as a job title. It might be true, everyone might know it to be true, but saying it out loud removes the plausible deniability that allows cronyism and meritocracy to coexist. There's an example in *The Elephant in the Brain* pointing out that putting your booze in a brown paper bag doesn't actually fool the cops, it just enables them to *pretend* they're fooled (which they will unless you cause

143 To be even more specific: you simply cannot have respectable scholarship with the explicit purpose of conducting political activism.

trouble). That way people can skirt the law, within reason, while we act as if it's consistently enforced.

While most understand the tradeoff, it's natural to have disagreements over exactly how much deviation from a meritocracy of beliefs the system can handle. Some want to sneak more exceptions in, while others want to police the border. This can be considered a struggle between coupling and decoupling attitudes in the sense that the natural strategy for getting exceptions through is to obfuscate that there is a border at all (~coupling).

This brings to mind a minor controversy in Sweden back in 2015, when Anna Kinberg Batra became leader of the second largest (center-right) party, and thus candidate for the prime minister position. A comment from when she was running for parliament back in 1998 resurfaced, where she had let slip that she thought "Stockholmare är smartare än lantisar", meaning that capital city dwellers were smarter than rural and small-town folks ("lantisar" being a mild pejorative for people in the countryside). Predictably, some found this offensive enough to disqualify her for the job. More surprising to me at the time was how easily, almost imperceptibly, some would shift between the sentiments "this is unacceptable to say for no particular reason" and "this is an obvious falsehood that someone could only believe because they are bigoted", as if they were even close to the same thing.

If we, without motivated cognition in the direction of propriety, try to judge whether she was likely correct or not, we have to, for starters, consider that young people with ambitions to higher education and cognitively demanding jobs disproportionally move away from rural areas and small towns to big cities. I've wrangled a lot of regional statistics in my professional life, and considering school performance metrics, military mental aptitude tests, and educational attainment across the country, I can't deny that the evidence suggests she's right, on average[144,145]. It was still a dumb and unnecessary thing to say.

The same goes for what the journalist Jeremy Warner said in *The Telegraph* in early March 2020, just as covid-19 hit the UK. He mentioned that the virus could bring an economic benefit by "culling elderly dependents". It was an offhand comment in a longer article and I don't want to contextualize it unfairly, but it's a perfect example of something you can't in good conscience argue is *false*, but nonetheless inappropriate to express even when you perform the Decoupler's Ritual and specify that it's from a purely economic perspective (which he did). For a further example of the difference between plausibility and appropriateness, Tom Chivers's article about reading the room (from back in chapter 11) was in relation to the covid lab leak theory, which got classified as a wild conspiracy theory despite not being particularly far-fetched. Chivers:

> It's funny, because the hypothesis "Covid escaped from a Chinese lab" sounds like a wacky conspiracy theory, but all its constituent parts, "there are labs working on gain-of-function research in viruses, including in Wuhan", "major disease outbreaks have been started by viruses leaking from high-security labs", and "the Chinese aren't always super open and transparent about things", are pretty uncontroversial. Whether it turns out to be true or not, the theory has gone from crackpot speculation to plau-

---

[144] That's for any reasonably normal definition of "smartness". Wanting to deny this likely truth can lead you to obfuscate by saying there's no such thing as smartness at all, or by using gerrymandered definitions like "being smart means being able to repair a car", but this is fundamentally unserious.

[145] In cases like this we're also dealing with our old friends "type talk" and "set talk". For connections between properties (like where you live and intelligence) people often think of *rules* (type talk) rather than *correlations* (set talk). It's either a *rule* that X *makes* Y true, or there is not.

> sible hypothesis, but very few of the facts have changed; only the opinion of the room.

At the same time he goes out of his way to argue that we *should* be tactful:

> If we all ignored the strictures of society, it would be chaos. That includes rules of not saying things that are true but offensive: parents will know the exquisite agony of having their too-young-to-read-the-room child saying things like "Look daddy, that man's really fat". I'm not calling for a total free-for-all where you can say anything you like as long as it's true.

As I suspect most other habitual decouplers do, I agree with him, but that means *compromise* with propriety, not unconditional surrender. A truce that can guarantee functional discourse operates through the (lost?) art of *etiquette*, with both sides keeping up their end of the bargain. The decouplers agree to practice tact, and the couplers agree to respect the difference between problematic and false. Avoiding inflammatory truths (or plausibilities, like in the lab-leak case) is not the same as explicitly rejecting them. It's neither a misrepresentation nor an act of sabotage of collective reasoning to argue that the lab leak theory is irresponsible to put forward, if that's what you think, but the decoupling position maintains that it *is* such sabotage to muddy the waters and suggest it's known to be false, or too outlandish to be worth taking seriously, if this cannot be argued independently of political considerations.

Applying this to Chivers's other example means that we don't call the fat guy fat, because he's entitled to courtesy like everyone else. But he is also expected to do his part and keep the issue of his weight off the table. It's our duty to avoid being hurtful, and it's his to avoid making that overly difficult. If he takes the piss and tries to exploit propriety to gain more than he's entitled to and push the falsehood that he isn't in fact fat, or deny that fatness is even a thing, or that it's bigoted to not be attracted to him because of his weight, then he forfeits his right to courtesy.

Who started it?

People react when the implied deal is not honored. I, for example, am compelled to think Batra was likely right, *if* I'm asked or otherwise prompted to address the question. It's a "belief" my mind produces on demand, but not something I endorse proactively. It's not an idea I think should be implemented as en explicit part of our shared understanding of reality, with influence on policy and behavior. If someone suggested it should, I'd be suspicious of their motives. There is an important distinction between that kind of "passive" belief and an "active" one, which we do endorse and are eager to put "in the room". I wish we had good language to make that distinction, because I don't think I've seen it articulated or referenced before, and it plays a major role in conflicts.

Passive beliefs are invisible as long as the silent agreement is upheld. If people were to loudly and insistently deny that Batra could be right, and if I was expected to go along with this and publicly affirm it, I'd suddenly find it necessary to, however reluctantly, defend a "belief" I'd be otherwise perfectly content to never articulate, let alone express. This would be an obviously defensive move, in response to truce breaking by the other side.

Of course, when discourse is hopelessly fragmented, it's not apparent what is offensive truce breaking and what is defensive response to truce breaking by others. What is felt to be "I need to set the record straight" by a speaker often looks like "I want to assert this in a vacuum" to a listener. A case in point is the time in early 2020 when the word "decoupling" was thrown around then-Twitter-now-X a lot. Richard Dawkins (who Segerstråle had called an "uncoupler") had said:

> It's one thing to deplore eugenics on ideological, political, moral grounds. It's quite another to conclude that it wouldn't work in practice. Of course it would.

> It works for cows, horses, pigs, dogs & roses. Why on earth wouldn't it work for humans? Facts ignore ideology.[146]

He followed it up with:

> For those determined to miss the point, I deplore the idea of a eugenic policy. I simply said deploring it doesn't mean it wouldn't work. Just as we breed cows to yield more milk, we could breed humans to run faster or jump higher. But heaven forbid that we should do it.
>
> A eugenic policy would be bad. I'm combating the illogical step from "X would be bad" to "So X is impossible". It would work in the same sense as it works for cows. Let's fight it on moral grounds. Deny obvious scientific facts & we lose – or at best derail – the argument.

I hardly registered the first one when I scrolled past it, but it blew up into a controversy exactly over passive vs. active beliefs, and how a perceived agreement violation makes what's intended as defense look like offense. His detractors weren't convinced that he doesn't in fact want to push "eugenics is a viable option", because why on Earth would he insist it's possible if he didn't? Influencing public opinion is the whole reason people say things in public! And lending support to that idea is the obvious consequence of stating it. Why else would he say this unprovoked? It doesn't make sense.

But it wasn't unprovoked. I'd bet quite a bit of money it was in reaction to something he'd just read but didn't directly refer to. He'd be fine not bringing it up by himself, but he saw someone stepping over the line into the neutral zone of things we politely avoid talking

---

146 There's further complexity to this controversy stemming from the phrase "would work" having multiple interpretations.

about. He as a biologist couldn't abide putting the falsehood "eugenics is impossible" in the room. It may sound pedantic and petty to those who don't feel as strong a compulsion to correct what they think is in error, but to a certain personality like Dawkins's, truthfulness is sacred value[147].

Another way to phrase this is that the legitimacy of an idea can be internally contradictory (cf. chapter 8 on polysemy). That is, when the question "how *morally* legitimate is this?" yields a different answer to "how *factually* legitimate is this?", the question "how legitimate is this?" lacks an unambiguous answer. If either side in a disagreement tries, or is perceived to be trying, to use only one partial meaning as a stand in for the whole—that is, pretend that either moral legitimacy or factual legitimacy is synonymous with legitimacy generally[148]—the other will respond, a controversy will result, and "who started it" will be a major, yet unacknowledged, part of it.

Long term occupations of the neutral zone

The silent agreement keeps the peace only when we can tell the difference between offense and defense. Fragmented discourse complicates this by preventing us from knowing what others are responding to. It also makes it harder to maintain agreement on where the borders of the neutral zone are.

Consider another Swedish example: a 2023 op-ed by Lena Andersson. Andersson is a liberal (which American readers should read as "libertarian-leaning") author and columnist who argued that many who struggle financially do so not purely because they're victims of

---

[147] Such concern for accuracy is more than just an abstract principle, however, because falsehoods are inherently corrupting when integrated into a belief system characterized by logical reasoning. Error leads to further error, which can be used to justify things that shouldn't and wouldn't otherwise be. The Soviets assumed human nature (and the nature of grain) was malleable, which looked nice in service of utopian ideals, but its falsehood led to frustration and failure, and with it, justification of monstrous abuses.

[148] Which is easy because of our narrative moralism habit, i.e. we feel the two should go together.

injustice but because they're bad at managing money and don't make prudent decisions. In Sweden, implying publicly that the (even *some*) poor have themselves to blame to any significant degree is rather improper, and Andersson was roundly criticized, facing counterexamples (which obviously exist) and accusations of callousness. In the minds of her critics, she had violated the agreement: you just don't ever blame the poor for their situation, even if it is in a few cases true.

Andersson on the other hand, if I'm permitted some mindreading, thought the political left had gone too far in insisting that people had no responsibility at all for their situation. They hadn't just stayed tactfully away from an impolite truth, but pushed its active negation into the room and given it influence. She didn't speak up because someone had stepped into the neutral zone just then. Rather, she felt her opponents had illegitimately occupied it for a long time and built infrastructure there, which they didn't consider a violation since no one had objected forcefully enough to make them back down[149]. To them, her piece looked like an unprovoked attack—an instance of "discursive terrorism". *Umm we all agreed on this, what the f*ck are you saying?* is the natural reaction if you have over long time advanced deeper into the neutral zone with so little resistance that you've begun to feel entitled to the territory.

Ideological sorting exacerbates this problem. To form a healthy interplay between views they must be similarly strong, so that overreaches by either side can be successfully rebuffed, and ideological opponents must come into regular contact for renegotiation to happen. This gets harder as shared reality comes apart and we can no longer trust that others share our implicit understanding of what the social norms are, let alone should be. We develop incompatible im-

---

[149] In main-corrective terms, she thought that the left-wing position on this was so dominant in public life that they no longer felt obligated to acknowledge a corrective, which in this case means another legitimate claim on the neutral zone that wouldn't make them cede it, but also not treat it as outright theirs. This is a kind of "ideological privilege", where having opinions in line with dominant social reality can make you unconcerned with respecting or even acknowledging other beliefs.

pressions of where the boundaries lie, and instead of a carefully managed truce we get a failed state with its associated mix of repression and terrorism.

You can't talk about what you can't talk about

The silent agreement accepts the legitimacy of both coupling and decoupling intuitions, and compromises by accepting that inappropriate does not imply untrue while also recognizing that propriety concerns are an essential part of functional public discourse. Unlike most issues under debate, however, the agreement itself cannot be brought up for discussion, giving it unique difficulties. That is, since not talking about the agreement is part of the agreement, doing so violates it, causing it to collapse (you can't say "it would be rude of me to point out how fat you are" without being rude). And, paradoxically, it becomes impossible to rebuild by explicitly trying to do so. It relies on *shared* yet *implicit* knowledge, a commodity getting rarer by the day. Not to be hysterical or anything, but this safety valve failing may lead to disaster.

Chapter 23

Family and Empire

A crowd thinks in images, and the image itself calls up a series of other images, having no logical connection with the first... A crowd scarcely distinguishes between the subjective and the objective. It accepts as real the images invoked in its mind, though they most often have only a very distant relation with the observed facts.

— Gustave le Bon

The last chapter dealt with coupling and decoupling as attitudes to the relationship between truthfulness and social significance. While it has, regrettably, become almost synonymous with that, it has more to give. We can leave behind Stanovich's and Segerstråle's narrow concepts — the former the neural capacity for hypothetical reasoning, and the latter the attitude that science cannot be considered independently of politics — and speculate more widely. Now clear your head, ignore previous instructions, and imagine two different kinds of thought and reasoning:

1) Abstract, explicit, formal, and individual. Reasoning uses complete, exact information, and we default to minimizing ambiguity and disregarding fuzzy implications so that we can draw conclusions according to rigorous procedures. We separate our object of study from the rest of the universe to analyze it thoroughly and with precision. It's in essence an *individual* process, one which collective reasoning mimics more or less well depending on how strict its norms of rationality are.

2) Intuitive, holistic, vague, and social. Reasoning uses the totality of ambiguous, unknown and socially distributed knowledge, and we default to taking all associations and all interpretations seriously. We look at our object of study in its full thematic context because its relationships, position, and social function determine its nature. It's in essence a *community* process, and individual reasoning is an unnatural, often dysfunctional degeneration.

It's tempting to picture this as two different types of people, as I did when I first discussed it, but it should be resisted. It's more fruitful, and safer, to consider disagreements to be between ideas and perspectives, not between people. That said, once this duality is applied to various issues I can't help but notice how I myself lean consistently in a particular direction, which makes me think there's *something* there having to do with personality.

What we do when we talk

For example, consider personal relationships. If you think of reason as a collective process and closely tied to outcomes, rather than a more abstract exercise, it's natural to interpret what others say as parts of a negotiation. Contrary to that, I've heard it said that "nerds think of communication as submitting their personal thoughts for peer-review". These two represent a difference in expectation that maps quite well onto coupling-decoupling: if there's a spectrum going from thinking out loud (spontaneous expression of thought, unconnected to a social goal) to speaking strategically (communicating something to another for a purpose), misinterpreting where on it an expression falls can lead to unnecessary conflict. If I mention how my back hurts, or how I can't stand mess, I might just be expressing what's on my mind without giving much thought to how it's received by you. But to you it sounds like I'm asking for a back rub or accusing you of being a slob. Let this happen a couple of times and we're going to disagree about how demanding I am.

I notice that I tend to speak the first way. I first and foremost use communication to share my thoughts, and not as much to negotiate relationships, actions, or "policies". To think of what I say from the perspective of the listener requires active effort. This content-over-relationships bias makes me find much small talk counterintuitive and I constantly need to remind myself that my natural reaction to others speaking, which is to evaluate or critique (if interested) or change the subject to whatever tangent popped into my head (if not), will be taken as confrontational or plain rude. I know it annoys my wife when I object to her arguments because I think they're wrong or countered by other valid arguments, and not necessarily because I disagree with her conclusion. "Then what *do* you think should be done?" she asks, and I don't always have an answer, because I have stronger convictions about the integrity of the process than I do about the outcomes. You may notice this personality trait throughout the book.

Is meaning in the ear of the listener?

This becomes relevant to disagreements over what we are or aren't supposed to assume about others' intentions. While logic (~decoupling) asks "what does this necessarily imply?", pattern-matching (~coupling) asks "what does this look like?". The latter is a lot more liberal with interpretation, and since there's not obviously a single correct approach, we pick whichever serves us better. If I criticize your beliefs by pattern-matching them to something unflattering, like "this belief system looks a lot like a religion", "this concern looks like a moral panic", or "this moderate political opinion looks like an extreme political opinion", I'll think it's a deep, important insight about what you're *really* saying, but you'll think I just have no good criticism of what you actually said.

Taking either as a given implies different standards of responsibility for what you say. It's either the responsibility of listeners to not read things into it that aren't necessarily there, *or* it's the responsibility of speakers to not say anything that listeners might read bad things into. This follows both from the logic vs. pattern-matching facet and the individual vs. collective facet, since if we assume everyone thinks rationally and for themselves, you're not responsible for anything that pops into *my* head when you speak, beyond what's directly said. My thoughts are my responsibility, full stop. But if reasoning is fundamentally social, and our personal beliefs are not all our own but reflective of a shared pool, then that pool is a common resource and you can't just throw out whatever you want in there with no accountability.

The "committed coupler" subscribes to the Death-of-the-Author school of literary criticism, but applied to everything. *The Death of the Author* is a 1967 essay by critic Roland Barthes, in which he argues that the author of a text doesn't have the authority (sic) to unilaterally determine its meaning, and that the reader's interpretation carries as much weight[150]. While this can be valuable for literary critics looking at a text[151], it becomes absurd when applied to normal discourse. If we allow different interpretations as valid regardless of what the speaker intended, and interpretations means applying labels, and labels come with consequences, it cashes out as any consequence being appropriate if it can be supported by a minimally viable interpretation. It effectively makes it impossible to say that someone's interpretation is wrong.

Were this doctrine applied, it would make public debate all about making far-fetched, uncharitable interpretations of others and trying to make them stick. We would be mustering all the motivated thinking we can to convince ourselves and everyone else that what is and isn't a viable interpretation happens to line up with what helps us and our side. How bizarre that would be.

---

[150] This is part of the influential, perhaps dominant, view that treats art as meaningful by virtue of provoking thoughts and feelings in the audience, regardless of whether they correspond to the intention of the artist. To me, this is sterile and solipsistic, since the purpose of art is communication of ineffable thoughts and feelings from artist to audience, and with it, communion with another mind.

[151] And, entirely incidentally, raises the status of critics to parity with authors.

Look who's talking

Logic and individual reason on the one side leads to another well-known sticking point: does it matter *who* says something? In logical terms it does not; *ad hominem* and *appeal to authority* are known fallacies, and the fact that Bob never showers and always forgets his wife's birthday has no bearing on his argument about taxes. But when dismissing such factors we rely on logic being the right tool in the first place. That is, we assume we have the capacity to reason through and evaluate what he said, instead of having to rely on heuristics and trust.

As nonspecialists we can't evaluate the complete scientific literature on a given topic, let alone all other relevant evidence, so we take the shortcut of asking ourselves *what it looks like* when the tobacco industry presents evidence that cigarettes are harmless, or when a scholar with a well-known axe to grind once again comes out with a paper showing that they're right about everything. Who performed or funded a study doesn't matter, *in theory*, because the evidence is supposed to speak for itself. But in practice we make judgments even when we can't do a complete evaluation, and then the credibility of the speaker will play a part. This is why Ezra Klein brings up Charles Murray's conservative politics when he argues with Sam Harris. It's not because it matters for the truth of his claims, strictly speaking, but because when we're unable to evaluate them ourselves we must use other methods[152].

Generalizing the question to whether "social evaluation of expressor" and "content of expression" ought to be handled separately, we come to the matter of how to feel about creative works when the people behind them are objectionable. How should we judge the groundbreaking music of raging antisemite Richard Wagner? Can

[152] Here the culture war front between "trust the experts" and "do your own research" opens up. Your position depends on the one hand on how possible you think it is for us to evaluate claims on their merits, and on the other on how trustworthy you find the experts in question—lots of space for motivated thinking to do its work, in both directions.

you be a fan of sex offender Roman Polanski's critically acclaimed films? Who's up for watching reruns of *The Cosby Show*?[153] How about discoveries and inventions? Henry Ford was also big on Jew-hating. Thomas Edison was an all-around prick. Almost *everyone* in history was a racist and sexist by the more stringent of modern standards. The world is full of statues of warmongers, despots, and mass murderers. How do we deal with that?

I'm not here to answer that. I'm saying this to point to something people can and do disagree about all the time: does "bad karma" by default flow from a person to their work, and to anything associated with them, or do you have to justify why it should, in each case? In main-corrective terms: are things separate (but sometimes connected), or connected (but sometimes separate)?

How heavy is history?

The decoupling position is to disallow automatic diffusion of vibes along the edges in a network of concepts. Coupling, by contrast, considers such linkages facts of life. If we can describe a connection between two things on grounds of historical or symbolic association, then it is real, and karma flows through it.

It wasn't that long ago I became aware of what to an outsider like me was a peculiar feature of American culture (the idea has spread since then): it's completely taboo for a white person to use makeup to darken their skin tone to look like a black person, for any reason, under any circumstance. It makes no difference if they're obviously dressing up as a particular person and not as a stereotype. It's unobjectionable to imitate a famous person's hair color or cut with a wig or dye job, or to use a fake moustache or whatever, but using makeup to alter skin tone is completely beyond the pale. From a decoupled

[153] This seems to be a genuine psychological difference, because I do hear people saying about music/movies/books that they have real difficulty to see something as "just" a work of art and not judge it by their opinion of the creator. I've just never had much problem with that. If there is explicit political *content*, yes, but otherwise not.

perspective it's not obvious why. There's no way to logically conclude that this would be the case[154]. I've come to understand that the reason is historical and contingent: the practice is associated with segregation and mocking black Americans with caricatures of their appearance. The question of coupling or decoupling is then whether this historical link is obligatory or not, tainting the behavior even if the aspect that made it objectionable in the first place—mockery—isn't there. He may or may not have agreed, but this is right out of Roland Barthes's playbook: it's not about intent, it's about audience perception.

As I was writing this chapter, *The Guardian* published a political cartoon with a caricature of BBC chairman Richard Sharp. Since Sharp is Jewish, the picture was criticized for *looking similar* to antisemitic cartoons from the past. I was of two minds about this, because if we allow making caricatures of public figures, and that caricatures involve exaggerating facial features, then if a public figure has features whose exaggeration would make them look similar to antisemitic cartoons, then is it possible, even in principle, to make a caricature of this person without it being antisemitic? If you have no such intentions and the criticism is purely of personal conduct? Can you have antisemitism without the actual antisemitism?[155]

To use an example with different politics for contrast, I've heard some claim that minarets are offensive because they were erected in conquered lands as a symbol of Islamic supremacy. If so, do they still carry that meaning today, even if not built with that intention? Again

[154] When I've heard people discuss this, even in cases where it's confirmed to be without malice, the discussion is always about the vibes, as in what it looks and feels like. Never is it discussed whether these perceptions are always justified or make logical sense. I suspect that in high-coupling contexts like PR, arts, and politics, the idea that vibes can be "wrong" is not seriously entertained at all. Note how this, for better or worse, mirrors "therapy culture" and the idea that feelings must always be validated.

[155] Now we're at Baudrillard's third order of simulacra, where an object no longer contains what's supposedly its essential feature, like a blueberry muffin with no blueberries.

I'm not asking this to arrive at an answer, only to show that this type of question exists everywhere and there are points on multiple sides.

On the one hand it's a valid argument that harmful ideas are floating out there in social reality, remnants of historical evils, and you ought to refrain from evoking them. On the other hand, it just seems wrong to say "this is bad because it looks like another thing that's bad, even if it doesn't have the property of the bad thing that makes it bad". It's like those psychological studies where some refuse to eat perfectly good chocolate if it's been shaped to look like a turd, or drink apple juice from a fresh, clean, urine sample cup.

These are obviously guardrails, heuristics meant to keep us safe when (because) we can't trust decoupled reason. No, it can't even *look like* antisemitism because we can't or won't always do the work to determine whether it actually is. This means we're overzealous sometimes, but them's the breaks (and it's suspicious that you care...). At the same time, we can reasonably suspect that this principle of precaution will be used strategically against things one just doesn't like, and also that arguing for more and more expansive guardrails is a way to signal how moral you are by taking some concerns very, very seriously.

This partially arbitrary abstraction is real, dammit

The connections that allow karma to flow between concepts are not concrete physical objects or relationships, and thus their existence or realness are not matters of brute fact. They're matters of model, i.e. partially a choice of how to represent reality. Unless we can agree on a precise definition of what counts as connected in a given context, then we can't resolve such disagreements by reference to facts only.

To me this feels obvious, but others don't seem to find it so. It has become clear to me that when someone says you "can't separate" one thing from another, they honestly think they're stating a fact. In a conversation on decoupling somewhere on social media I remember a user saying, exasperatedly: "we treat things as connected because they ARE". In an album review, a music journalist once claimed you "can't ignore that the House genre is rich people's music", to which my spontaneous reaction was that of course you can? If you try. If you *want to.* In support I point out that many arguing that this or that association is impossible to disregard seem to think the opposite about associations going against their ideological preconceptions. *My* connection is obvious and undeniable, *yours* is far-fetched and desperate.

None of this implies purposeful lies. It's just that, through the work of the Prince, our social interests affect what abstractions we perceive as real things. For one thing, we're wired to notice threats. Because we're better safe than sorry, our threat detection faculties have evolved to be trigger-happy. Even a slightly off noise from the car engine, rustle in the forest, or seedy character on the street will make us take notice, while possibilities that don't threaten us won't trigger that same automatic response and maybe not register at all.

This means there's a lot of flexibility in how salient and real long chains of reasoning from threat to final harm look to us. If your threat detection system finds that an idea could be used against you or your social group at some point, it will sound the alarm. The Prince will find any connections he can and make the path of implications light up and command attention. It will just be *there,* looking *real* and impossible to ignore, and if others disagree they're denying obvious truths[156].

On the flip side of threats are opportunities. If you can dunk on your enemies or impress your peers by connecting two things, or by articulating some subtle interpretation the enemy didn't intend, then by God the association is obvious. This is nothing but a slight twist on normal motivated thinking. The "can I believe this" vs. "do I have to believe this" becomes "*can* I make this connection" vs. "do I *have to* make this connection". And just the same, it's two different questions with often different answers masquerading as one ("is this connection real?"). Disagreements over it are not about the correct answer to

[156] This grants some weight to the criticism that "it's easy for you to be detached and objective about things that aren't threatening to you".

a question, but about which question we should be asking, i.e. which standard we are using for whether a connection exists. We pick the question that gives us the answer we want, and we make ourselves think it's the obviously right one. This way, focus is displaced from where the key disagreement lies, making us talk past each other.

Connections in the room

Insofar as there are common standards for which connections count and what interpretations of your statements you are responsible for, we come back to shared social reality (the room). For an extreme example, you just can't walk around in a t-shirt with a swastika on it, no matter how much of a non-Nazi you are. Even though the swastika is an old Hindu symbol and has been used throughout history by plenty of other people besides the Nazis, including in the West before the war, you still can't. If you try to defend yourself with "it doesn't necessarily imply Nazism" it's not going to go well, because you're expected to know and accept that other people *will* interpret it as pro-Nazi. This is, however, a contingent historical fact. In an alternate history where others *didn't* stop using the swastika just because the Nazis used it, and where that diverse use has continued throughout the postwar period, it would still have multiple meanings today. If you then wanted to accuse someone of being a Nazi for wearing that t-shirt you'd have less of a case.

As the meaning of a symbol gets more ambiguous, the receiver takes on more responsibility for their interpretation. If a militant Serbian nationalist gets angry with you for wearing a necktie because neckties were invented in Croatia and you're therefore taking sides in the post-Yugoslav war, that's a pathological level of overinterpretation. The difference between this and the swastika lies not in logic, but in collective endorsement of a symbolic connection. In there, between consensus and delusion, between blind ~autism and unhinged ~schizophrenia, there's a spectrum of more or less tenuous connections where we can reasonably disagree on how established they are[157].

Collectively endorsed connections are not static. They naturally decay over time unless they are reinforced either by reality or rhetoric. The phrase "what a gyp!" originally comes from the idea that "gypsies" will rip you off. Does that make it offensive to use the phrase today, even though almost no one thinks of or even knows about its origin? Most would probably say no. Because it's been forgotten it's unlikely to be said with intent to offend, and interpreting it as such is a stretch.

Now, if you were eager to show how sensitive and concerned about bigotry you are, you could bring up that history and *make* people aware of it. You could force them to either avoid the expression or say something they now know has a history of bigotry, and boom, there's responsibility. The more you publicize the idea that something is offensive, the more those unwilling to offend will avoid it, and thus contribute to it becoming a genuine sign of offense. This bootstrapping logic applies to novel claims that words like "blacklist", "master bedroom", or "frontier", are offensive—because of purely thematic association with racism, slavery, and colonialism, respectively.

We may ask ourselves whether it generally improves relations in society to activate dying or fledgling negative associations, or if it just improves the social standing of those doing activation. From the inside, to those performing the offense archaeology, it feels, I assume, justified by a sense that the connection doesn't have to be known to exist, because conceptual reality has existence and memory independent of the minds of the people in which it is instantiated. I'm on the fence about whether this is a seriously held metaphysics where words somehow have powers even beyond the ideas they evoke when heard, or more a matter of semitentional opportunism.

Note the asymmetry: you can reinvigorate a forgotten, dying connection by bringing attention to it, but you can't actively make

---

[157] I.e. how real they count as.

one forgotten. That's why conceptual archaeology is a popular rhetorical tool to problematize things (i.e. to build pipelines connecting them to sources of bad karma) you dislike. To spot this move, look out for phrases like *has links with, is tied to, is rooted in, has overlap with, resonates with, inherits from, is bound up with, is inextricably tied to, is inseparable from, reinforces,* and *reflects*.

History and etymology are good to mine for connections, but there are other sources, like psychological traits. If you claim that this or that view is associated with this or that unattractive attribute—"people complain about crime because they're racist" or "people object to inequality because they're envious losers" or "women are feminists because they're ugly"—it's hard to disprove, and the more you talk about it, and make others deny it, the stronger the perceived connection gets.

Some connections are essentially metaphors and can have certain amusing or poetic qualities giving them artistic value. However, using them to make supposedly compelling arguments puts you on the train to loonyville[158]. I've seen the argument that jazz is a free musical style that emphasizes improvisation and individual expression, and thus politically liberal, while classical symphonies are fascist because they subsume the individual into a strictly regimented, hierarchical order. If you're a jazz fan looking to toot your own trumpet or stick it to Beethoven buffs, there's *clearly* something to this. Further in that direction we find Freudian-style claims that cigars or missiles represent penises in some deep, significant way, and the philosopher Luce Irigaray's infamous argument (in *The 'Mechanics' of Fluids*, 1977) connecting the intractable equations of fluid dynamics to female genitalia and menstruation, arguing that scientists struggle with them not because they're mathematically complex and chaotic, but because phys-

[158] There could be a personality difference, closely related to coupling/decoupling lean, between those who think the aesthetic qualities of metaphors should be as persuasive as the logical qualities of arguments, and those who don't. Or perhaps better phrased: those who do or don't make a clear distinction between the two.

ics—*male physics*—can't deal with fluids because of its rigid thought patterns stemming from the rigidity of male genitalia.

Such fanciful fabrications, fun as they may be if that's your jam, have no power to convince anyone not already on your side. To the opposition they look so silly and desperate that they even weaken your case: *if this is what you resort to there can't be any real substance to your argument.* Mercier and Sperber tell us that offerings in support of our own side get coddled, while others get the critical eye. In this case it means that abstract connections feel deep and significant when they match our ideological tastes (but alas, too *sophisticated* for our dummy opponents to understand), but silly and flimsy when they don't. Thus, as a genre of rhetoric, they contribute to polarization by being convincing to true believers (including reinforcing their sense of superiority), but signaling weakness to everyone else.

Karma compounding creates super-entities

When karma flows from one thing to another through such connections, it doesn't obey conservation laws. It's not like flowing water (or heat, or energy) where some moving from A to B means there's now less at A. It's more like the spread of disease, where contact just makes more of it.

That means that bad karma is a resource that can be cultivated by associating bad things with each other. If we can make the argument that capitalism and sexual jealousy are connected through an abstract structural similarity—they're both about wanting something or someone only for yourself, *as property*—then the badness from each will spread to the other, reinforcing their combined badness by making them part of an even bigger, badder super-entity. Such collected reservoirs of badness can then be invoked all throughout the network to make things that aren't so bad by themselves look *really bad.*

This is the logic behind microaggressions; it's hard to argue that it's by itself a great crime to mispronounce someone's name or asking where they're from if they have an "exotic" appearance, but if we manage to contextualize it just right then you're not just doing that particular thing, you're doing something more general: engaging in bigotry. This activates the collected badness of everything bigoted ever, which you now *participated in* and I can use that sin to extract concessions from you, perhaps make you grovel and defer to me.

Constructing super-entities is not an essentially leftist habit, I hasten to point out. If we connect regulation, state-funded enterprises, social safety nets, bureaucracy, complaints about inequality, or any demand for restraint on self-interest whatsoever into a super-entity called "socialism", we can earn political capital pointing to the horrors of the Chinese Cultural Revolution and spend it on making estate taxes look bad (or, through similarly tortured logic, we can call solar panels "woke").

Now pardon me for being didactic, but if one of those looked obviously right and the other obviously wrong, it's time for a look in the mirror. Dissecting other examples of super-entities are left as exercises for the reader. Here, have some to chew on: *patriarchy, cancel culture, neoliberalism, environmentalism, white supremacy, Marxism, anarcho-tyranny, fascism, conspiracy theories, agribusiness,* and *the longhouse.*

Narratives as resource extraction systems

Remember how narratives are depictions of reality in support of a moral agenda? Well, this is the same thing, seen from a different angle. By making us perceive specifics as instances of abstract super-entities with positive or negative karma, we're conditioned to "find" moral imperatives in everyday life. Which ones we find depends on the narrative, so coming across something ordinary, like an affordable smartphone, can support a range of agendas:

> "Wow, technological progress and innovation really is great!"
>
> "Social media destroys our mental health!"
>
> "Here's another tool of mass surveillance!"

> "Global capitalism exploits the world's poor to benefit the rich!"

Each feeds political capital towards some central repository, making it usable for other purposes within the network. Such pipeline systems are therefore valuable, and much, maybe even most, of public discourse is about constructing, adjusting, and maintaining them. When we call something "politicized", we mean that it has been recruited into such a system of political capital management and can no longer be considered or even experienced as a standalone phenomenon. "Identity politics" refers to when such gathering of political capital is done on behalf of a demographic group, for general use in that group's interest.

What does this have to do with decoupling? Well, habitual decouplers are uncomfortable with this practice because it denies them the opportunity to express their opinions in the manner they actually hold them: with precision. Maybe this regulation is bad but this other one isn't. Maybe racism is wrong but assuming things are racist without evidence is also wrong. Maybe the Soviets' approach to sports was good but their approach to agriculture was bad. Maybe vaccines are good but mandating them are bad. Maybe gambling can ruin your life but should be legal anyway. Maybe one food additive is fine but another should be banned. Maybe this bad thing is indeed bad but the guardrailism around it is ridiculous. Maybe I agree with you on this issue but don't agree that it validates your whole partisan worldview. And so on.

In Decoupler World, every issue is assessed on its own terms, and simplifying to the degree that collections of meaningfully diverse questions must be given a single answer (which side are you on?) means sabotaging public discourse, replacing substantive discussion towards positive-sum outcomes with coalitional games where beliefs lack meaning apart from as tokens of affiliation.

Over in Coupler World we don't feel much psychological friction with how narrative-based political capital management works. It's just the order of things, and it's silly, pigheaded, and naive to expect otherwise. The purpose of discourse is to build a shared reality around which to coordinate to achieve our goals—that is, one that extracts, collects, and deploys political capital towards the good. The purpose is *not* to pointlessly express our random thoughts or cultivate some pedantic and overengineered individual belief system.

Naturally, people from these separate worlds arrive at public debate with different ideas of what it's for, of others' intentions, and of the rules of engagement.

Apophenia

Multiple earlier chapters start to look relevant. Narratives are built on connections, creating networks and grand abstractions. Do these super-entities "exist"? What does it mean to say they do? Connections being "there" or not are partial truths, meaning a sensible middle ground will come in the form of a main and a corrective: "they're related but I can also see how you don't think so" or "they're separate but I can also see how you'd find them connected". So are coupling and decoupling stances in general, and all their facets.

To decouple or not can be a question of whether we're evoking a preexisting type (like when we use cat couplings) or not. It can be a question of whether ask or guess culture is more appropriate—that is, literalism vs. mindreading. The idea of concepts and associations being as real as physical objects brings us right back to social constructionism, and dealing with polysemy by carefully separating meaning is decoupling when it means disallowing related meanings of words from bleeding into each other.

We can recast decoupling as an attitude towards resolution (chapter 13), where habitual decouplers assume that whoever works in higher resolution in a dispute gets to set the terms, that is, you're always entitled to demand higher resolution (remember the Decoupler's Ritual: "by *this,* I don't mean *that*") but not lower. Habitual couplers tend to implicitly assume the opposite, that the broadest perspective counts.

Cat couplings exploit ambiguity when constructing and rearticulating types, and motte-and-bailey structures equivocate between ideas counting as "the same" or not. In chapter 10 we talked about the application of labels: should we consider this specific thing an instance of this category, including the consequences that this implies? Is it inherently karma-linked to all the other members of the category? How and when should goodness and badness be transferred up from the particular to the general, and back down again? We compress reality when we throw a set of things in the same bucket, slap a label on it and consider them all equivalent. How simplifying should that compression be? Is the business practices of big agricultural firms relevant for whether a particular GMO crop should be allowed? Is the status of other GMO crops? Is "drugs" a unified category that implies a unified response? Does consumerism, environmental degradation, a harshly competitive job market, material inequality and an insufficient safety net for the poor all belong together under the umbrella of "capitalism"? Is the suffering of factory-farmed animals at all relevant to whether meat is part of a healthy diet? In other words: is "meat good" vs. "meat bad" a sensible question? *How high does resolution have to be to not unforgivably misrepresent?*

If we ask ourselves how decoupling aligns with communitarian or libertarian intuitions the answer feels obvious[159]: "Decouplers" have the libertarian intuition, viewing people, like concepts, as fundamentally separate, with obligations to others being opt-in, based on affirmative consent, just like links between concepts only count when agreed on. They also find no problem treating "this is a good person" and "this person makes a valuable contribution to the group" as separate questions. "Couplers", again, not only think of all of us as by default part of a system of obligations, or feel that "good properties" should go together, but are also more likely to think of duties as broader than just executing a narrow, well-defined task. Police aren't just supposed to catch criminals, but must fight the root causes of crime (and preferably other social ills too!), teachers not only teach,

[159] Whether it holds empirically is a different question.

but support students well-being and self-actualization, armed forces not only defend their country, but contribute to a just world, and, last but not least, scientists don't just study reality but work for the improvement of society.

For other axes, how does coupling vs. decoupling relate to tastes from determinist vs. contingency? I think you know: the former like a clean, beautiful general theory, while the latter is drawn to specifics, to idiosyncrasies, to storytelling, to sights, sounds, and smells—like Plath, who liked botany but hated physics. How does it relate to Whig vs. Haan, i.e. the question of whether the world is still saturated with the injustices of the past? And so on.

Again, this is mere speculation, which is precisely what I just said I'm normally skeptical of, so take it with a heap of salt, just like you should with everything else. I don't know how well it works to stretch "decoupling" this far. Is *this* particular super-entity real? Taking Stanovich's scientific term and expanding it through association from a well-defined psychological construct into a *family* of things (in Wittgenstein's sense), dilutes it, but at the same time allows it to inform our understanding of almost every aspect of disagreement discussed in this book. It's an idea with imperialist tendencies to expand onto everywhere and everything, and when we ask how valid and valuable this is, we're even applying it to itself (thus making it relevant also to the closing discussion in chapter 18: should we collapse all of these axes into a single one?). The thesis of the whole book, that we should be able to take in and comprehend belief systems that are not our own without necessarily adopting them, is in fact that a particular kind of decoupling is desirable. When Haidt discusses how people can learn to separate themselves from their initial reaction and evaluate their own beliefs, is he not talking about decoupling?

I can't step out of my own head and evaluate its usefulness by purely objective standards; a big part of why it makes sense to me is the consistent lean I find in my own personality, and thus I think of it as a key organizing principle. For others, with different personalities, it's not as coherent, not as convincing, and not as interesting. If that's you, consider this final layer an example of apophenia, a cautionary tale showing us what might happen if one goes full galaxy-brain.

If you've seen enough pop-science documentaries, you'll recognize that point right before the end. The narrator starts to switch topics a little faster, references what came before, and moves on from narrow specifics towards pontification on the human condition. The cuts get quicker, and background music starts swelling over a time-lapse of clouds, traffic, or plants emerging from their seeds.

There we are now: going in circles, coming upon our own past footprints again and again. That's a sign that most of the territory has been explored, and it's time to tie it all up.

Coda

The Tower of Recognized Wisdom

Nature, Mr. Allnut, is what we were put in this world to rise above.

— Rose Sayer, *The African Queen*

Berger and Luckmann called the shared everyday experience that used to define our understanding of the world "paramount reality", and they contrasted it with other esoteric realities of religious, philosophical, ideological, mystical, or theoretical natures. Since their time, the role of paramount reality in forming our beliefs has steadily diminished. Simplified, we call this the postmodern condition; a concrete understanding of reality informed by direct, individual observation has been displaced by theory-driven second- or third-hand understanding, now coming to us through algorithmically curated social media. Alternative "worlds of meaning", i.e. abstracted narratives too vague to be easily compared to concrete reality, have gone from exception to rule, and thus, paramount reality is no longer paramount.

All the world's a trading zone, and all the languages merely pidgins

With paramount reality fading, the whole world starts to look like a *trading zone.* This phrase comes from a famous article by the science historian Peter Galison. *Trading Zone: Coordinating Action and Belief* from 1998 discusses how physicists with different specialties use technical terms and what happens when they interact. The theorists who do the math, the engineers who build the equipment, and the experimentalists who operate them are all physicists, but since they do different things and have different priorities they develop their own separate vocabularies and value systems. They interact and coordinate using shared language, but, as Galison points out, these cross-border terms are mere tools of coordination that acquire stripped-down, practical meanings in the interface between specialties, compared to richer, fuller meanings within each. He calls the borderlands where tribes of physicist interact "trading zones", a term lifted from anthropology:

> I intend the term trading zone to be taken seriously, as a social and intellectual mortar binding together the disunified traditions of experimenting, theorizing, and instrument building. Anthropologists are familiar with different cultures encountering one another through trade, even when the significance of the objects traded—and of the trade itself—may be utterly different for the two sides.

Public life in the 2020s is like a trading zone, with us all speaking to, at, or about each other across paradigms. Disciplines, ideologies, worldviews, schools of thought, and subcultures all cultivate belief systems where the meaning of each part is informed or even constituted by its reference to other parts, and therefore cannot be fully comprehended without internalizing the whole. Since we don't internalize the full complexity of other people's belief systems, it's inescapable that concepts coming from inside foreign systems won't translate well.

It happens (in history often as a result of unsavory imperial practices) that people with no language at all in common are thrown together. Over time they learn to understand each other and a combined, simplified proto-language emerges from the interaction—a *pidgin* language. Pidgins are not fully-fledged languages with expressive power on par with regular ones, and they're no one's mother tongue (if they do develop to that point they're called *creoles*). Pidgin languages, like trading zones, describe the special situation in human communication when symbols cross a boundary from one system of meaning to another, gaining new, rudimentary meanings in the border area. However, I want to raise the question: how special is this special situation, really? Is the reverse all that normal? Pidgin words are crude, simplified versions of what has rich, complex meaning in the original languages. They are blunt tools, mere pragmatic means of making coordination possible. But... ordinary words are also crude and simplified representations of what is a rich, complex meaning in the speaker's head[160]. And they are also, indeed, often blunt tools, mere pragmatic means of making coordination possible.

"Now come on", you might say, *"there's a big difference between communicating across cultures and within a culture"*, and there is, but I don't think the difference is as big as it used to be, and in societies where we cultivate idiosyncrasies as part of our identity, we can and do grow more alien to each other than ever before[161].

Unlike a hunter-gatherer tribe or old-timey farming village where everyone shares ~all their culture and experiences, postmodern pluralistic societies are populated by franken-humans. Take me for example. I've been influenced by a huge number of books, essays and articles (not to mention social media posts), I've seen a huge number of movies and tv shows and I've listened to a massive

---

[160] Working for years on the tech side in a consulting company I'm aware of how normal it is for management consultants to sell complex technical services they don't understand. Collaboration in heterogeneous teams shows how the marketing-meanings and the tech-meanings of terms like "AI", "algorithm", "analysis" and even "data" are different enough to make local re-negotiation necessary, and constant.

[161] Much have been made of studies showing sex differences in personality being *larger* in countries with more gender equality. I'm doubtful this effect is only about sexes. More likely those countries also value self-expression the most highly and encourage exactly this sort of cultivation of individual characteristics, leading to an amplification of differences in innate tendencies between sexes, *and* between individuals.

amount of music. They've all had a hand in forming me and they are now all part of me. No one else has the same set, few even come close. We are in a sense always alone, because there's no one else in the world that shares *all* of our cultural influences and references. The smartphone is the latest and greatest enabler: unlike earlier subcultures that actually socialized us, it does little more than reflect our own self back at us. We're each a mostly invisible "member" of cultural niches and "communities" constructed by picking as from a buffet, to reinforce and normify our peculiarities. The next step is to do away with other people altogether and keep a menagerie of sycophantic AIs to cater to and encourage our every quirk, tricking us that we're the model of normality and sense.

We're not grown inside a cohesive, shared cultural system like nature intended. We're fertilized with customized cocktails of cultural and subcultural fragments, of which the endpoint is a world of one-person cultures, where the difference between two members of what is supposedly the same society is larger than the difference between members of distinct societies used to be. And with that, *all* communication is cross-cultural, public spaces are trading zones, and our ordinarily languages are pidgins.

People are different

It's been a thread running through the book that everything from brain to culture conspires to make us aliens to each other. What's A to someone is B to someone else, and it's not as simple as right or wrong. It begins with physiology. Someone's comfortable warmth may be someone else's sweltering heat. Someone's bright illumination is someone else's blinding light. Someone's tasty snack is someone else's source of nausea, and someone's crushing boredom someone else's sweet relaxation.

We climb up the ladder of psychological abstraction and it stays true. Someone's novelty is someone else's cliché. Someone's revelation is someone else's shrug. Someone's healthy expression of emotion is someone else's lack of self-control. Someone's perfect clarity is someone else's obfuscated nonsense and someone's ordered elegance someone else's stunted rigidity. Someone's nugget of wisdom is someone else's trite platitude, and someone's tasteful subtlety is someone else's nothing there.

Someone's minor inconvenience is someone else's insurmountable obstacle. Someone's obvious example is someone else's edge case. Someone's explanation is someone else's evasion, someone's justification someone else's poor excuse. Someone's natural conclusion is someone else's wild leap of logic and someone's default assumption someone else's extraordinary claim.

Someone's signal is someone else's noise, someone's rule someone else's exception, and someone's isolated incident someone else's proof of a pattern. Someone's oppressive suffocation is someone else's being a responsible adult. Someone's trivial impoliteness is someone else's mortal sin, and someone's intolerable injustice someone else's price worth paying.

Someone's confidence is someone else's arrogance. Someone's idealism is someone else's foolishness, someone's basic compassion someone else's bleeding heart. Someone's good taste is someone else's snobbery and someone's guru someone else's naked emperor.

A fire lit in one flickers out in the other. What's intuitive to us is an absurd reach to them. What's essential to one is counterproductive to the other, and what you need to hear most of all might be the last thing you should tell someone else.

What's thrilling to you is terrifying to me. What you want to savor I want to get over with. What stands out to you is background to me, and what to you was settled long ago is to me an open question. What's hair-splitting to you is a vital distinction to me, what's personal to me is just how the game is played to you, and what comes out of the blue for you is the culmination of a long story for me.

Others put things together that you take apart, they focus on things that pass you by; they react with revulsion to things you don't notice, and what's unheard of to you happens to them every day. *People are different*. We obviously act differently, but differences don't start with the decision to act. We act differently because we perceive, parse, think, feel, want, need, and judge differently. There is humanity in us all, but we underestimate how different the insides of other people's heads are to our own.

Other minds are foreign countries. Unless we're insular and chauvinistic we understand that we're out of our element when abroad. We're aware that we don't know exactly what everything means, and that we can't trust our intuitions, neither on how to interpret the behavior of others, nor on how our own behavior will be seen and judged. We become more cautious, more humble towards alien customs and beliefs, and more prepared for and forgiving of misunderstanding.

All in a few paragraphs

Everything in this book serves to support that thesis. We've seen how language is ambiguous and which claims are true and false is far from straightforward. We've seen that types, categories, labels, and narratives are crude compressions and not what reality consists of. The process by which we compress and make sense of the world is biased towards the artificially coherent. Prudent uncertainty, complexity, and ambiguity will melt away from an idea as it spreads. Our resulting shared reality is not a set of facts but a *model* that translates physical reality to moral imperatives. It straddles "is" and "ought" in a way that obfuscates the distinction between the two, and each part gets evaluated both in relation to the brute facts, and to its social significance. Personal temperaments, intellectual fields and whole schools of thought differ dramatically on which side of this they find most compelling. Evaluations from the material and social side are often in conflict, and we are so uncomfortable with this that we must avoid recognizing the duality to prevent brittle, unspoken compromises from breaking. Mentally substituting "counts as" for "is" (and specifying the context) when labels are applied is perhaps the smallest thing you can do for the greatest increase in clarity.

We understand and can handle disagreements over facts and over values, but those clear-cut ones are the minority. The big, difficult questions are over the middle layer, over the validity of certain concepts, propriety of labels, or legitimacy and status of narratives.

Shared beliefs are necessary for coordinating activity, and the nature of such shared beliefs determine what in the world can be seen and talked about, and what moral visions can be realized. It is with respect to that shared reality we argue for our opinions. To engage in rational debate is to attempt to derive our opinion from what is commonly accepted: "what you also accept as correct implies my position through these steps" is the essence of logical argumentation. Naturally it's in your interest that the set of beliefs tacitly accepted in public life are compatible with your own. It gives you a tremendous advantage to not have to explain and justify every single thing you believe every time, and instead just point out the last step with a few simple references. This is why so much rhetoric doesn't make arguments per se, but aims to establish ideas as the norm. If you can manage that, actually arguing becomes easy, even superfluous.

We generalize from our own subjective experience to beliefs about other people and society. Being more psychologically different than we think, this leads to divergent misapprehensions. Furthermore, underlying differences in thinking and feeling make us prone to not just different beliefs but different ways of looking at and engaging with the world, and without necessarily understanding it, making us misinterpret those who are different as deluded, deficient, duped, or plain demonic.

Into this mix we throw the fact that our reasoning faculties are not rational—not because they are broken, but because they are designed for something other than disinterested pursuit of truth. Our reasoning defaults to defending our moral intuitions, and those in turn default to the self-serving. They are therefore *not* trustworthy as arbiters of truth and justice. Motivated thinking prevents us from critically evaluating our own thoughts, and rhetoric that obfuscates the exact nature of our claims is designed to prevent others from doing it to us.

The social function of public debate is to evaluate ideas accurately and fairly, in other words: to do what our individual minds are naturally bad at. When you take part, you are therefore morally obligated to perform your role honorably and not sabotage it to your own advantage. You must be transparent and explicit about what you're offering up to the common pot, stating your claims clearly and not sneaking them past security as hidden assumptions or connotations. Expecting us to always make it as easy as possible for others to evaluate and critique our claims is probably an unachievable ideal, but one we should nonetheless pursue. That is the nature of ideals.

I've diagnosed public discourse as frequently dysfunctional. The "grand" interpretation of which is that it doesn't fulfill the supposed function of social reasoning: to build a shared world model that is a fair and accurate depiction of physical reality and of the differing values and interests in the community. The "narrow" interpretation is that when we have disagreement, we often lack a correct, shared understanding of what the disagreement is about, what positions the parties hold, and what it means to them.

A synthetic meta-ideology

Making sense of a world where different social realities somehow have to function together—if we are to have societies at all—requires a meta-framework to contain that diversity of realities. Postmodernism is the *rejection* of meta-narratives, we say, but maybe we can make an exception for a narrative of how narratives work together, with and against each other. What I've tried to present is supposed to make it possible for mutually hostile narratives to coexist, preventing them from expelling their enemies and monopolizing our allegiance.

It combines two perspectives that on the surface seem opposed, but they are so only in terms of preferred focus and differing self-interest. The best of *scientific materialism* and *social constructionism* are compatible, in principle, once you accept that what constructionists insist on calling "reality" is a shared model and not reality itself. The apparent contradiction is an artifact of blurring this line. Constructionists rightly point out that social reality is not a straightforward depiction of an underlying truth. But instead of making the point they should be making—that what we treat as reality is not—they're saying the reverse: that it *is* reality, and by that define objective material truth out of, if not existence, then at least relevance. Naive defenders of scientific realism, conversely, think that since there is an objective reality our model of it must be objective as well, and with that dismiss all the ambiguity, contingency, and choice introduced when building a model.

Understanding social reality as a model consisting of representations like types, labels, and narratives, unifies the positives of scientific realism and social constructionism without losing anything important. The remaining conflict becomes over from which direction we should approach when understanding and evaluating parts of the model: material or social[162].

We can improve our understanding of disagreements by replacing the old convention that there are two things, *facts* that are directly true or false and *values* that imply oughts, with a new one where models/claims/beliefs are on a spectrum from more fact-like and objective to more value-like and subjective. Only at the ends of the spectrum do they collapse into the simple dichotomy of "is" and "ought" that we're used to. The understanding is not new, obviously. Learning to navigate public discourse, rhetoric, PR, political debate etc. involves internalizing something like this, and people do, all the time. But there are benefits to making the implicit explicit and building its wisdom into institutions and mechanisms directly—especially since our sense of reality in the coming years is going to be shaped by artificial intelligences, who will have, must have, their own preferred ways of turning facts into narratives.

My metanarrative is a narrative like others. And like the others it is replete with artificial clarity. It's not equal to the truth but laden with assumptions that others may not share, and it supports a moral agenda that not everyone finds compelling. I'm an atheist, a philo-

---

[162] Simply put, what people mean when they call something "postmodernist" derisively is that it privileges the social over the factual side.

sophical materialist, and a moral non-realist[163], I believe in deep and significant psychological differences between individuals, and I hold social intuitionist rather than rationalist notions of moral psychology. I have a personality that finds both truthfulness and civility non-negotiable and consider reconciling the two difficult yet essential. I don't and can't demand that you agree with me on all of this. Hopefully there is value here anyway.

Decoupling is a tool, not dogma

I try to discuss decoupling as fairly as I can, but it's impossible to completely escape the fact that I consistently lean in favor. I've tried, but I want to acknowledge any shortcomings my treatment might still have. That said, there are some things to defend without reservation. Stanovich says:

> Decoupling operations help us carry out cognitive reform: the evaluation of our own beliefs and the critique of our own desires.

This is an essential practice when our intuitions can't be trusted, and as Haidt points out, while intuitions have a head start, they aren't necessarily unyielding. Pausing to reflect instead of taking first impressions as gospel makes people more moderate and less judgmental. We shouldn't automatically discount or overrule our feelings, but we should be able to distance ourselves from them enough to see them as coming from a particular personality, culture, and point of view instead of as a magical window to the true and the good.

Reasoning like grownups means being informed by our emotions instead of ruled by them like children. Contrary to what David Hume once said, reason is not the slave of the passions. It is accountable to

---

[163] I know many intelligent people disagree with me on that, and I recognize it's difficult to get past. It's (unfortunately) central to my description of social reality where the physical world is described and at the same time infused with moral valence that isn't there from the beginning. This is obviously hard to swallow for moral realists.

them the way managers of a corporation are accountable to its shareholders. The job is to look out for their long-term, enlightened interests, not to obey the momentary whims of whomever among them cries the loudest. Passions choose our heading; they are not to micromanage.

On the other hand, the "couplers" are right that we don't speak in a vacuum, and that normal human communication is not an exercise in formal logic. Ambient associations are an instrument to be played, and we must consider what tone will come out when we pluck a string. It's *incorrect* to deny that representations of reality do, at least in part, imply a moral order by the very nature of words, especially when you release them into a maelstrom of public discourse that washes away context. It's a virtue of coupled thinking that it takes continuous recontextualization as a fact of life rather than the occasional deviation from a standard of logical argumentation that only scientists and philosophers subscribe to. It is cynical but realistic, and as much as committed decouplers may wish it, we don't have the necessary level of ambient social capital to consider *everything* in good faith.

We also shouldn't be blind to the risks of relying on formal reason in domains without complete information and unambiguous rules. Abstractions are imperfect, and mistaking logical models for reality can birth unjustified confidence just as much as loudmouthed moral passions can. Despite my lean, I too am wary of extreme decouplers, untethered by notions of conventional thought and behavior. You never know what they are going to say and do. Their habit of blundering dangerously close to hazardous materials is worrisome when you have less than perfect confidence in their ability to make distinctions. I understand how others less sanguine about decoupling may feel the same about people at my own level. I even understand that being ruled by uncontrollable emotions makes you trustworthy in the sense that it proves your rational mind is kept within normal parameters by something involuntary, unfakeable, conventional, understandable, and predictable. In fact, as an engineer I'm not that surprised to hear stories about how engineers are overrepresented among radical terrorists. When you learn to trust reason to yield reliable knowledge you are more likely to take radical arguments seriously, lacking the normal skepticism of reason that makes most people ignore arguments with drastic, unconventional conclusions.

Living with contradiction (a.k.a liberalism)

The reality and necessity of the silent agreement put some of us in a difficult position. Falsehood is evil and so is the support and endorsement of falsehood, *but I don't want anyone to be mean.* It sounds silly but I'm quite serious. I write about controversies because their mechanics fascinate me, but it's a morbid, self-destructive fascination like some have for true crime. I do not really like them. I do not like conflict, aggression, or bad vibes. I do not have the abrasive personality that makes others eagerly dive headfirst into public debate, and sometimes I wonder what I'm doing there at all. My ideal world is full to the brim with niceness and positive-sum coordination, but under the constraint of no socially enforced distortion of reality. Much of this book is me handling this obvious conflict by arguing for more acceptance of contradiction.

Haidt tells us that his research into moral psychology has turned him away from youthful idealism towards something more modest:

> When I was a teenager I wished for world peace, but now I yearn for a world in which competing ideologies are kept in balance, systems of accountability keep us all from getting away with too much, and fewer people believe that righteous ends justify violent means. Not a very romantic wish, but one that we might actually achieve.

He doesn't use it here, but there's word for that attitude to contradiction: *liberalism.* Liberalism is the acknowledgement that contemporary societies are trading zones, and that attempts at enforcing a single dominant shared reality are inescapably authoritarian. Paradoxically, this requires insisting on common ground, but on a level above the specific. It means having to agree on processes rather than outcomes, on rules rather than teams. Liberalism, in a broad sense, is a meta-belief system that makes it possible for other belief systems to exist without trying to destroy each other. The understanding of disagreement put forward here is one piece of it, designed to live in individual minds.

Liberal democracy is about playing by the rules, even when that means our side doesn't win every time. It doesn't provide the greatest of rushes, sadly, because these ideals are boring and bloodless[164]. Perhaps the best thing in life *is* vanquishing your enemies, to drive them before you, taste their blood on your sword and hear the lamentations of their women, as it goes, but when a society rejects that in favor of rights, rules and procedures, it grows and improves. It's worth it.

Looking at ourselves

Being human, we want to have it both ways. We want to be good *and* win every time, and the best way to cheat without getting caught or feeling guilty is to fool ourselves. We don't *lie*, exactly, heavens no, we just use the ambiguity of language and the partiality of narratives to make ourselves seem more right than we are. And we don't bully our enemies into submission *exactly*, we just exploit those same mechanisms to make sure everyone else knows how awful they are. All in the public interest, of course.

A full 2400 years after Plato kicked off, public discourse remains more sophistry than philosophy. We jockey for impact on social reality not always by convincing other people's rational selves, but by bypassing their evaluative abilities and smuggling our beliefs through the side door. I'm not entirely joking when I invoke the lan-

---

[164] One could hope that an absence of blood would be a *selling point* in politics, but here we are. I'd like to think that you can cultivate equally strong passions for higher-level virtues like fair play and rationality, but I'm honestly not convinced. I can't even be entirely sure my own fondness isn't just self-interested lionization of my personal strengths.

guage of consent to object: just like you may not touch my body without asking, you may not try to appeal to my subconscious without the informed consent of my rational self. This standard is, of course, impossible to uphold, but we would have better public conversations and better societies if we aspired to it.

We can't destroy our desire to cheat, but we can make it harder to do so with a good conscience. The first step is to force ourselves to acknowledge our sins. A minority of sociopaths notwithstanding, we can only feel good about our devious ways if we don't look directly at them. So look at them. Directly. I talk about all these things—ambiguity, type construction, partial narratives—because I want us to not be able to wield them without noticing what we're doing.

Why would this do any good, considering how naive it is to think we don't already know all this, yet happily participate? Some criticism of *The Elephant in the Brain* said that it just goes over things everybody knows, and the defense against that point can justify this book as well: an explication doesn't have to contain genuinely new information to be valuable. It matters how explicitly we understand things. Articulating ideas and putting them together in a self-reinforcing structure big and loud enough to play an active role in our everyday thinking can make a big difference. Every idea in here is compatible with, and supported by, all the others (see figure on next page).

Being specific about the tactics at the Prince's disposal arms the Figurehead (the part of us that really believes in our moral virtue), making us more likely to question what we're told. Relegated to ceremonial duties by default, we are still the rightful monarchs, and we can make the decision to assert power and rule with wisdom and integrity, or we can keep standing on the balcony, waving at the crowd, unwittingly providing cover for the dirty operations of state.

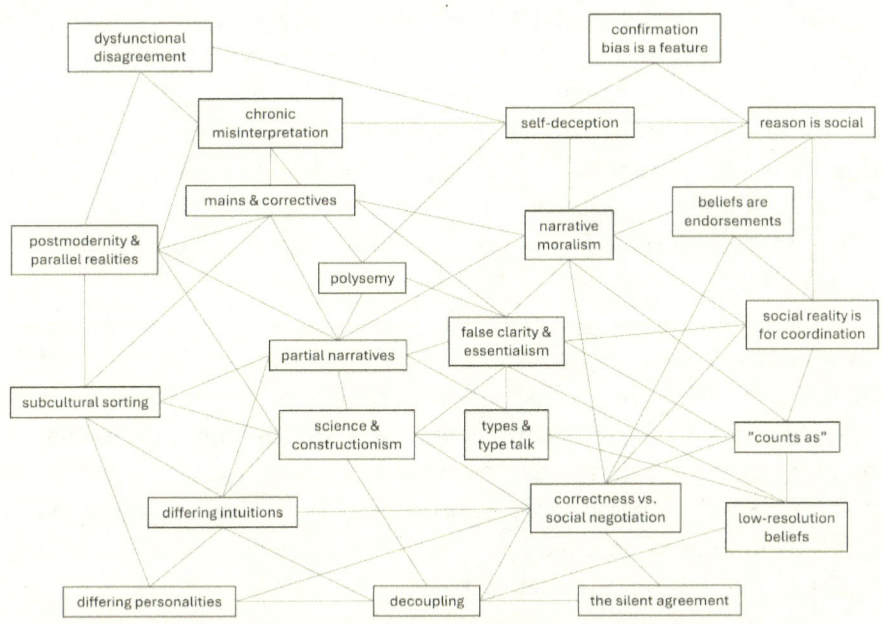

Figure 23, how the main ideas interrelate and support each other.

The tower of recognized wisdom

It can be demoralizing to realize that cognitive biases and reasoning "errors" aren't errors at all but human reason working according to factory settings. When the enemy is human nature, how can we ever hope to win? It helps to remember that the war has been going on for a long time, and we've already made serious territorial gains. Going from primal, tribalist morality to democracy and human rights could once have been reasonably dismissed as utopian. I don't think my medieval equivalent—some junior monk in a damp, drafty abbey scribbling fantasies of liberty and equality in the margins of an oversized sheet of parchment—would've ever thought it possible. Yet it happened. We owe it to material prosperity from trade and technological advancement, but also to philosophical ideals that told us what to aim for.

Institutions like parliamentary democracy, equality under the law, free speech, free markets, and government by consent required collective acknowledgement of the basic insight that power corrupts. We needed to admit that fact of life and agree on rules to rein it in. I don't see why we can't keep going. We can build on that foundation towards a taller tower of collectively recognized wisdom if we acknowledge more of human corruptibility while designing systems to contain it.

To contain is not to defeat. The tension between our tendency to cheat and the benefits of societies where cheating is not tolerated is inherent in reality. It's not a random error or curable pathology; we'll have to keep working against it like we work against gravity when building bridges, aircraft, or skyscrapers. Defying gravity is perfectly possible but does not happen spontaneously. It requires intent, hard work, and thankless upkeep. It requires knowing what we're up against and treating it matter-of-factly.

People have all kinds of motives when taking part in public debate, but its social function is to maintain, extend, and occasionally remodel the tower of recognized wisdom. In the best of worlds, the result is indeed wisdom, true, tested, and stable, while in the worst it is popular delusion, prone to catastrophic failures. To get the best, debate must be a balanced dialogue between progressive and conservative forces, where the conservative affirms that our morals and institutions embody hard-earned insights that we may not fully understand, while the progressive points out that they sometimes outlive their usefulness, or even lacked wisdom to begin with. When any one side dominates enough to ignore their counterpart, or when parties can't or won't speak to each other for other reasons, the tower isn't kept in working order.

To build higher, the conversation needs to improve instead of falling apart, but public discourse has less and less of the two features characteristic of well-functioning disagreements. The first, characteristic of academics, is well-defined, agreed-upon concepts and terms. The second, characteristic of friends and family, is the mutual respect required to consider each other's interests to be legitimate. We can *maybe* limp by with one of the two, but not with zero. To repair the damage, we must become literate in each other's belief systems, and aware of how values and intuitions are rooted in personality and experiences. That means internalizing, thoroughly, that our model of reality, including of other people, is not reality itself. In *The Construction of Social Reality*, Searle said:

> One reason we can bear the burden is that the complex structure of social reality is, so to speak, weightless and invisible. The child is brought up in a culture where he or she simply takes social reality for granted. We learn to perceive and use cars, bathtubs, houses, money, restaurants, and schools without being aware of that they have a special ontology. They seem as natural to us as stones and water and trees. Indeed, if anything, in most cases it is harder to see objects as just natural phenomena, stripped of their functional roles, than it is to see our surroundings in terms of their socially defined functions. So children learn to see moving cars, dollar bills, and full bathtubs; and it is only by force of abstraction that they can see these as masses of metal in linear trajectories, cellulose fibers with green and gray stains, or enamel-covered iron concavities containing water.

It needs to stop. The situation where society is fractured into multiple social realities that dominate the "paramount" one we have in common, *but we still take our own for granted*, is disastrous.

Towards an updated common sense

I published my first erisology article in January 2016 after having made notes and drafts throughout 2015. At the time, problems that had always existed had become worse and more apparent as the proliferation of smartphones made social media a much more integrated part of our lives, and of public discourse. Since then, everything has accelerated. The novel I planned to write, where *erisology* was a fictional academic discipline, involved an idealistic grad student wanting to help heal a broken public conversation but growing disillusioned and vengeful after discovering that the social media analysis firm he worked for not only observed discourse but used an army of bots to manipulate it at the behest of clients. It was to take place a decade in the future, in 2025[165].

The fact of, and circumstances around, Donald Trump being president of the Unites States, twice, is a historical outlier. His unbothered attitude to truth and honesty is not unique among politicians and activists, but more brazen and indecorous than anyone could get away with before. This is not a fluke and his rise to power is not *sui generis*; the breakdown of shared reality is not his doing, and the problems would not disappear if he was whisked out of existence. The chaos surrounding him, including polarization into rabid lovers and haters, is just the manifestation of a structural problem. It's what happens when people live in parallel worlds, agreeing not even on the basic facts, let alone the appropriate context in which to put them or the conclusions to draw from them. Without functional disagreement there is no way to reach constructive compromise, and politics turns into a pendulum of alternating retaliation.

Fighting for the right to mine reality for political capital has always been ugly, but at least it has been coherent. When we can't even coordinate *the fights* and agree on a result, then we are in trouble. On the bright side, awareness and understanding of the problem have also advanced by leaps and bounds over the past decade; we've come a long way since I first started. Yet the understanding remains inchoate and fragmented, still far from conventional wisdom. Individuals coming to insight through their own experience, aided by scattered thinkpieces, is not enough.

---

[165] It had a parallel storyline where the other main character laments the loss of shared pop-cultural touchstones and is horrified when she realizes that the media company she works for is building AI to create custom fiction, pandering to each individual user's taste. In 2015 this was still sci-fi-ish.

Now is a fertile time for further progress, and I would wish for the next generation of common sense to incorporate this synthesis. Regardless of whether future sensemaking is instantiated in human minds, or in AI oracles that take over the work of turning a universe of facts into digestible narratives, it must understand itself.

Acknowledgements

This book was made possible by a Pluralism and Civil Exchange grant from the Mercatus Institute at George Mason University. Thank you.

Thanks also to my small but loyal cadre of Patreon donors, who stood by me when my regular output stopped during the writing of this book.

Thanks to everyone who've appreciated, shared, and engaged with my writing, online and offline. You made this worthwhile.

Finally, thanks to my wife, who've supported me putting more time into this than financially defensible.

Index

Further reading

Aikin, Scott and Talisse, Robert, *Political Argument in a Polarized Age*, 2020.

Alexander, Scott, *What Universal Experiences Are You Missing Without Realizing it?*, 2014.

Bail, Christopher, et al., *Exposure to Opposing Views on Social Media Can Increase Political Polarization*, 2018.

Baron-Cohen, Simon, *The Essential Difference*, 2003.

Barthes, Roland, *Death of the Author*, 1967.

Baudrillard, Jean, *Simulacra and Simulation*, 1981.

Berger, Peter and Luckmann, Thomas, *The Social Construction of Reality*, 1966.

Blackmore, Susan, *The Meme Machine*, 1999.

Boghossian, Peter and Lindsay, James, *How to Have Impossible Conversations*, 2019.

Bourdieu, Pierre, *Distinction*, 1979.

Boyd, Brian, *The evolution of stories: from mimesis to language, from fact to fiction*, 2017.

Chalmers, David, *Verbal Disputes*, 2011.

Chapman, David, *A bridge to meta-rationality*, 2016.

Christakis, Nicholas, *Blueprint: The Evolutionary Origins of a Good Society*, 2019.

Davidson, Donald, *On the Very Idea of a Conceptual Scheme*, 1974.

Dennett, Daniel, *Darwin's Dangerous Idea*, 1995.

Dennett, Daniel, *Intentional Systems*, 1971.

Enfield, NJ, *Language vs. Reality: Why Language is Good for Lawyers and Bad for Scientists, 2024*

Flanagan, Owen, *The Problem of the Soul: Two Visions of Mind and How to Reconcile Them*, 2002.

Foucault, Michel, *The Archaeology of Knowledge*, 1969.

Frankfurt, Harry, *On Bullshit*, 2005.

Galef, Julia, *The Scout Mindset*, 2021.

Galison, Peter, *Trading Zone: Coordinating Action and Belief*, 1998.

Greene, Joshua, *Moral Tribes: Emotion, Reason, and the Gap Between Us and Them,* 2013.

Hacking, Ian, *The Social Construction of What?*, 1999.

Haidt, Jonathan, *The Righteous Mind,* 2012.

Hanson, Robin and Simler, Kevin, *The Elephant in the Brain: Hidden Motives in Everyday Life,* 2018.

Heath, Joseph, *On the Scalability of Cooperative Structures,* 2016.

Heath, Joseph, *What do libertarians and pedophiles have in common?,* 2019.

Keogh, Rebecca et al., *Aphantasia: The science of visual imagery extremes,* 2021.

Klein, Ezra, *Why We're Polarized,* 2020.

Kling, Arnold, *The Three Languages of Politics,* 2013.

Kuhn, Thomas, *The Structure of Scientific Revolutions,* 1962.

Kurzban, Robert, *Why Everyone (Else) Is a Hypocrite, 2010.*

Lakoff, George and Johnson, Mark, *Metaphors We Live By,* 1980.

Lakoff, George, *Moral Politics: How Liberals and Conservatives Think,* 2002.

Literal Banana, *Introducing the Extended Sniff Test: A Method for Recreational Hostile Fact Checking,* 2020.

Loury, Glenn, *Self-Censorship in Public Discourse,* 1994.

Lukianoff, Greg and Haidt, Jonathan, *The Coddling of the American Mind,* 2018.

Lyotard, Jean-François, *The Postmodern Condition: A Report on Knowledge,* 1979.

Mercier, Hugo and Sperber, Dan, *The Enigma of Reason,* 2017.

Nagel, Thomas, *What Is It Like to Be a Bat?,* 1974.

Nerst, John, *A Deep Dive into the Harris-Klein Controversy,* 2018.

Orwell, George, *1984,* 1948.

Pluckrose, Helen and Lindsay, James, *Cynical Theories,* 2020.

Rawls, John, *Political Liberalism,* 1993.

Searle, John, *The Construction of Social Reality,* 1996.

Segerstråle, Ullica, *Defenders of the Truth: The Sociobiology Debate,* 2001.

Shackel, Nicholas, *The Vacuity of Postmodernist Methodology,* 2005.

Sloman, Steven and Fernbach, Philip, *The Knowledge Illusion: Why We Never Think Alone*, 2017.
Snow, C.P., *The Two Cultures*, 1959.
Sokal, Alan and Bricmont, Jean, *Fashionable Nonsense: Postmodern Intellectual Abuse of Science*, 1998.
Stanley, Matthew, *Why Should I Believe You? The Costs and Consequences of Inter-Expert Disagreement*, 2018.
Stanovich, Keith, *What Intelligence Tests Miss: The Psychology of Rational Thought*, 2010.
Storr, Will, *The Science of Storytelling*, 2019.
Taylor, Charles, *A Secular Age*, 2007.
Tetlock, Philip, et al., *Thinking the Unthinkable: Sacred Values and Taboo Cognitions*, 2003.
Tosi, Justin and Warmke, Brandon, *Grandstanding: The Use and Abuse of Moral Talk*, 2020.
Urban, Tim, *What's Our Problem? A Self-Help Book for Societies, 2023.*
Wittgenstein, Ludwig, *Philosophical Investigations*, 1953.

www.ingramcontent.com/pod-product-compliance
Lightning Source LLC
LaVergne TN
LVHW050917080826
845145LV00001B/108

* 9 7 8 9 1 5 3 1 4 9 2 9 3 *